"In *Mediation & Popular Culture*, Jennifer L. Schulz weaves together insights on how mediation is portrayed in TV and movies, prodigious research on mediation practice, ethics and theory, and a discussion of the practical choices that mediators face every day of their working lives. The result is an enjoyable, thought-provoking, creative and very useful discussion of the defining characteristics of mediation. For mediators who want to understand the gap between what the public expects of us and what we actually deliver, this is essential reading."

Bernie Mayer, Ph.D., Professor of Conflict Studies, Negotiation and Conflict Resolution (NCR) Program, Creighton University; author of The Conflict Paradox *and* The Dynamics of Conflict

"Dr. Schulz has written an interesting and impressive book. *Mediation & Popular Culture* brings together theory, practice, gender insights and popular culture in order to highlight the differences between how we imagine mediation and how it is actually practiced. I highly recommend it."

Deborah M. Kolb, Ph.D., Deloitte Ellen Gabriel Professor for Women in Leadership (Emerita); Co-founder of the Ford Foundation-funded Center for Gender in Organizations at Simmons College School of Management; and Co-Director of the Negotiations in the Workplace Project at the Program on Negotiation at Harvard Law School

"*Mediation & Popular Culture* provides a valuable lens to understand messages about mediation sent to the general public, which can affect how disputants react to mediation in real life. Analyzing films and television programs, empirical and other scholarly literature and her own experience as a mediator, Jennifer L. Schulz shows that both the popular media and the espoused theory of the mediation field distort the reality of mediation. In so doing, she presents a thoughtful, interesting and more realistic portrait of mediation as it actually is practiced."

John Lande, Isidor Loeb Professor Emeritus, University of Missouri School of Law

Mediation & Popular Culture

This book examines mediation topics such as impartiality, self-determination and fair outcomes through popular culture lenses. Popular television shows and award-winning films are used as illustrative examples to illuminate under-represented mediation topics such as feelings and expert intuition, conflicts of interest and repeat business, and deception and caucusing. The author employs research from Australia, Belgium, Canada, China, Denmark, France, Germany, Greece, India, Israel, Japan, the Netherlands, New Zealand, Singapore, South Africa, Spain, the United Kingdom and the United States of America to demonstrate that real and reel mediation may have more in common than we think. How mediation is imagined in popular culture, compared to how professors teach it and how mediators practise it, provides important affective, ethical, legal, personal and pedagogical insights relevant for mediators, lawyers, professors and students, and may even help develop mediator identity.

Jennifer L. Schulz is Professor in the Faculty of Law, University of Manitoba, Canada, and Fellow of the Winkler Institute for Dispute Resolution, Osgoode Hall Law School, Toronto. She is the author of many articles and chapters on mediation and co-editor of *A Transnational Study of Law & Justice on TV* (2016) and *Ethnicity, Gender, and Diversity: Law and Justice on TV* (2018). Dr. Schulz has won four teaching awards, a national ADR service award, and is a federal and international research grant recipient. She has been a visiting scholar at the University of Cambridge; Birkbeck, University of London; the University of Toronto; and a research fellow at the Program on Negotiation at Harvard University.

Routledge Research in Media Law

Available titles in this series include:

Public Service Broadcasting 3.0
Legal Design for the Digital Present
Mira Burri

Photography and the Law
Rights and Restrictions
Michael O'Flanagan

Mediation and Popular Culture
Jennifer L. Schulz

Forthcoming titles

Journalists, Anonymous Sources and the Law
A Comparative, Theoretical and Critical Analysis
Damian Carney

Public Service Media and the Law
Theory and Practice in Europe
Karen Donders

Mediation & Popular Culture

Jennifer L. Schulz

Routledge
Taylor & Francis Group
LONDON AND NEW YORK

First published 2020
by Routledge
2 Park Square, Milton Park, Abingdon, Oxon OX14 4RN

and by Routledge
605 Third Avenue, New York, NY 10017

Routledge is an imprint of the Taylor & Francis Group, an informa business

First issued in paperback 2021

British Library Cataloguing-in-Publication Data
A catalogue record for this book is available from the British Library

Library of Congress Cataloging-in-Publication Data
Names: Schulz, Jennifer L., author.
Title: Mediation and popular culture / Jennifer L. Schulz.
Description: London ; New York : Routledge, 2020. |
Series: Routledge research in media law |
Includes bibliographical references and index. |
Identifiers: LCCN 2019056986 | ISBN 9780367181055 (hardback) |
ISBN 9780429059551 (ebook)
Subjects: LCSH: Mediation on television. | Mediation in motion pictures. |
Law on television. | Law in motion pictures.
Classification: LCC PN1992.8.M388 S38 2020 |
DDC 791.45/653--dc23
LC record available at https://lccn.loc.gov/2019056986

ISBN 13: 978-0-367-18105-5 (hbk)
ISBN 13: 978-1-03-223813-5 (pbk)
ISBN 13: 978-0-429-05955-1 (ebk)

DOI: 10.4324/9780429059551

Typeset in Galliard
by Taylor & Francis Books

Jack and Max,
I love you
so very, very much
so very, very much.
You are the BEST boys
in the whole, wide world.

Contents

Figures

Acknowledgements

I would like to recognize Robson Hall Faculty of Law at the University of Manitoba where I am a Professor and the Winkler Institute for Dispute Resolution at Osgoode Hall Law School where I am a Fellow. At the time of researching I was a Research Fellow at Birkbeck School of Law, University of London, and a Faculty Visitor at the Faculty of Law, University of Cambridge. I acknowledge the Association of Commonwealth Universities and especially the Gordon and Jean Southam Fellowship for financial support that made my research trips to the UK possible, and the cities of London and Cambridge for inspiration when I needed it most. At the time of writing I was on sabbatical from Robson Hall and benefitted from research support from the University of Manitoba's Legal Research Institute. Thanks go to Elliott for love, Lisa, Sandra and Cheryl for friendship, and to my Mom for her unwavering enthusiasm for this book.

1 Mediation & popular culture

Research from: Australia, Canada, China, Germany, Israel, New Zealand, UK and USA

Mediation is the focus of my life in the law – both as a scholar and as a practitioner – and it is the focus of this book. I do two things in this book that have not been done before: I delve into mediation matters that are under-represented in the literature, and I illustrate and examine them using popular culture examples. How mediation is imagined in popular culture – compared to how professors teach it and how mediators practise it – provides important affective, ethical, legal, personal and pedagogical insights. These will be the focus of this book.

I adopt Lon Fuller and Christopher W. Moore's definitions of mediation. Fuller describes mediation as a process with the "capacity to reorient the parties toward each other, not by imposing rules on them, but by helping them achieve a new and shared perception of their relationship, a perception that will redirect their attitudes and dispositions toward one another."[1] Moore describes mediation as the intervention into a dispute or negotiation by an acceptable, impartial and neutral third party who has no authoritative decision-making power. This third party, the mediator, assists the disputing parties in voluntarily reaching their own mutually acceptable settlement.[2] I adopt these classic definitions because they highlight the fact that the mediator controls the process but the disputants retain ultimate control over the outcome. The mediator helps the parties identify and evaluate their interests and options as they proceed to design and craft their own agreement. As succinctly put by Robert A. Baruch Bush and Joseph P. Folger: "A mediator is someone who intervenes to help when people are in the middle of conflict."[3]

The mere presence of a third party will alter the substance, tone and course of negotiations between two people. If that third party is a trained mediator, she or he will be able to assist the parties to negotiate more productively with each other than they could alone. Mediation is in this way connected to negotiation, but is of course different because the parties are not reaching their agreement on their own

1 Lon Fuller, "Mediation: Its Forms and Functions" (1971) 44 *Southern California Law Review* 305 at 328.
2 Christopher W. Moore, *The Mediation Process: Practical Strategies for Resolving Conflict*, 2nd edn (San Francisco, CA: Jossey-Bass, 1996) at 15.
3 Robert A. Baruch Bush & Joseph P. Folger, *The Promise of Mediation: The Transformative Approach to Conflict*, 2nd edn (San Francisco, CA: Jossey-Bass, 2005) at 41.

as negotiators; they have the third-party mediator's help. The fact that the third party, the mediator, does not render a decision is what distinguishes mediation from arbitration. In arbitration, arbitrators make binding decisions. Mediators do not. Mediators proactively facilitate the negotiations of the parties, and they do so very differently than arbitrators or lawyers do. Lawyers ask themselves: "how should I frame this case in law?" or "how does the law apply to these facts?" Mediators ask: "why are these people stuck?," "what needs to happen to make a difference?," and "will they be able to work together again?" Mediators use their skills and experience to help facilitate a process of dispute resolution, reality testing along the way. Mediators also have a training function, helping the parties learn more productive ways of negotiating with one another in the future. The beauty of mediation lies in its flexibility. Mediators can choose their process and their style and mediation can happen in community, court-connected, mandated or private settings. The disputants and mediator work together to reach creative resolutions that are unattainable in the courtroom. In mediation, parties' contexts, histories and socio-economic positions can be taken into account more than is possible in courts of law. Disputants' needs and interests, not just their legal positions, can be examined. Disputants can tell their stories, express their emotions and control the outcome of their disputes. In so doing, they often find their relationships are less damaged than they would be after a court process. All this, plus mediation is more informal than court, is confidential, can be undertaken without a lawyer and is faster and cheaper than litigation.

Given all the benefits of mediation it is not surprising that it is used across North America, Europe and China for an ever-widening array of disputes. Writers have described mediation applications in many contexts, such as business, commercial and workplace,[4] public law,[5] environmental,[6] and criminal and restorative

4 M. Watkins, *Breakthrough Business Negotiation: A Toolbox for Managers* (San Francisco, CA: Jossey-Bass, 2002); A. Stitt, *Mediating Commercial Disputes* (Toronto: Canada Law Book, 2003); D. Corry, *Negotiation: The Art of Mutual Gains Bargaining* (Toronto: Canada Law Book, 2000); D. Lipsky, R. Seeber & R. Fincher, *Emerging Systems for Managing Workplace Conflict* (San Francisco, CA: Jossey-Bass, 2003); B. Kuretzky & J. MacKenzie, *Mediating Employment Disputes* (Toronto: Canada Law Book, 2001); P. Bishop, *Winning in the Workplace: ADR Strategies for Employment Disputes* (Toronto: Carswell, 1995); D. Lax & J. Sebenius, *The Manager as Negotiator: Bargaining for Cooperation and Competitive Gain* (New York: The Free Press, 1986); D. Kolb & J. Williams, *The Shadow Negotiation: How Women Can Master the Hidden Agendas that Determine Bargaining Success* (New York: Simon & Schuster, 2000); R. Linden, *Working Across Boundaries: Making Collaboration Work in Government and Non-Profit Organizations* (San Francisco, CA: Jossey-Bass, 2002).

5 S. Carpenter & W. Kennedy, *Managing Public Disputes: A Practical Guide for Government, Business, and Citizens' Groups* (San Francisco, CA: Jossey-Bass, 2001); E. Dukes, *Resolving Public Conflict: Transforming Community and Governance* (Manchester: Manchester University Press, 1996); J. Poitras & P. Renaud, *Mediation and Reconciliation of Interests in Public Disputes* (Toronto: Carswell, 1997).

6 L. Susskind, *Environmental Diplomacy: Negotiating More Effective Global Agreements* (New York: Oxford University Press, 1994); L. Bacow & M. Wheeler, *Environmental Dispute Resolution* (New York: Plenum, 1984).

justice contexts.[7] In Canada, 10.1% of people report spending money on mediators for their everyday legal problems.[8] Mediation scholarship is wide-ranging.[9] Scholars have focused their attention on online dispute resolution initiatives,[10] designing dispute resolution systems,[11] and the lawyer's role in dispute resolution endeavours.[12] Researchers have addressed their minds to international disputes and peacekeeping,[13]

7 S. Sharpe, *Restorative Justice: A Vision for Healing and Change* (Edmonton: Edmonton Victim Offender Mediation Society, 1998); D. Cayley, *The Expanding Prison: The Crisis in Crime and Punishment* (Toronto: House of Anansi Press, 1998); W. Derksen, *Confronting the Horror: The Aftermath of Violence* (Amity, 2002); R. Ross, *Returning to the Teachings: Exploring Aboriginal Justice* (Toronto: Penguin, 1996); M. Yantzi, *Sexual Offending and Restoration* (Toronto: Herald Press, 1998).

8 Trevor C.W. Farrow, Ab Currie, Nicole Aylwin, Les Jacobs, David Northrup & Lisa Moore (2016) "Everyday Legal Problems and the Cost of Justice in Canada: Overview Report," *Canadian Forum on Civil Justice*, https://tinyurl.com/v4ug92z

9 Gemma Smyth, "Mediation," in Julie Macfarlane, ed., *Dispute Resolution: Readings and Case Studies* (Toronto: Emond Montgomery, 2011); S. Goldberg, F. Sander & N. Rogers, *Dispute Resolution: Negotiation, Mediation, and Other Processes*, 3rd edn (Gaithersburg, MD: Aspen Law and Business, 1999); C. Moore, *The Mediation Process: Practical Strategies for Resolving Conflict*, 3rd edn (San Francisco, CA: Jossey-Bass, 2003); M. Deutsch & P.T. Coleman, eds, *The Handbook of Conflict Resolution* (San Francisco, CA: Jossey-Bass, 2000); K. Arrow, R. Mnookin et al., eds, *Barriers to Conflict Resolution* (Cambridge, MA: PON Books, 1999); K. Cloke, *Mediating Dangerously: The Frontiers of Conflict Resolution* (San Francisco, CA: Jossey-Bass, 2001); J. Winslade & G. Monk, *Narrative Mediation: A New Approach to Conflict Resolution* (San Francisco, CA: Jossey-Bass, 2000).

10 E. Katsh & J. Rifkin, *Online Dispute Resolution: Resolving Conflicts in Cyberspace* (San Francisco, CA: Jossey-Bass, 2001); C. Rule, *Online Dispute Resolution for Business* (San Francisco, CA: Jossey-Bass, 2002).

11 C. Costantino & C. Merchant, *Designing Conflict Management Systems: A Guide to Creating Productive and Healthy Organizations* (San Francisco, CA: Jossey-Bass, 1996); W. Ury, J. Brett & S. Goldberg, *Getting Disputes Resolved: Designing Systems to Cut the Costs of Conflict* (Cambridge, MA: PON Books, 1993).

12 M. Silver, *Mediation and Negotiation: Representing Your Clients* (Toronto: Butterworths, 2001); C. Noble, L. Dizgun & P. Emond, *Mediation Advocacy: Effective Client Representation in Mediation Proceedings* (Toronto: Emond Montgomery Publications, 1998); G. Chornenki, *The Corporate Counsel Guide to Dispute Resolution* (Aurora, ON: Canada Law Book Inc., 1999); N. Atlas, S. Huber & W. Trachte-Huber, *Alternative Dispute Resolution: The Litigator's Handbook* (Chicago, IL: ABA Publishing, 2000), Julie Macfarlane, *The New Lawyer: How Settlement is Transforming the Practice of Law*, 2nd edn (Vancouver: University of British Columbia Press, 2008).

13 J. Lederach & J. Jenner, eds, *A Handbook of International Peacebuilding: Into the Eye of the Storm* (San Francisco, CA: Jossey-Bass, 2002); A. Chayes & M. Minow, eds, *Imagine Coexistence: Restoring Humanity After Violent Ethnic Conflict* (San Francisco, CA: Jossey-Bass, 2003); L. Fisk & J. Schellenberg, *Patterns of Conflict, Paths to Peace* (Peterborough: Broadview Press, 2000); M. Watkins & S. Rosegrant, *Breakthrough International Negotiation: How Great Negotiators Transformed the World's Toughest Post-Cold War Conflicts* (San Francisco, CA: Jossey-Bass, 2001); R. Fisher, A. Schneider, E. Bogwardt & B. Ganson, *Coping with International Conflict: A Systematic Approach to Influence in International Negotiation* (Upper Saddle River, NJ: Prentice Hall, 1997); B. Kellerman & J. Rubin, *Leadership and Negotiation in the Middle East* (New York: Praeger, 1988).

and to the connections between conflict resolution, transformation and spirituality.[14] There is an extremely large family mediation literature[15] and an expanding school conflict resolution scholarship.[16] This huge body of mediation literature, despite its diversity, tends to be in agreement regarding the hallmarks of mediation, which include the self-determination of the parties,[17] the impartiality of the mediator,[18] the importance of voluntary participation[19] and the lack of decision-making power of the mediator.[20] These hallmarks form the core of what I call the quintessential mediation story.

14 Robert A. Baruch Bush & Joseph P. Folger, *The Promise of Mediation: Responding to Conflict Through Empowerment and Recognition* (San Francisco, CA: Jossey-Bass, 1994); E. Worthington, *Five Steps to Forgiveness: The Art and Science of Forgiving* (Crown Publishers, 2001); K. Cloke & J. Goldsmith, *Resolving Personal and Organizational Conflict: Stories of Transformation and Forgiveness* (San Francisco, CA: Jossey-Bass, 2000); J. Lederach, *The Journey Toward Reconciliation* (Harrisonburg, VA: Herald Press, 1999); M. Hadley, *The Spiritual Roots of Restorative Justice* (New York: State University of New York Press, 2001).

15 A. Taylor, *The Handbook of Family Dispute Resolution: Mediation Theory and Practice* (San Francisco, CA: Jossey-Bass, 2002); B. Landau et al., *Family Mediation Handbook*, 3rd edn (Toronto: Butterworths, 2000); C. Noble, *Family Mediation: A Guide for Lawyers* (Toronto: Canada Law Book, 1999); H. Irving & M. Benjamin, *Therapeutic Family Mediation: Helping Families Resolve Conflict* (Thousand Oaks, CA: Sage Publications, 2002). Examples of family mediation in popular culture include the opening scene of the American film *Wedding Crashers* and episode one of season two of the Showtime series *The Affair*. See also Jennifer L. Schulz, "Using Film to Teach ADR," in Christine Corcos, ed., *The Media Method: Teaching Law With Popular Culture* (Durham, NC: Carolina Academic Press, 2019).

16 W. Kriedler & L. Furlong, *Adventures in Peacemaking: A Conflict Resolution Guide for School-Age Programs* (Cambridge, MA: Educators for Social Responsibility, 1995); L. Eggert, *Anger Management for Youth: Stemming Aggression and Violence* (Bloomington, IN: National Education Service, 1994); A. Beane, *The Bully Free Classroom* (Minneapolis, MN: Free Spirit Publishing, 1999); H. Van Gurp, *Peer Mediation: The Complete Guide to Resolving Conflict in our Schools* (Winnipeg: Portage and Main Press, 2002); W. Warters, *Mediation in the Campus Community* (San Francisco, CA: Jossey-Bass, 2000).

17 Canadian Bar Association – Ontario, Model Code of Conduct for Mediators, III Principle of Self-Determination: 1. "Self-determination is the right of parties in a mediation to make their own voluntary and non-coerced decisions regarding the possible resolution of any issue in dispute. It is a fundamental principle of mediation which mediators shall respect and encourage."

18 Maureen E. Laflin (2000) "Preserving the Integrity of Mediation Through the Adoption of Ethical Rules for Lawyer-Mediators," 14 *Notre Dame Journal of Law, Ethics & Public Policy* 479 at 483–484; and Canadian Bar Association – Ontario, Model Code of Conduct for Mediators, IV Impartiality: 1. "Mediators shall serve only in those matters in which they can remain impartial"; and 3. "If mediators become aware of their lack of impartiality, they shall immediately disclose to the parties that they can no longer remain impartial and shall withdraw from the mediation."

19 Andrew J. Pirie, *Alternative Dispute Resolution: Skills, Science, and the Law* (Toronto: Irwin Law, 2000) at 208.

20 Manel Canyameres & Anne Catherine Salberg, "Historical Contribution to the Ethical and Methodological Principles of Mediation," in Jacques Faget, ed., *Mediation in Political Conflicts: Soft Power or Counter Culture?* (Oxford: Hart Publishing, 2011) at 39.

Individual mediators of course practise differently. They practise interest-based,[21] transformative,[22] narrative,[23] insight,[24] social norm,[25] restorative,[26] critical moment[27] and on-the-spot[28] mediation. However, they all endorse the hallmarks of the quintessential story. They stress that disputants are in charge of their resolutions and that a facilitative mediation approach is usually preferred to a directive, evaluative approach. Mark Umbreit describes the facilitative nature of mediation as follows: "Mediators do not impose any binding decisions but instead work on empowering the parties in conflict to construct their own settlement."[29] Authenticity, transparency and honesty are thought to be good traits in a mediator, and deceptive techniques are not endorsed. This quintessential mediation story is found throughout mediation scholarship, practice and training. Scholars, trainers, law professors and mediators stress that mediation should be voluntary, party self-determination is vital, mediators should be neutral, a facilitative orientation to mediation is preferred, and deceptive practices are unethical. Finally, a common theme in the literature is the idea that mediation, especially in contrast to litigation, provides space for disputants' feelings and cultural identities.

The importance of culture to mediation, therefore, cannot be overestimated. Culture comprises the enduring norms, values, customs and behavioural patterns common to a group of people. It can manifest itself in shared knowledge, beliefs, art, law, morals, attitudes, customs, behaviours and habits. Culture is a dynamic meaning-making system that directs thinking and suggests appropriate emotions and behaviours. Each culture contains subcultures and each individual may identify with more than one cultural group. Culture is important to conflict because it makes meaning for disputants, and thus conflict can be said to be influenced by culture. Yet one can never definitively say what "the culture" does or believes, nor conclusively predict what a particular disputant will do based on her or his cultural

21 R. Fisher, W. Ury & B. Patton, *Getting to Yes*, 2nd edn (Sydney: Century Business, 1991); Christopher Moore, *The Mediation Process: Practical Strategies for Resolving Conflict* (San Francisco, CA: Jossey-Bass, 1986); and D. Lax & J. Sebenius, *The Manager as Negotiator: Bargaining for Cooperation and Competitive Gain* (New York: Simon & Schuster, 1986).

22 Robert A. Baruch Bush & Joseph P. Folger, *The Promise of Mediation: The Transformative Approach to Conflict*, 2nd edn (San Francisco, CA: Jossey-Bass, 2005).

23 John Winslade & Gerald Monk, *Narrative Mediation: A New Approach to Conflict Resolution* (San Francisco, CA: Jossey-Bass, 2001).

24 Bernard Lonergan, *Insight: An Essay in Human Understanding* (San Francisco, CA: Harper and Row, 1957); and Cheryl Picard, *Insight Mediation: Mediating Interpersonal and Small Group Conflict* (Toronto: Dundurn Press, 2002).

25 Ellen Waldman, "Identifying the Role of Social Norms in Mediation: A Multiple Model Approach" (1997) 48:4 *Hastings Law Journal* 703.

26 M.S. Umbreit, *Mediating Interpersonal Conflicts: A Pathway to Peace* (West Concord, MN: CPI Publishing, 1995).

27 This is an emerging approach to mediation, advocated by scholars affiliated with Harvard Law School's Program on Negotiation.

28 N. Milner, "Linda Colburn: On-the-Spot Mediation in a Public Housing Project," in Deborah M. Kolb and Associates, *When Talk Works: Profiles of Mediators* (San Francisco, CA: Jossey-Bass, 1994) 395 at 397.

29 M.S. Umbreit, *Mediating Interpersonal Conflicts: A Pathway to Peace* (West Concord, MN: CPI Publishing, 1995) at 4.

background. No culture is characterized by one specific conflict style that all its members exhibit. Some scholars, like Bernard S. Mayer, believe that cultures may be described in terms of predominant approaches to conflict – for example, tendencies to avoid or engage.[30] Also, whether a cultural group can be said to be more collectivistic or individualistic can have an impact on behaviour in conflict and in the mediation chamber.[31] What mediators know is that culture is important and disputes are rarely about only one thing. Mediators working in legal settings, the focus of this book, know that the law is not necessarily the only thing at issue between disputing parties. History, money, culture and a host of other things can be equally important. Mediators recognize this in a way that lawyers typically do not.

Mediation and culture do not exist separately from one another. Paraphrasing Lawrence Friedman, there is more explanatory power, more richness, more bite in exploring the connections between mediation and culture than in treating mediation as an isolated domain.[32] However, to date, mediation scholarship on culture has focused on national culture, cultural sensitivity and tips on how to mediate cross-culturally. Mediation scholars have not examined popular culture. This is a significant omission given the prevalence of popular culture media and its enormous influence around the world. In this book I explicitly engage with popular culture, something that has not been done before.

Law and popular culture scholars are very interested in depictions of lawyers and legal processes in popular culture. But that is where their understanding of "law" stops. Despite the reality that the vast majority of all legal cases settle, even in the very litigious United States, the almost exclusive focus of law and popular culture scholarship has been on the trial and the lawyer. I reject this narrow conception of law and include dispute resolution and the mediator. This book therefore links two fields and broadens the subjects of study in both. Mediation is widened to include popular culture, not just national culture, and cultural legal studies is extended to include mediation, not just litigation. The relationship between law and popular culture strengthens the law, it does not undermine the law.[33] Likewise, thinking about mediation and popular culture together strengthens mediation.

Thus the culture this book concerns itself with is popular visual culture, specifically television and films made for entertainment and commercial purposes. Films and TV shows are social artefacts, texts and examples of culture that reflect, reproduce and create meaning. Popular culture matters. It is pervasive, unavoidable and interesting.

30 Bernard S. Mayer, *The Dynamics of Conflict Resolution: A Practitioner's Guide* (San Francisco, CA: Jossey-Bass, 2000).

31 Collectivist cultures value the group over the individual and emphasize the importance of harmonious relationships within the group. Conflict is viewed as a social failure. Individualist cultures value the individual over the group and prize independence. Conflict is inevitable on the road to individual success, which is the ultimate goal.

32 L.M. Friedman, "Law, Lawyers, and Popular Culture" (1988–89) 98 *Yale Law Journal* 1579 at 1582.

33 Naomi Mezey, "Law's Visual Afterlife: Violence, Popular Culture, and Translation Theory," in Austin Sarat, ed., *Imagining Legality: Where Law Meets Popular Culture* (Tuscaloosa, AL: The University of Alabama Press, 2011) at 87.

For diverse, young mediation students – whether in Canada, the USA, the UK, Australia, Europe, Africa or Asia – popular culture may be their shared culture. Neal Feigenson notes that movies and television provide the opportunity to be more integrated with fellow members of our shared culture.[34] They invoke membership in a common popular culture because we all – students and disputants alike – intuitively understand the conventions of television and movie storytelling.[35]

American, Israeli, Australian and Canadian scholars agree that popular culture contains jurisprudence. Anthony Chase suggests a cinematic jurisprudence whereby we look at law through the lens of the cinema and see an alternative view of legality.[36] Jessica Silbey notes that TV shows and films about law can shape our expectations of justice by persuading us of a particular view.[37] Orit Kamir notes that one of the fundamental premises of a study of law and film is that some films contain jurisprudence.[38] Alison Z. Young says that "cinema is jurisprudence"[39] and so does William P. MacNeil, including television as well.[40] Rebecca Johnson writes that "film and TV not only represent the world, but participate in the making of that world."[41] Here, when I write about television and film's depictions of mediation, I further this process of world-making. You, as reader, engage in it with me, and we begin to develop mediation jurisprudence together. This is vital because, as Austin Sarat states, "mass-mediated images are as powerful, pervasive, and important as are other early twenty-first-century social forces – for example, globalization, neocolonialism, and human rights – in shaping and transforming legal life."[42]

Thus, for many students and disputants, television, film and other forms of popular culture teach them what they think they know about law. Americans Michael Asimow and Shannon Mader note: "Most people learn most of what they

34 Neal Feigenson, "The Visual in Law: Some Problems for Legal Theory" (2011) *Law, Culture and the Humanities* 1 at 7, http://ssrn.com/abstract=2145585

35 Richard K. Sherwin, "Law in the Digital Age: How Visual Communication Technologies are Transforming the Practice, Theory, and Teaching of Law" (2006) 12 *Boston University Journal of Science and Technology Law* 227 at 250.

36 Anthony Chase, *Movies on Trial: The Legal System on the Silver Screen* (New York: New Press, 2002) at xiii.

37 Jessica Silbey, "Images in/of Law" (2012–13) 57 *New York Law School Law Review* 171 at 177–178.

38 Orit Kamir, "Cinematic Judgment and Jurisprudence: A Woman's Memory, Recovery and Justice in a Post-Traumatic Society (A Study of Polanski's *Death and the Maiden*)," in A. Sarat, L. Douglas & M. Merrill Umphrey, eds, *Law on the Screen* (Stanford, CA: Stanford University Press, 2005) at 29.

39 Alison Young, "Murder in the Eyes of the Law" (1997) 17 *Studies in Law, Politics and Society* 31 at 31.

40 William P. MacNeil, *Lex Populi: The Jurisprudence of Popular Culture* (Stanford, CA: Stanford University Press, 2007).

41 Rebecca Johnson, "Television, Pleasure and the Empire of Force: Interrogating Law and Affect in *Deadwood*," in Peter Robson & Jessica Silbey, eds, *Law and Justice on the Small Screen* (Oxford: Hart, 2012) at 37.

42 Austin Sarat, "What Popular Culture Does For, and To, Law," in Austin Sarat, ed., *Imagining Legality: Where Law Meets Popular Culture* (Tuscaloosa, AL: The University of Alabama Press, 2011) at 1.

think they know about law and lawyers from consuming popular legal culture."[43] Australian researchers have found that parties' perceptions of the law play an important role in framing their expectations, and their perceptions are primarily based on informal sources, not professional legal advice.[44] Many Canadian students, clients and disputants believe that law is what they see demonstrated on American legal television programmes and films. They see lawyers in fancy suits walking around courtrooms, talking to "your honour" about Miranda rights. Canadians are amazed to discover that Miranda rights do not exist in Canada, and that our lawyers must wear black legal robes over their suits, stand still, and address the judge as "my lady" or "my lord." However, using popular culture in the classroom is not just about pointing out when TV shows portray law or mediation inaccurately. David Black has written about the tendency of lawyers, when watching legal films, to conduct processes of forensic criticism,[45] and then to stop their analyses there. In other words, some legal academics who write about law as depicted in popular culture only write about what popular culture gets wrong. I agree with Black that this is not especially interesting, given that we know that visual media must exaggerate stories about law and mediation in order to appeal to viewing audiences and to sell commercial products. If movies and TV shows about mediation were actually accurate – demonstrating polite, non-adversarial conflict resolution – viewers would be bored, so all popular culture visual media storylines must be "juiced up" with drama and conflict. Once we move beyond the idea of merely criticizing popular culture for mediation inaccuracies we can mine it for the new ideas and questions it suggests.

German scholars Stefan Machura and Michael Böhnke state that there are at least three effects of legally themed popular culture.[46] First, it familiarizes us with the legal systems of other countries – predominantly the American court system. Second, it enjoins viewers to put their trust in legal authority. Finally, it heralds social change; for example, by portraying more ethnically diverse law firms than actually exist in reality. Does mediation-themed popular culture do the same thing? What kind of mediation popular culture is available? There is surprisingly little mediation on TV or in film, despite mediation's popularity as a dispute resolution process. Although scholars, lawyers and judges agree that mediation is the future of legal practice,[47] mediators and mediative processes are seldom portrayed in popular culture. One of my students

43 Michael Asimow & Shannon Mader, *Law and Popular Culture: A Course Book* (New York: Peter Lang, 2004) at 7.

44 R. Crowe, R. Field, L. Toohey, H. Partridge & L. McAllister, "Bargaining in the Shadow of the Folk Law: Expanding the Concept of the Shadow of the Law in Family Dispute Resolution" (2018) 40 *Sydney Law Review* 319 at 322.

45 D. Black, *Law in Film: Resonance and Representation* (Urbana and Chicago, IL: University of Illinois Press, 1999) at 126 and 145.

46 Stefan Machura & Michael Böhnke (2018) "The Legal System in German Popular Culture," in Nicole Rafter et al., eds, *Oxford Encyclopedia of Crime, Media, and Popular Culture* (New York: Oxford University Press) at 451–468.

47 Julie Macfarlane, *The New Lawyer: How Settlement is Transforming the Practice of Law*, 2nd edn (Vancouver: University of British Columbia Press, 2008) and R.H. Mnookin, S. Peppet & A. Tulumello, *Beyond Winning: Negotiating to Create Value in Deals and Disputes* (Cambridge, MA: Harvard University Press, 2000).

asked: "Do so few people know about alternatives to the judicial system (such as mediation), or want to take advantage of them, because they are so rarely depicted in an obvious way in popular culture?"[48] As scholars, we need to take this question seriously. I know about mediation because I have personal experience as a co-mediator, mediator, mediation trainer, university professor and mediation disputant. I am also very familiar with mediation research, have authored publications and frequently attend and speak at conferences. However, what about the public? What about students? Where can they get mediation information? Popular culture is one answer because television and film are very accessible. The shows and movies that millions of people watch have cultural import, provide information about dispute resolution and can be used as teaching tools.

Popular culture can help us understand mediation differently from the way we understand it in law school. We can study movies and television shows, as well as cases and codes of mediator conduct, in order to find out more about mediation. Just as no one would say a city's road map provides the entire picture of that city, so too codes, regulations and textbooks do not provide the entire picture of mediation.[49] In watching a film or a TV show, we see, hear, feel and experience mediation differently than when we read a textbook or attend a lecture. Therefore in this book I look to TV and movies as unique places to fill in the gaps and to gain a fuller understanding of mediation. All the films and TV shows studied in this book:

i are fictitious narratives;
ii depict mediative processes as defined by Fuller and Moore;
iii contain at least one character in a mediative role; and
iv showcase interpersonal as opposed to international conflict.

I found five American television shows, *Fairly Legal, The Good Wife, The Office, Orange is the New Black* and *Star Trek: The Next Generation* and one American film, *Wedding Crashers*, that meet all of these criteria – namely fictional movies and TV shows including a character expressly identified as a mediator, who mediates interpersonal conflict according to Fuller and Moore's definitions. I also found one Australian film, *Face to Face*. Almost all of these television shows have won Emmy awards, the American film won a People's Choice Award, and the Australian film won Best Dramatic Feature at the 2012 Byron Bay International Film Festival. While winning awards does not guarantee viewership, it definitely increases the chances that audiences will watch, or have watched, the show or film, thereby providing more shared popular culture mediation reference points.

Additionally, there are popular culture characters who perform mediative roles although they are not expressly called mediators. These characters help disputants identify and evaluate their interests and options and design their own agreements. So, for example, many teachers, counsellors, members of the clergy, parents and

48 Student comment from 2017/2018 academic year.
49 John Denvir, ed., *Legal Reelism: Movies as Legal Texts* (Urbana, IL: University of Illinois Press, 1996) at xii.

lawyers in popular culture and in real life perform mediative interventions in disputes. As Deborah Kolb notes, "Everyone, in one way or another, can claim to act as a mediator at some point in time."[50] Therefore in this book I also include mediators who are third party interveners in conflict, even though they are not explicitly labelled mediators. These "mediators" come from Hollywood films such as *The Break-Up* (People's Choice Award for Jennifer Aniston) and Bollywood, such as *Bajrangi Bhaijaan* (third highest-grossing Indian film and second highest-grossing Bollywood film of all time). They also come from European films, such as *Amélie* from France (2002 European Film Award, 2002 César Award for best film in France, and the people's choice award at the Toronto International Film Festival), and China, namely *The Story of Qui Ju* (1994 National Society of Film Critics Award for best foreign language film and 44th in *Time Out's* 100 best Chinese Mainland movies). These are popular, well-watched movies that have something to say about mediation.

In 1979 Americans Robert Mnookin and Lewis Kornhauser referred to the fact that substantive law is always in the background of every mediation, exerting influence by predicting what will happen if a court decides instead of the parties in mediation. They famously deemed this "bargaining in the shadow of the law."[51] In 2018 Australian researchers Jonathan Crowe, Rachael Field, Lisa Toohey, Helen Partridge and Lynn McAllister found that popular culture forms part of the "folk law" that informs disputants' decisions in mediation.[52] The Australian research team found that while we do bargain in the shadow of the law, as Mnookin and Kornhauser said, we probably bargain more "in the shadow of the folk law," which includes more popular culture and less legal advice. Folk law is pluralistic and comprises what we hear from our friends and family, what we find online and what we watch in popular media. The researchers note that in the Australian family law context, where parties are trying to negotiate or mediate post-separation parenting, most people rely upon folk law, while professional legal advice "plays a relatively minor role."[53] Parties prefer informal folk law sources of information because they are accessible, immediate and familiar,[54] not to mention free. So most legal inquiries begin online and are followed up with

50 Deborah M. Kolb and Associates, *When Talk Works: Profiles of Mediators* (San Francisco, CA: Jossey-Bass, 1994) at 356. At 355 Kolb states:

> In ongoing situations of conflict and dispute, people get involved and try to help parties deal with their differences. These people are mediating, even though they do not necessarily align themselves with the profession. … this part of the field [is] important because it represent[s] probably the most extensive application of mediation. While these informal practitioners might lack the training and professional experience of the other two groups, they may have more of an impact.

51 Robert H. Mnookin & Lewis Kornhauser, "Bargaining in the Shadow of the Law: The Case of Divorce" (1979) 88:5 *Yale Law Journal* 950.

52 J. Crowe, R. Field, L. Toohey, H. Partridge & L. McAllister, "Bargaining in the Shadow of the Folk Law: Expanding the Concept of the Shadow of the Law in Family Dispute Resolution" (2018) 40 *Sydney Law Review* 319.

53 Ibid., at 322.

54 Ibid., at 330.

conversations with friends and family or counsellors and clergy members. All the while, news reports, popular media and TV further inform parties involved in legal disputes. The 2018 Australian research demonstrates that legal advice is "merely one source among others"[55] that parties rely upon. The researchers conclude that: "The law that people follow in their everyday lives bears more resemblance to what we call the folk law than to the positive law found in statutes and cases."[56] If the researchers are correct, that means popular culture visions of mediation, such as those found in the shows and movies listed above, could have more influence on disputants than mediation texts and manuals.

Clearly a TV show or movie cannot stand in the place of a mediation training manual or a mediation course, as obviously they are designed and created for different purposes. However, TV shows and films can be used as illuminating case studies through which to more fully understand mediation, and that is the use to which I put them in this book. Popular culture media have pedagogical insights to offer and these insights are especially salient in the mediation classrooms of today, where visual learners come to class with laptops and iPhones, and have multiple screens, images, conversations and tweets going while taking notes at the same time. Using television and film in mediation classrooms around the world just makes sense. Indeed, the United Nations Educational, Scientific and Cultural Organization (UNESCO) states, "empowerment of people through information and media literacy is an important prerequisite for fostering equitable access to information and knowledge, and building inclusive knowledge societies."[57] Therefore, law and mediation students should be media literate. According to Marin Dell, students must be educated not only in critical thinking but also in media literacy. Lawyers and mediators must be able to think critically about the ways the media and popular culture communicate to clients and how that shapes our societies.[58] Dell argues that the American Bar Association's requirement that law students be taught critical-thinking skills should also encompass media literacy education. In the current American climate of fake news and alternative facts, lawyers – who deal in truth, lies, facts and the search for justice – need to be popular-culture literate. Katherine Kruse outlines six steps to lawyering as problem solvers: problem identification; gathering and evaluating information and raw materials; solution-generation; solution-evaluation; decision; and action.[59] Dell takes Kruse's steps and notes that "media literacy skills are a necessary part of gathering and evaluating information and raw materials effectively and are currently a missing part of

55 Ibid., at 333.
56 Ibid., at 337.
57 "What is Media Literacy" 1 *Media Literacy Now*, https://medialiteracynow.org/what-ismedia-literacy/ and www.unesco.org/new/fileadmin/MULTIMEDIA/HQ/CI/CI/pdf/media_and_information_literacy_curriculum_for_teachers_en.pdf
58 Marin Dell, "Fake News, Alternative Facts, and Disinformation: The Importance of Teaching Media Literacy to Law Students" (November 5, 2018), https://ssrn.com/abstract=3002720 at 7–9.
59 Katherine Kruse, "Biting Off What They Can Chew: Strategies for Involving Law Students in Problem-Solving Beyond Individual Client Representations" (2002) 8 *Clinical Law Review* 405 at 407.

legal education."[60] Putting media literacy together with mediation instruction makes further sense for visual learners who are often millennials (those born between 1980 and 1995). Shawna Benston and Brian Farkas argue that mediation appeals to many millennials' financial risk-aversion and interdisciplinary educations.[61] In mediation there is rarely a "scary," all-or-nothing financial result, and non-legal and extra-legal information is welcomed. Therefore mediation is attractive to risk-averse and interdisciplinary-educated millennials, especially when they are also technologically interconnected and thus well exposed to cross-cultural and international differences, as such exposure lowers the barriers to collaborative conflict resolution.[62]

When using mediation from popular culture in the classroom, meanings have to be made. John Storey, like many others, notes that meaning is always in process.[63] My interpretation of the mediation shows and movies discussed in this book are only mine. You will have your own. As Marcel Danesi notes: "Signs never really tell the whole truth. They mediate reality for us, because they necessarily constitute convenient selections from the infinite realm of the knowable. … The representation of anything is, thus, a mediational process."[64] Movies and TV shows mediate meanings, mediators and audiences in any number of ways. Throughout this book I draw on research findings, popular culture examples, stories from my own mediation practice and students' comments. Such a multifaceted approach provides richer insights and comports with new paradigms for writing on conflict resolution that integrate theory, research, practice and teaching, as advocated by Noam Ebner and Jennifer Parlamis.[65] I also pay attention to gender.

Writers in the dispute resolution field typically write separate chapters on gender and culture. I have not done that because gender and culture cannot be separated out; they permeate everything. The culture this book concerns itself with is popular culture. The gender this book concerns itself with is the female gender. The mediators I have studied in television and film are often women and the mediation sessions I am most familiar with are the ones in which I served as mediator, and I am a woman. (Having said that, most of the mediators who are actually making a really good living mediating are men. Women's disproportional representation in popular culture as mediators makes sense vis à vis the portrayal of men as lawyers, but not with respect to the actuality of women in lucrative private mediation

60 Marin Dell, "Fake News, Alternative Facts, and Disinformation: The Importance of Teaching Media Literacy to Law Students" (November 5, 2018), https://ssrn.com/abstract=3002720 at 55.

61 Shawna Benston & Brian Farkas, "Mediation and Millennials: A Dispute Resolution Mechanism to Match a New Generation" (2018) 2 *Journal of Experiential Learning* 166 at 171.

62 Ibid., at 174–175.

63 John Storey, *Cultural Theory and Popular Culture*, 3rd edn (Harlow: Pearson Education Limited, 2001) at 71.

64 Marcel Danesi, *Understanding Media Semiotics* (London: Arnold, 2002) at 17; emphasis added.

65 Noam Ebner & Jennifer Parlamis, "Weaving Together Theory, Research, Practice and Teaching: A Four-Dimensional Approach to Negotiation and Conflict Management Work" (2017) 10:4 *Negotiation and Conflict Management Research* 245.

practice.) Most of the female mediators depicted in popular culture are white, able-bodied, educated and heterosexual. I acknowledge this at the outset because it is important to be clear that the gender discussed in this book is female, yet not inclusive of all women. David Black notes that "the least robustly documented and least confidently asserted area of influence and connection – is the matter of the influence of representations of women lawyers on the public and the profession."[66] Likewise, there is no way to really know what influence, if any, Kate Reed, North America's first TV mediator protagonist (on the now off-the-air primetime American dramedy *Fairly Legal*) had on the public and on mediators, but I do note that she was a woman. Due to the proliferation of male lawyer images in popular culture, and sexism in society in general, the image of a "lawyer" that first pops into most people's minds is of a male lawyer. While reading this book it is perfectly fine with me if readers immediately think of a female mediator – however she may look to them.

When employing my popular-culture examples I follow Naomi Mezey and Cassandra Sharp's approaches, which focus on ethnographic method. Mezey's method requires us to interpret law in cultural terms using anthropology's ethnographic method of thick description, as does Sharp's, which recommends ethnographic approaches in order to put qualitative understandings of cultural activities such as mediation in context.[67] I will do some of that here, on occasion thickly describing television shows and films, with a view to understanding mediation better. A true ethnographic approach for an entire television series spanning many years is beyond the scope of this book, but thick description does work. As Neal Feigenson says, "all of this matters not just ethnographically but jurisprudentially."[68] I have spent countless hours researching, reflecting, writing and watching movies and television shows. I watch at home, which means I can pause at any time to facilitate note-taking and dialogue-transcription. My method is neither scientific nor a coding process, but rather a drawing out of themes, images and ideas. As in all ethnographically inspired work, the influence of one's self on descriptive and interpretive processes must be acknowledged. Like a legal anthropologist I am a participant-observer of mediation in popular culture, but I must be clear that in this book I write about the things that interest me most.

The American Bar Association Section on Dispute Resolution's 2017 Task Force on Research on Mediation Techniques stressed the importance of strengthening the links between researchers and mediators.[69] As both a researcher and a mediator I

66 D. Black, *Law in Film: Resonance and Representation* (Urbana and Chicago, IL: University of Illinois Press, 1999) at 118.

67 Cassandra Sharp, "Let's See How Far We've Come: The Role of Empirical Methodology in Exploring Television Audiences," in Peter Robson & Jessica Silbey, eds, *Law and Justice on the Small Screen* (Oxford: Hart, 2012) at 121.

68 Neal Feigenson, "The Visual in Law: Some Problems for Legal Theory" (2011) *Law, Culture and the Humanities* 1 at 8, http://ssrn.com/abstract=2145585

69 Task Force on Research on Mediation Techniques, commissioned by the ABA Section of Dispute Resolution (June 12, 2017), www.americanbar.org/groups/dispute_resolution.html

know books like this one are only a first step. Researchers must do more to include the insights of practitioners, and mediators must disseminate what they do and have learned from practice. We must collaborate. My first example of mediation in popular culture comes from the People's Republic of China, where there is governmental and cultural collaboration with respect to mediation. The government actively promotes the traditional Chinese cultural ideal of mediation rather than adversarial litigation, as demonstrated by 2010's *People's Mediation Law*. Chinese TV producers promote the governmental goal of harmony through reality TV mediation shows, which are currently very popular on Chinese primetime television. Chinese reality TV mediation shows first appeared in 2008. By 2011 there were 38 mediation shows broadcast by 34 local TV stations and four provincial satellite networks. Most of them deal with interpersonal and neighbourhood disputes in local communities, are broadcast daily, given primetime slots right before or after the national evening news, and are often repeated during the day.[70] Colin S. Hawes and Shuyu Kong describe the Chinese mediation shows as "a kind of Oprah Show meets Judge Judy with Chinese characteristics."[71] Hawes and Kong believe the shows' popularity has to do with the demands of official censors for TV programming that promotes a harmonious society, and the requirement for courts to publicly demonstrate their support for mediation as the most appropriate method for resolving interpersonal and neighbourhood disputes.[72] These shows comply with government censors' demands to promote harmony while also broadly appealing to TV viewers. Hawes and Kong believe that TV mediation shows can help educate viewers about the benefits and drawbacks of mediation:

> It is true that these shows combine some of the negative features of [Laura Nader's] "harmony ideology," such as a heavy focus on social stability and propaganda ... but ... they can act as an important educational tool to remind viewers that litigation may not always be the best or most cost-effective method to resolve their disputes.[73]

Mediation forums have actually been set up for Chinese citizens as real-life spinoffs from reality TV shows.[74] They are called mediation studios and they have full-time staff mediators and law firms on retainer to provide legal advice when necessary. Popular culture has a direct and real effect on mediation in China and it could in other countries too.

In the next chapters of this book I focus on important matters in mediation: impartiality, self-determination and fair outcomes; feelings and expert intuition; conflicts of interest and repeat business; deception and caucusing; and mediator

70 Colin S. Hawes & Shuyu Kong, "Primetime Dispute Resolution: Reality TV Mediation Shows in China's 'Harmonious Society'" (2013) 47 *Law & Society Review* 739 at 759.
71 Ibid., at 764–765.
72 Ibid.
73 Ibid., at 742.
74 Ibid., at 765.

identity. I use popular culture examples wherever possible. Whether you are a lawyer, mediator, educator, researcher or student you will find some of my TV and film examples good (for example, seeing disputant relationships transformed) and some bad (such as mediators who engage in deception), but all will be interesting. Using popular culture to think about mediation will open up space to consider tensions in our field and discuss them in an accessible way, learning things about ourselves along the way.

2 Impartiality, self-determination and fair outcomes

Popular culture: *Fairly Legal* (TV show, USA) and *Amélie* (film, France)
Research from: Australia, Canada, France, India, Israel, Japan, New Zealand, South Africa, UK and USA

Impartiality

Conflict resolution literature states that mediators should be neutral, impartial and unbiased.[1] The idea that mediators will operate neutrally is a cornerstone of conflict resolution theory. Hilary Astor argues that mediation gains its legitimacy not from law but from mediator neutrality and the parties' consensual decision-making.[2] North America's largest conflict resolution organization, the Association for Conflict Resolution, has Model Standards of Conduct for Mediators that outline proper mediation behaviour. Standard II refers to impartiality and states:

> The concept of mediator impartiality is central to the mediation process. A mediator shall mediate only those matters in which she or he can remain impartial and even-handed. If at any time the mediator is unable to conduct the process in an impartial manner, the mediator is obligated to withdraw.[3]

So when mediation scholars write that mediators should be neutral, and when mediators introduce themselves to disputants saying they are neutral, they mean they are impartial, unbiased and non-partisan. They have no financial interest in the matter in dispute, no personal connection, no prior knowledge of the dispute or the disputants and no conflicts of interest. They also mean they will provide process equality so that nothing in their mediation process favours one party over the other.

Although mediation literature focuses on the term "neutrality," I prefer "impartiality." Neutrality suggests remaining above the fray or staying out of

1 See for example: C. Morris, "The Trusted Mediator," in J. Macfarlane, ed., *Rethinking Disputes: The Mediation Alternative* (Toronto: Emond Montgomery, 1997); A. Taylor, "Concepts of Neutrality in Family Mediation" (1997) 14 *Mediation Quarterly* 215; and J. Rifkin, J. Millen & S. Cobb, "Toward a New Discourse for Mediation" (1991) 9 *Mediation Quarterly* 151.
2 Hilary Astor, "Mediator Neutrality: Making Sense of Theory and Practice" (July 2007) 07/46 Legal Studies Research Paper, http://ssrn.com/abstract=998202 at 3.
3 Association of Conflict Resolution, *Model Standards of Conduct for Mediators*, http://acrnet.org/about/initiatives/QualityAssurance/standards-conduct.htm

things, which mediators do not do. Impartiality, to my mind, means not unfairly favouring one party over another, which mediators should do. Rick Russell argues that "impartial" is the better term because it focuses on how mediators intervene, as opposed to whether or not they should. Importantly, impartiality is not a goal in and of itself. It is a tool that mediators promise to use in their interventions.[4] Russell states that: "Impartiality means treating all equally in the sense of offering each party what we believe they need to arrive at an informed decision about settlement. It does not mean treating the parties identically."[5]

Mediators also need to ensure they can maintain impartiality with respect to the disputants' personal characteristics, backgrounds, beliefs and performance in the mediation session.[6] It can be hard when the mediator believes she has a legal, moral, ethical, religious or conscientious duty to act in a way that is inconsistent with the interests of one of the disputants.[7] Ellen Waldman poses the question well: "Can I approach each party with equal openness, curiosity, and respect?"[8] If the mediator is concerned that maybe she cannot, she must so disclose. A study by Christine Rack raises concerns about mediators operating with "insider bias" and "Anglo-protective" behaviours that could put minority disputants at a disadvantage[9] by favouring disputants from the mediator's in-group and devaluing the stories of disputants from out-groups. Carol Izumi notes that disputants from out-groups that are "foreign" can more easily be conceptualized as the enemy and therefore be less credible to certain mediators.[10] Gary LaFree and Rack demonstrate "the strongest evidence of ethnic and gender disparity in the treatment of minority claimants in mediation,"[11] and Izumi also alerts mediators to be aware of accent discrimination.[12] Mediators concerned about their ability to remain impartial should:

- be self-aware, self-conscious and self-monitoring;
- learn how our own perspectives situate us and impact us;
- show empathy and be respectful; switch judgment to curiosity;

4 Rick Russell, "The Principle of Impartiality: Is it relevant to dispute resolution practitioners?" (2019) 27:2 *Canadian Arbitration and Mediation Journal* 9 at 10.
5 Ibid., at 12.
6 Model Standards of Conduct for Mediators, II(B)(1).
7 Omer Shapira, *A Theory of Mediators' Ethics: Foundation, Rationale, and Application* (Cambridge: Cambridge University Press, 2016) at 189.
8 Ellen Waldman, ed., *Mediation Ethics: Cases and Commentaries* (San Francisco, CA: Jossey-Bass, 2011) at 297–298.
9 Christine Rack, "Negotiated Justice: Gender & Ethnic Minority Bargaining Patterns in the MetroCourt Study" (1999) 20 *The Mitchell Hamline Law Journal of Public Policy and Practice* 211 at 273.
10 Carol Izumi, "Implicit Bias and the Illusion of Mediator Neutrality" (2010) 34 *Journal of Law and Policy* 71 at 118–119.
11 Gary LaFree & Christine Rack, "The Effects of Participants' Ethnicity and Gender on Monetary Outcomes in Mediated and Adjudicated Civil Cases" (1996) 30 *Law and Society Review* 767 at 789.
12 Carol Izumi, "Implicit Bias and the Illusion of Mediator Neutrality" (2010) 34 *Journal of Law and Policy* 71 at 120.

- know our own biases and assumptions – they can be unconscious, implicit or explicit;
- be aware that the first story heard can colour mediators' views, and our own stories have impact too;
- remember that the closer we are to the dominant culture the harder it is to see others' perspectives, because the dominant culture's views present as normalcy;
- increase our exposure to people different from ourselves;
- increase mediator diversity;
- accept that we have influence and police ourselves for essentialist assumptions;
- terminate the mediation if we know we cannot combat our personal views/biases;
- attend anti-bias or anti-prejudice mediation training programmes;
- debrief, reflect and provide constructive feedback to one another.

The reality is, of course, that no one is completely impartial. Izumi states that "the veneer of neutrality is stripped away by research findings that show convincingly that mediators fall far short of the ethical duty to treat parties impartially and without bias."[13] Sara Cobb and Janet Rifkin, Linda Mulcahy and Hilary Astor have all shown that neutrality in mediation is a rhetorical device that obscures the operation of power.[14] In this chapter I delve into three crucial mediation matters – impartiality, party self-determination and fair outcomes – illustrating and examining them using popular culture examples. The now off-the-air American TV dramedy *Fairly Legal* allows us to consider the tensions between balancing our duty to practise impartially and ensuring disputants make their own decisions. The 2001 French film *Amélie* reminds us that, as mediators, we may also have to consider what is fair and decide whether or not we have a duty to ensure fair settlements. Both of these popular culture examples feature a white, able-bodied, heterosexual woman in the role of mediator. That is not an accident. As Jocelyn Turnbull and I have argued, mediation is gendered. Mediation is primarily gendered female and litigation is primarily gendered male, and, as a result of its female gendering, mediation is often devalued as "soft law" or "law-lite" as compared to hard, tough, "manly" litigation in North America.[15] However, we will see that trying to mediate impartially, enhancing party self-determination and facilitating fair outcomes is hard work indeed.

Fairly Legal was the first American primetime television series focused on mediation to air in North America. The show debuted on January 20, 2010, and the final episode aired on June 15, 2012. The series told the story of a Caucasian

13 Ibid., at 155.

14 Sara Cobb & Janet Rifkin, "Practice and Paradox: Deconstructing Neutrality in Mediation" (1991) 16 *Law and Social Inquiry* 35; Linda Mulcahy, "The Possibility and Desirability of Mediator Neutrality: Towards an Ethic of Partiality" (2001) 10 *Social and Legal Studies* 505; and Hilary Astor, "Mediator Neutrality: Making Sense of Theory and Practice" (July 2007) 07/46 Legal Studies Research Paper, http://ssrn.com/abstract=998202

15 Jennifer L. Schulz & Jocelyn Turnbull, "Mediation: The 'Girly' Litigation?" (2012) 2 *Journal of Arbitration and Mediation* 43.

woman lawyer turned mediator, Kate Reed, who mediates disputes in a decidedly non-neutral fashion. A close analysis of mediation as depicted in this TV show demonstrates the usefulness of popular culture for thinking through the important mediation issues of impartiality and party self-determination.[16] We could watch Kate mediate every week on television or now on Amazon.com whenever we like. This is one of the pleasures of serial television and binge-watching; getting to know characters and watching them grow and change: "TV in this respect is much more like 'life'."[17] Kate does not bring an overtly feminist approach to her mediations, but each episode of *Fairly Legal* portrays her as a strong, effective, likable protagonist, which in and of itself sends a powerful message about women mediators. In early episodes of *Fairly Legal* Kate reveals some of her thoughts about mediation, which resonate with how we teach mediation: "The advantage of mediation is you can all avoid a long and costly trip to court. But, in order for mediation to work, we have to be open and honest."[18] Kate also says, "Mediations can be a little bit squishy. You get a grip on one end and then they just squish out on the other."[19] This reflects the reality of mediation practice.

Each episode of *Fairly Legal* begins in roughly the same way. Kate engages in an impromptu "mediation" session and resolves it, before the "real" mediation of the episode is revealed. This serves to demonstrate Kate's mediation prowess and to show viewers how quickly she can "think on her feet." As Robert D. Benjamin notes, "A mediator, by definition, must have a high tolerance for ambiguity and be capable of operating less formally and often in the middle of great confusion."[20] Kate does this very well in the chaotic opening mediation sequences. Then, later in the show, when the more complicated, planned or assigned mediation is depicted, viewers are primed to root for Kate, whom they assume to be competent based on her earlier success in the impromptu mediation. The assigned, planned or court-connected mediations Kate facilitates range over a wide legal terrain – family, environmental and commercial law. Indeed, her wide-ranging mediation repertoire provides some support for those who argue that the skill set of being a good mediator is more important than subject matter expertise.[21]

While Kate's impromptu mediations are informal, and traditional mediation training stresses the informality of the process as compared to litigation, in reality most mediators operate in fairly structured, inflexible ways, in mediation

16 David Sutton, "*Arrival*: Anthropology in Hollywood" (February 2018) 34:1 *Anthropology Today* 7, suggests that a careful parsing of the anthropological concepts in the film *Arrival* provides ideas about the usefulness of popular culture for thinking through contemporary anthropological issues and conveying them to a wider audience.

17 Rebecca Johnson, "Television, Pleasure and the Empire of Force: Interrogating Law and Affect in *Deadwood*," in Peter Robson & Jessica Silbey, eds, *Law and Justice on the Small Screen* (Oxford: Hart, 2012) at 45.

18 Episode 105, "The Two Richards."

19 Ibid.

20 Robert D. Benjamin, "The Mediator as Trickster: The Folkloric Figure as Professional Role Model" (1995) 13:2 *Conflict Resolution Quarterly* 131 at 133.

21 Michael P. Carbone, "The Unimportance of Subject Matter Expertise" (November 2009), www.mediate.com/mobile/article.cfm?id=5403

chambers, with signed terms of mediation and articulated ground rules. Kate does too. After each informal opening sequence she mediates, pursuant to contract and often at the behest of a judge, in the boardroom of her law firm. In the pilot episode, for example, Judge Nicastro assigns a case to Kate to mediate. As the judge assigns the case to Kate, he says to her, "A mediator is a referee in a game with no rules except for the ones the parties make themselves." This is true. However, then he gives Kate only one day to find a resolution, which requires her to breach many mediation tenets in order to do so. So, instead of speaking respectfully to disputants to ask them to remain quiet, Kate whistles and shouts at them. Although Kate appears to understand what mediation is, and says things such as "lawyers burn bridges – mediators build them," she does things mediation scholars would not approve of. Chief among them is her lack of neutrality and the way she takes self-determination away from her disputants.

In "Believers" (Season 1, Episode 6) Kate demonstrates her lack of neutrality and her penchant for acting more like an advocate than a mediator. She is hired to mediate a wrongful dismissal case between a computer prototype designer named Marcus and Marsden Technologies, the corporation that fired him. During the mediation session Kate dismantles the prototype Marcus designed for Marsden and puts all the pieces in an envelope. Then, each time Marsden agrees to a termination clause that Kate either suggests or deems fair, she hands Marsden one piece of the prototype. This approach demonstrates without a shadow of a doubt that Kate is not neutral. She is totally and completely on Marcus' side. Kate is not an unassuming, neutral third party. She is the star of the mediation show. She actively engineers a process of resolution that gets Marcus a favourable deal and results in an agreement with Marsden Technologies. The mediation is about her and her control over the outcome. Later, when Marsden's engineers reassemble the prototype and discover that it does not work, Kate steps in and advocates on Marcus' behalf, convincing Marsden Technologies to rehire him so that he can take the bugs out of his own invention. Thus, throughout the episode Kate appears more like Marcus' lawyer or advocate, not an impartial mediator.[22] This is well represented in a promotional image for the show (see Figure 2.1). Kate the mediator is pictured alone, as the star, with no human disputants to consider. Instead she smiles as she alone controls small, mute lawyer figures, ready to topple them at any moment.

Mediators might rightly be appalled by Kate's behaviour, but we must remember there are many examples of mediators from anthropological and historical records who were chosen as mediators precisely for the perspective they could bring to the dispute. These mediators – usually respected, often elder, members of the community – were not necessarily neutral in their mediation work, and in fact were usually chosen specifically so they could opine on the conflict. Dean G. Pruitt et al. noted in 1989 that "powerful mediators are quite common in many settings … they also tend

22 See discussion in Jennifer L. Schulz, "Fairly Legal: A Canadian Perspective on the Creation of a Primetime Mediator," in M. Asimow, K. Brown & D.R. Papke, eds, *Law and Popular Culture: International Perspectives* (Newcastle Upon Tyne: Cambridge Scholars Publishing, 2014) 43 at 47.

Figure 2.1 Sarah Shahi as Kate Reed in *Fairly Legal*

to be powerful in many non-Western societies. … [and] there is evidence from the international arena … that more powerful mediators are more popular and more successful."[23] For example, article 22 of *The People's Mediation Law* of the People's Republic of China states that mediators may adopt various means to mediate disputes, including explaining the relevant laws, regulations and state policies, patiently persuading the parties, and proposing solutions.[24] In Japan the mediator may, at any stage of the proceedings, make proposals for settlement.[25] India and South Africa have both adopted the International Mediation Institute's Code of Conduct. As such, in both countries the existence of circumstances potentially affecting, or appearing to affect, a mediator's impartiality will not automatically imply unfitness to act as a mediator, provided these circumstances have been fully disclosed and addressed to the satisfaction of the parties.[26] According to J.G. Merrills, while neutrality is important in international mediation, acceptability of a mediator does not hinge on neutrality. It can just as likely depend on what a mediator can offer.[27] Our insistence upon neutral mediators is a modern-day, Anglo-American, legally inspired obsession, likely stemming from the law's purported adherence to neutrality and

23 D. Pruitt, G. Welton, W. Fry, N. McGillicuddy, L. Castrianno, C. Ippolito & J. Zubeck, "The Process of Mediation: Caucusing, Control and Problem Solving," in Rahim M. Afzalur, ed., *Managing Conflict: An Interdisciplinary Approach* (Westport, CT: Praeger, 1989) at 204.

24 www.cspil.org/Uploadfiles/attachment/Laws%20and%20Regulations/

25 Japan International Mediation Center, The Institutional Mediation Rules, www.jimc-kyoto.jp/rules

26 Indian Institute of Arbitration and Mediation's Mediation Rules, 2017, section 2.B.ii, www.arbitrationindia.com/pdf/rules_mediation.pdf and section 2.2 of Mediate Africa's Code of Professional Conduct for Mediators, www.mediateafrica.com/panellists/code-of-conduct

27 J.G. Merrills, *International Dispute Settlement*, 5th edn (Cambridge: Cambridge University Press, 2011) at 32.

objectivity. But, of course, neutrality is situated, fluctuating and contextual. Feminist and critical race scholars have shown us how the law is neither neutral nor objective. There is no reason to suspect otherwise from mediation. Benjamin states: "The mediator needs to be free to engage or challenge any party in a conflict. Neutrality is a holdover concept from the technical-rational thinking frame of traditional professionals. … At best, [mediators] strive to be balanced, not neutral."[28] Linda Ippolito notes that: "To work effectively in the world of relationships means being able to act outside, as well as inside, the rational-logical realm of traditional legal practice."[29] Kate Reed is working outside the traditional realm of legal practice and theoretical understandings of mediation, preferring instead to emulate social network mediators,[30] First Nations mediators[31] or the mediators of yore.[32]

Mediation texts, trainers, teachers and professors do not endorse advocacy as part of the mediator's role, yet popular culture validates Kate in such a role; *Fairly Legal* has viewers cheering when the mediator is partial. Rebecca Johnson asks us to try to understand "television's affect-based tools of persuasion" and realize that, if we do not question them, they can "rationalise and sustain the underlying ways of thinking, talking and imagining law."[33] In other words, if we do not interrogate pop culture's way of validating non-neutral mediation practice we may find our field changing its understanding of impartiality or falling out of step with disputants' desires. That is why Bernard S. Mayer's term "aspirational neutrality"[34] makes sense, and is the only kind of neutrality a mediator can actually promise. Mayer says:

> When I say that I am acting as a neutral third party, I mean that my goal is to help disputants have the conversation they need to have, and that I will not intentionally advocate for one person's legitimate interests at the expense of another. I will be transparent about any connection I have with the parties and any way I may stand to benefit from a particular outcome.[35]

28 Robert D. Benjamin, "The Mediator as Trickster: The Folkloric Figure as Professional Role Model" (1995) 13:2 *Conflict Resolution Quarterly* 131 at 143.
29 Linda Ippolito, "ADR has lost its 'alternative' way" (September 14, 2012) *The Lawyers Weekly*, www.lawyersweekly.ca
30 C. Picard, P. Bishop, R. Ramkay & N. Sargent, *The Art and Science of Mediation* (Toronto: Emond Montgomery, 2004) at 106.
31 R. Ross, *Returning to the Teachings: Exploring Aboriginal Justice* (Toronto: Penguin, 1996).
32 Sally Engle Merry (1984) "Anthropology and the Study of Alternative Dispute Resolution," 34 *Journal of Legal Education* 277; and Clifford Geertz, *Local Knowledge: Further Essays in Interpretive Anthropology* (New York: Basic Books, 1983).
33 Rebecca Johnson, "Television, Pleasure and the Empire of Force: Interrogating Law and Affect in *Deadwood*," in Peter Robson & Jessica Silbey, eds, *Law and Justice on the Small Screen* (Oxford: Hart, 2012) at 34.
34 Bernard S. Mayer, "What We Talk About When We Talk About Neutrality: A Commentary on the Susskind-Stulberg Debate, 2011 Edition" (Spring 2012) 95:3 *Marquette Law Review* 859.
35 Bernard S. Mayer, "Are We Ever Neutral? Should We Be?" (January 2018) *ACResolution: The Quarterly Magazine of the Association for Conflict Resolution* 19, www.acresolution-digital.org/acresolutionmag/january_2018?pg=19#pg19

We may use *Fairly Legal* as an illustrative popular culture text to interrogate our commitment to impartiality. When we do, we come to Izumi's conclusion:

> We should accept that mediator neutrality is elusive and shape-shifting; it is neither a condition nor characteristic that one possesses or lacks. It is a complex, multi-layered relationship and a system of interaction with the parties that requires constant vigilance.[36]

Greg Rooney argues that mediators should "detach from the concept of neutrality as a core element of mediation practice."[37] Aspirational theoretical constructs such as neutrality and balanced power do not really exist. They are constructs that can only be assessed once a mediation is complete. "The only assessment can be whether, in all the circumstances, the results of the process and outcome were good enough."[38] Rooney further argues that: "The mediator's presence in the room changes the dynamics in the relationship between the parties."[39] Bronwen Gray says, "neutrality is perhaps better understood as the power that the mediator can access or choose not to access at any given point during the mediation."[40] Anthropologists and ethnographers have long known that the participant-observer is always implicated in the creation of the world observed. The mediator is a participant in the mediation process and, together with the disputants, jointly creates a collective experience. This experience is more than the sum of its parts – mediator and disputants – and it is subjectively experienced differently by each one. All parties are influenced by each other. They all work together to construct the reality of the mediation chamber. Barbara Wilson argues that mediation is a group process wherein the mediator is not only involved but also serves as the leader.[41] As such, she argues, we should bring the extensive literature on leadership in group contexts into our mediation work, because understanding mediation as a group process lets us think about it in new ways. Impartiality is an aspirational goal for mediators, who know that their very presence in the room changes conflict dynamics and influences the disputants. Robert A. Baruch Bush and Joseph P. Folger state that "neutrality means that the mediator's only interest is the interest in using his or her influence to make sure the parties maintain control of decisions about outcomes."[42] In other words, that it is the mediator's job

36 Carol Izumi, "Implicit Bias and the Illusion of Mediator Neutrality" (2010) 34 *Journal of Law and Policy* 71 at 121.

37 Greg Rooney, "Rebooting Mediation by Detaching from the Illusions of Neutrality, Just Outcomes, and Balanced Power" (February 2015), www.mediate.com//articles/RooneyFutures.cfm

38 Ibid.

39 Ibid.

40 Bronwen Gray, "Mediation as a Post-Modern Practice: A Challenge to the Cornerstones of Mediation's Legitimacy" (2006) 17:4 *Australasian Dispute Resolution Journal* 208 at 216.

41 Barbara Wilson, "Leave No Footprints": On the Role of Influence in Mediation (June 13, 2017), https://ssrn.com/abstract=2985387 or http://dx.doi.org/10.2139/ssrn.2985387

42 Robert A. Baruch Bush & Joseph P. Folger, *The Promise of Mediation: The Transformative Approach to Conflict*, 2nd edn (San Francsico, CA: Jossey-Bass, 2005) at 105.

to prioritize party self-determination. In this way, impartiality and self-determination are closely linked.

Self-determination

Rachael Field argues that the pursuit of party self-determination is the foundational tenet of mediation,[43] and Bush and Folger describe self-determination as the central and supreme value of mediation.[44] Quite simply, the distinguishing feature of mediation is that the parties, not an arbitrator, not a judge, and not the mediator, make the final decisions and decide on the settlement. Classic mediation stresses a facilitative orientation or approach wherein mediators facilitate disputants' negotiations, attempting to help them reach a settlement on their own terms, based on the parties' own sense of what works for them. Christopher W. Moore underlines this by noting that the mediator has no authoritative decision-making power but, rather, assists the parties in voluntarily reaching a mutually acceptable settlement.[45] The notion of party self-determination is universally accepted in the mediation field and relates predominately to the outcome of the mediation – the disputants decide the matter, not the mediator. The self-determination of disputants is simply fundamental to mediation. It is a core principle in all mediator codes of conduct and has long been established in the mediation literature and in mediation training programmes. Self-determination is the first ethical standard listed in the American Model Standards of Conduct for Mediators[46] and is the first ethical principle listed in the ADR Institute of Canada's Code of Conduct for Mediators.[47] As Michael Moffitt notes: "A hallmark of mediation is that the mediator cannot impose terms on the parties. Instead, mediation parties retain the ultimate say on whether the settlement terms are acceptable."[48] While there may be debate within the mediation community about other aspects of mediation practice, the proposition that mediation parties are to have self-determination is universally accepted.[49] For example, in 2016–2017 the Global Pound Conference Series, in conjunction with the International Mediation Institute,

43 Rachael Field, "Proposing a System of Contextual Ethics for Mediation for a Range of Mediation Models and in Both Ad Hoc and Institutional Environments" (2017) 10 *Contemporary Asia Arbitration Journal* 293.

44 Robert A. Baruch Bush & Joseph P. Folger, "Reclaiming Mediation's Future: Re-Focusing on Party Self-Determination" (2015) 16 *Cardozo Journal of Conflict Resolution* 741 at 742.

45 Christopher W. Moore, *The Mediation Process: Practical Strategies for Resolving Conflict*, 2nd edn (San Francisco, CA: Jossey-Bass, 1996) at 15.

46 www.americanbar.org/content/dam/aba/migrated/2011_build/dispute_resolution/model_standards_conduct_april2007.pdf

47 See http://adric.ca/rules-codes/code-of-conduct/ section 3:

> Principle of self-determination: It is the right of parties to a Mediation to make their own voluntary and non-coerced decisions regarding the possible resolution of any issue in dispute. Every Mediator shall respect and encourage this fundamental principle of Mediation.

48 Michael Moffitt, "Suing Mediators" (2003) 83 *Boston University Law Review* 147 at 178.

49 Ibid., at 178 note 116.

conducted a global survey of 2,878 people – including dispute resolution professionals, counsel, educators and other individuals who derive a livelihood from the resolution of conflict – in 31 countries. Next to reducing costs and expenses, permitting parties to retain control over the outcome was viewed as the most important result of mediation.[50]

In order to control the outcome or exercise self-determination, mediation parties must have the necessary, relevant information. Omer Shapira says it is the mediator's responsibility to ensure the parties have the relevant information, otherwise party self-determination cannot be said to exist in the mediation.[51] Shapira states that three conditions must be met for the exercise of party self-determination: (i) the parties must have mental capacity to decide; (ii) the decision must be voluntary and uncoerced; and (iii) the decision must be informed and made on the basis of relevant information.[52] This means that if one party does not have proper information, the mediator cannot allow that party to settle. Therefore the mediator can help one disputant by creating the conditions in the session that allow that party to make an informed decision, thereby exercising her or his right to self-determination. We see examples of this in *Fairly Legal* when Kate provides information necessary to secure one of the disputant's ethical rights. When a disputant does not have all the information he requires to make a proper decision and exercise self-determination, Kate helps him. In real life, mediators provide this kind of help more indirectly than Kate does. While Kate makes bold, general statements in joint session, many mediators provide more directed statements in private caucus. Diane Mainville recommends comments such as: "I am noticing a pattern that may be getting in the way of you achieving your objective. Are you interested in hearing more?"[53] If the disputant says yes, the mediator provides more details. Mainville also says mediators can say things such as "I have seen many instances when using this negotiating strategy has backfired," as long as they do so in a private setting.[54] Mediators must be wise about when they provide information. If a mediator provides crucial information at the eleventh hour, tired disputants may just accept it without truly exercising self-determination. Disputants must make decisions when they have energy, and with informed consent. Julie Macfarlane notes that new lawyers, like mediators, employ decision-making processes with their clients that ensure all settlement decisions are made with informed consent.[55] Finally, Shapira reminds us that a disputant may make an informed decision to make what the mediator might think is an uniformed decision,[56] and in those situations the mediator must live with that decision.

50 Thomas J. Stipanowich (November 27, 2017), http://mediationblog.kluwerarbitration.com/2017/11/27/learned-global-pound-conferences/
51 Omer Shapira, *A Theory of Mediators' Ethics: Foundation, Rationale, and Application* (Cambridge: Cambridge University Press, 2016) at 159.
52 Ibid., at 366–367.
53 Diane Mainville, "What is Good Faith Negotiation and Mediation?" (2018) 27:1 *Canadian Arbitration and Mediation Journal* 10 at 15.
54 Ibid.
55 Julie Macfarlane, *The New Lawyer: How Clients are Transforming the Practice of Law*, 2nd edn (Vancouver: University of British Columbia Press, 2017) at 208.
56 Omer Shapira, *A Theory of Mediators' Ethics: Foundation, Rationale, and Application* (Cambridge: Cambridge University Press, 2016) at 371.

However, by helping one party make an informed decision is the mediator favouring that party? If so, has the mediator lost her impartiality? Conflicts between the disputant's right to self-determination and the mediator's duty to act impartially can easily arise. This leads to a crucial tension or balancing act in mediation: attempting to ensure both mediator impartiality and party self-determination. What is a mediator to do? I would resolve the tension on the side of party self-determination. A mediation party cannot truly exercise self-determination without full information, and thus mediators sometimes need to provide some "extra" information. If that is extra help, and therefore not strictly impartial, it does not concern me, as long as it is done mindfully and transparently. James H. Stark and Douglas N. Frenkel correctly note that, in most professional contexts, explicitness and directness are considered desirable. Many mediators, however, will not be explicit due to fears of offending party self-determination.[57] This leads to the paradoxical situation where, out of a desire to best help parties make decisions, mediators do not provide the best information, choosing vaguer statements and replies in order to "help preserve" impartiality and party self-determination. Stark and Frenkel's review of the social science literature on persuasion leads them to argue for the wisdom of directness in, for example, describing the severity of the consequences of not settling.[58] When mediators are not clear, mediation disputants may not truly perceive the seriousness of court, other interpretations of their dispute, etc. Stark and Frenkel conclude that highly suggestive rhetorical questions are not as helpful as direct statements, especially if the direct statements are detailed and substantively grounded.[59]

Once we agree that in order to facilitate party self-determination, mediators may provide information, the next obvious question is: can they also provide suggestions? Or does that encroach too much upon mediator impartiality? Some mediators make it a policy to never provide suggestions, either because they believe very strongly that they should remain neutral or because they are concerned about crossing the line over to providing legal advice. Other mediators are in favour of giving suggestions. Anecdotally I can attest to the fact that some lawyers will not hire a mediator unless the mediator provides suggestions. We need to openly acknowledge that mediators make suggestions. Mediators try to convince the parties to maintain their optimism. Mediators help the parties realize that their goals may not be achievable, highlight weaknesses and reality-test. Mediators also make "just between us" statements and suggestions in private caucus.

Mediators who openly acknowledge that they make suggestions commonly fall on the evaluative side of the mediation spectrum. Leonard Riskin first outlined the facilitative and evaluative mediator approaches and later renamed them elicitive and directive approaches.[60] (Ten years earlier Susan Silbey and Sally Engle Merry

57 James H. Stark & Douglas N. Frenkel, "Changing Minds: The Work of Mediators and Empirical Studies of Persuasion" (2013) 28 *Ohio State Journal on Dispute Resolution* 263 at 312.

58 Ibid., at 319.

59 Ibid., at 351.

60 Leonard L. Riskin, "Understanding Mediators' Orientations, Strategies and Techniques: A Grid for the Perplexed" (1996) 1 *Harvard Negotiation Law Review* 7 and,

described mediation styles as falling along a continuum between bargaining and therapy.[61]) Facilitative, integrative or elicitive mediation focuses on the mediation process itself, is future-oriented and says "law is not necessarily relevant." Evaluative, advisory or directive mediation focuses on results, what happened in the past and what a court would likely decide. Kimberlee Kovach and Lela P. Love argue that evaluative mediation is an oxymoron.[62] Evaluative mediation is not true mediation because true mediation is facilitative, and that is certainly what Canadian law professors teach their students. Common-law professors stress classic mediation, which has a facilitative orientation or style wherein mediators facilitate disputants' negotiations, attempting to help them reach a settlement on their own terms. Evaluation, argue Kovach and Love, "may be a form of third party assisted conflict resolution, but it is not a form of mediation."[63]

Deborah Kolb notes there is a difference between mediators who act as orchestrators or as dealmakers,[64] the latter working much like evaluative or directive mediators, trying hard to convince the parties to settle. David Greatbatch and Robert Dingwall's study of divorce mediators demonstrates that mediators try to make certain outcomes more likely, calling this process selective facilitation.[65] These mediators provide greater opportunities to discuss the favoured option, encourage discussion in that direction and inhibit other less-favoured conversations. Other family mediators have also noted they are more likely to use evaluative styles when they are mediating high-conflict divorces.[66] When mediators use their power in these ways not only does it limit party self-determination, it also shows that different mediators mean different things when they say they are facilitative mediators. Indeed, Cheryl Picard found that there is no agreement on the meaning of the words "evaluative" and "facilitative" amongst Canadian mediators.[67] Mediators use the words to describe their approach to their practice, yet these words mean different things to different mediators. This is borne out in New Zealand research, which shows there is a difference between the style mediators claim to use and the style(s) they actually use.[68] The authors conclude

later, Leonard L. Riskin, "Decision-making in Mediation: The New Old Grid and the New Grid System" (2003) 79 *Notre Dame Law Review* 1 at 12–13.

61 Susan S. Silbey & Sally E. Merry, "Mediator Settlement Strategies" (1986) 8:1 *Law and Policy* 7.

62 Kimberlee K. Kovach & Lela P. Love, "Evaluative Mediation is an Oxymoron" (1996) 14:3 *Alternatives to High Cost Litigation* 31.

63 Ibid.

64 Deborah M. Kolb, *The Mediators* (Cambridge, MA: MIT Press, 1983) at 25.

65 David Greatbatch & Robert Dingwall, "Selective Facilitation: Some Preliminary Observations on a Strategy Used by Divorce Mediators" (1989) 23 *Law & Society Review* 613 at 618.

66 R. Baitar, A. Buysse, R. Brondeel, J. De Mol & P. Rober, "Styles and Goals: Clarifying the Professional Identity of Divorce Mediation" (2013) 31:1 *Conflict Resolution Quarterly* 57 at 59, referencing C. Beck & B. Sales, *Family Mediation: Facts, Myths and Future Prospects* (Washington, DC: American Psychological Association, 2001).

67 Cheryl Picard, "Common Language, Different Meaning: What Mediators Mean When They Talk About Their Work" (2002) *Negotiation Journal* 251 at 261–262 and 264.

68 Grant Morris, "Eclecticism versus Purity: Mediation Styles Used in New Zealand Employment Disputes" (2015–2016) 33 *Conflict Resolution Quarterly* 203.

that mediators are mixing and matching styles and there are benefits to a directive style. As Kenneth Roberts points out, the evaluative-facilitative mediation debate is a false dichotomy[69] because most mediation involves a combination of facilitative and evaluative methods.[70]

Mediation that falls closer to the evaluative side is not necessarily bad. Kenneth Dunham notes that "directive mediation allows a mediator the freedom to assess the parties' positions and actively help parties craft settlement proposals that work, rather than awaiting creativity to strike the parties or proposing solutions the parties should accept."[71] Robert Rubinson alerts us to the importance of socio-economic factors. The vast majority of people cannot afford lawyers, and therefore they also cannot afford private mediation. This means they get court-connected mediation, which tends to be evaluative in style and extremely variable in terms of quality. Stephen B. Goldberg and Margaret L. Shaw note that the more directive type of mediation that takes place in court-connected mediation programmes is likely to increase and become even more routinized.[72] Rubinson notes:

> Evaluative mediation, however, tends to be the most efficient, and efficiency is a primary goal of court-connected mediation, even if the rhetoric of such programs suggests otherwise. The "best" mediation [facilitative, resource-rich, choosing your mediator], then, is not, for many litigants, a possible one. The debate about best practices of mediation thus must be informed by an understanding of the socioeconomic contexts in which many mediations take place.[73]

Rubinson points out that most low-income wage-earners are hourly workers who do not get paid if they do not work. So the time involved in taking public transportation to a mediation session, plus the session itself, represents lost wages and mitigates in favour of shorter mediation sessions.[74] Facilitative, narrative and transformative mediation take longer than evaluative mediation, so "the end result is that one model – the evaluative model – must become the predominant model in a world of scarce resources for mediation."[75]

69 Kenneth M. Roberts, "Mediating the Evaluative-Facilitative Debate: Why Both Parties are Wrong and a Proposal for Settlement" (2007) 39:1 *Loyola University Chicago Law Journal* 187 at 189.
70 Ibid., at 201–208.
71 Kenneth F. Dunham, "Practical Considerations in Medication Training: Should Mediators be Trained to Adapt to the Circumstances of Each Case?" (2012) 11 *Appalachian Journal of Law* 185 at 189.
72 Stephen B. Goldberg & Margaret L. Shaw, "The Past, Present, and Future of Mediation as Seen through the Eyes of Some of Its Founders" (April 2010) 26:2 *Negotiation Journal* 237 at 248.
73 Robert Rubinson, "Of Grids and Gatekeepers: The Socioeconomics of Mediation" (2016) 17 *Cardozo Journal of Conflict Resolution* 873 at 875–876.
74 Ibid., at 892.
75 Ibid., at 893.

Roberts argues that "evaluative elements need to be utilized, even within a facilitative process."[76] For example, evaluative techniques such as offering assessments about whether an agreement is fair in a non-legal sense are useful and important to many disputants. Other disputants need reality testing, and there is an ambiguous boundary between "reality testing" and "evaluation." Stark and Frenkel note that "most mediators engage pervasively in persuasion activities,"[77] and that both facilitative and evaluative mediators "engage in at least some form of 'substantive' or 'outcome-oriented' persuasion."[78] For example, mediators may be chosen for their wisdom, which implies that the mediator's ideas and suggestions may be solicited. For the budget-conscious disputant, and to increase access to justice, a mediator who can in fact provide useful suggestions may well make the most sense. If a mediator can provide disputants with information or common options, that can be very helpful. Mediators can say things like "there are four popular ways to value small businesses" or "teenagers typically follow one of three methods to make changes to custodial arrangements."[79] Mediators can use knowledge gained in pre-mediation sessions to move the parties toward settlement. For example, the mediator might say to one disputant, "you have told me that this is important to you, therefore why … ?"[80] Or, "given your goals as you have shared them with me, are you willing to lose them for $50,000?" Mediators can also give suggestions by guessing at the parties' life or business goals, quoting statistics (for example, "More than 95% of cases settle. I see no reason why you are in the other 5%."), predicting what might happen in court ("the vast majority of litigants are deeply disappointed with the process"), telling stories about other mediations, or saying things like "in my experience."[81] Many disputants find it comforting if a mediator confirms that their agreement is in the "normal" range.[82] These types of mediator interventions and suggestions are well received. They restore hope and choice for disputants who may be running out of both.

Persuasive, evaluative, suggestion-giving mediation is what we see in popular culture, but interestingly is not what we teach. Dwight Golann and Marjorie Aaron argue that the field of mediation would benefit if we acknowledged that mediators do evaluate and began to teach students how to evaluate effectively.[83] Stark and Frenkel argue that most mediators who are comfortable mediating

76 Kenneth M. Roberts, "Mediating the Evaluative-Facilitative Debate: Why Both Parties are Wrong and a Proposal for Settlement" (2007) 39:1 *Loyola University Chicago Law Journal* 187 at 213.
77 James H. Stark & Douglas N. Frenkel, "Changing Minds: The Work of Mediators and Empirical Studies of Persuasion" (2013) 28 *Ohio State Journal on Dispute Resolution* 263 at 266.
78 Ibid., at 268.
79 John Wade "Evaluative Mediation – Elephants in the Room?" (February 20, 2019), www.mediate.com/pfriendly.cfm?id=14034 at 9.
80 Ibid., at 4.
81 Ibid., at 6.
82 Ibid., at 11.
83 Dwight Golann & Marjorie Aaron, "Beyond Abstinence: Safe and Impartial Evaluation Can Be Effective in Mediation" (2019) *Dispute Resolution Magazine* 24.

persuasively do so based on a combination of intuition, normative views about what is "good," personal style and a sense of mastery of specific persuasive techniques.[84] Providing suggestions or persuading are active mediation roles that I believe can be appropriate, if designed to help disputants evaluate options more objectively or to better exercise self-determination. For example, Kate Reed in *Fairly Legal* evaluates disputes, makes judgments and pushes the parties toward her solutions. She is clearly not impartial, nor does she preserve party self-determination, yet she is still perceived to be a good mediator. Watching Kate mediate may inspire law professors to adjust how they teach mediation. Golann put it as follows in an email message to a dispute resolution listserv I subscribe to. Golann said:

> Indeed, it sometimes seems that we in law schools are teaching classical music, while the world of legal practice embraces jazz and hip hop. Without suggesting that one form is more valuable than another, it's not surprising that if students look for jobs and Deans for donations in a hip hop world, classical approaches may seem less attractive.[85]

Similarly, the persuasive, evaluative mediation styles we see in film and in real life may be prevalent because that is what disputants want.

Disputants want the mediator to actively help them reach a resolution. They want help, and that involves making suggestions, reality checking and evaluating options. This is the style of conflict intervention we see in the 2001 French film *Amélie*. *Amélie* was nominated for the 2002 best foreign language film at the Academy Awards, the Golden Globes and the BAFTAs. It won the European Film Award, the London Critics' Circle Film Award for foreign language film of the year, the 2002 César Award for best film in France, and the People's Choice award at the Toronto International Film Festival.[86] While winning awards does not guarantee viewership, it increases the chances that people have watched the film; and thus it is reasonable for me to argue that *Amélie* may contribute to people's perceptions about conflict resolution.

In *Amélie* the heroine protagonist Amélie Poulain, played by actress Audrey Tautou, operates with her own sense of justice and helps those around her, her way. Amélie is a gamine, with all of that word's "connotations of mischievousness,

84 James H. Stark & Douglas N. Frenkel, "Changing Minds: The Work of Mediators and Empirical Studies of Persuasion" (2013) 28 *Ohio State Journal on Dispute Resolution* 263 at 269.

85 Dwight Golann, Professor of Law and Director, Center for Representation in Dispute Resolution, Suffolk University Law School, Boston, MA, in a February 4, 2019 email to DRLE@po.missouri.edu

86 "The wilfully provocative analogy between *Amélie* and a commercial for France ('an advertising brochure') may actually be nothing more than a simple statement of fact." Carolyn A. Durham, "Finding France on Film: *Chocolat*, *Amélie* and *Le Divorce* (2008) 19:2 *French Cultural Studies* 173 at 175. Indeed, the French Ministry of Culture noted that 62% of its foreign tourists decided to vacation in France after having viewed France in a film (*Le Nouvel Observateur* (2005) 77).

frivolousness and, especially, femininity."[87] Carolyn Durham says she is "the new ideal of Frenchness."[88] Gamine is a word used to describe a thin, young, attractive woman with a short pixie haircut and a mischievous air about her. Images of Audrey Hepburn are often used to capture the style of the gamine; Audrey Tautou was deliberately styled in order to provide the look of the gamine to Amélie in the film (see Figure 2.2). This was important because the character of Amélie is an impish, quintessentially French fixer. Amélie is an orchestrator who fixes problems. In that sense she is a conflict resolver, but she is not a traditional mediator because she is not at all impartial, nor is she interested in party self-determination. She is very interested in fair outcomes but she achieves them in mischievous ways. Amélie is a young waitress in Paris who focuses on the lives of others instead of her own, becoming a conflict resolver in her neighbourhood.[89] One day she finds a small box of childhood mementos behind her bathroom wall. She anonymously returns the box to its owner and witnesses his happiness. Amélie's act inspires the man to visit his estranged daughter and meet his grandson for the first time. Delighted by her success, Amélie next encourages her emotionally distant father to travel for the first time in his life. She steals his beloved garden gnome and gives it to her friend, who is a flight attendant. The flight attendant takes pictures of the gnome in famous tourist locations around the world. Amélie anonymously sends the pictures to her father, eventually inspiring his first trip outside of France.

87 Carolyn A. Durham, "Finding France on Film: *Chocolat*, *Amélie* and *Le Divorce*" (2008) 19:2 *French Cultural Studies* 173 at 176. Amélie is a *gamine*, with all of that word's "connotations of mischievousness, frivolousness and, especially, femininity." She is the "the new ideal of Frenchness" and "will almost certainly reinforce America's traditional conception of France as a feminised nation." Ibid., at 176.

88 Ibid., at 176.

89 The film *Amélie* has, on the one hand, been found to "fit specific expectations of what a French film should look like" (Diane Barthel-Bouchier, "Exportability of Films in a Globalizing Market: The Intersection of Nation and Genre" [2012] 6:1 *Cultural Sociology* 75 at 88). And on the other hand, the character "Amélie does not encounter the real Paris, afflicted as it is with racial and religious division, socio-economic hardship and crime" (Michelle Scatton-Tessier, "Le Petisme: flirting with the sordid in Le Fabuleux destin d'Amélie Poulain" (2004) 4:3 *Studies in French Cinema* 197 at 199). "The film's ethnic whitewashing of Paris triggered a spiteful debate in France." (Dudley Andrew, "Amélie, or Le Fabuleux Destin Du Cinéma Français" (2004) 57:3 *Film Quarterly* 34 at 45, www.jstor.org/stable/10.1525/fq.2004.57.3.34). And:

> There were two opposite opinions to choose from: (a) The film was too nostalgic to be true. The film shows Paris like it does not exist anymore: village-like, serene, romantic. This romantic view is false and morally wrong, it is a dangerous fraud, because it neglects the raw reality Paris has to face like any other western capital, and the film has an all-white cast, and is therefore unrepresentative. (b) The film is very nostalgic, but is very sincere about being a romantic film, and shows how ordinary people always have hope available to help them, to help them out of their misery. The film is not about present-day Paris, but universal human capacities.
>
> (G. Van der Pol, "The fabulous destination of a cultural tourist in Paris: Games of make-believe in Amélie [2001]" [2004] 2:2 *New Review of Film and Television Studies* 257 at 258)

Figure 2.2 Audrey Tautou as Amélie Poulain in *Amélie*

Amélie's conflict resolution effort, otherwise known as the playful theft of the garden gnome, leads her father to broaden his horizons.

Amélie embarks upon deceptive schemes to achieve conflict resolution. In so doing she is not impartial and not interested in party self-determination, but she is interested in fairness. The concierge in Amélie's building is very grumpy and still mourns her long-deceased husband who cheated on her. Amélie steals the concierge's old letters from her husband, using them to create a new letter in which he apologizes to his wife for cheating. The concierge, though surprised that a letter could arrive decades late, is overjoyed with the news that her husband loved her after all. Amélie's deception brings the concierge peace and happiness. Finally, the grocer on Amélie's street, a horrible man named Collignon, has employed a mentally challenged young man named Lucien. Collignon is routinely cruel and derogatory to Lucien, so Amélie avenges Lucien by breaking and entering Collignon's home and setting up practical jokes in his apartment.

Amélie operates with her own sense of justice and helps those around her in her own way. She fixes problems and resolves conflicts (even while breaking and entering). However, in spite of her desire to help others, Amélie has trouble helping herself. (This provides some support for Linda Babcock and Sara Laschever's research on women negotiators. They found that women negotiators do better negotiating on behalf of others than they do when negotiating for themselves.[90]) Amélie changes others' perspectives so that they enjoy their lives more.[91] Mediation scholars would

90 Linda Babcock and Sara Laschever, *Women Don't Ask: Negotiation and the Gender Divide* (Princeton, NJ: Princeton University Press: 2003).

91 G. Van der Pol, "The fabulous destination of a cultural tourist in Paris: Games of make-believe in Amélie [2001]" (2004) 2:2 *New Review of Film and Television Studies* 257 at 264.

characterize her as extremely interventionist, or as an evaluative conflict intervener. When we watch *Amélie*, and when we observe what is actually going on in mediation practice in Europe and North America, what we see are evaluative interventions.

How do we explain the difference in mediation practice, both reel and real, from mediation teaching? I think it may have something to do with pragmatism. Disputants are practical. Their time is money and they value closure and reaching agreements. In 2004 Bernard S. Mayer provided a list of what he thinks mediation disputants want:

- Clients want to be told who is right and who is wrong;
- They seek vindication;
- They want to be told whether a solution being suggested is fair and reasonable, or whether they are being played for a fool;
- They want help in convincing other parties of the merits of their case or the reasonableness of their proposals;
- They want substantive information and advice;
- They want to know how other people have solved the same problem;
- They want the mediator to guide the process with a firm hand, making sure that they do not waste time and are not subject to attacks, dirty tricks or a level of emotional engagement that they are not prepared for;
- They want to get out of the room.[92]

While Mayer's list has not been empirically tested, it certainly stands up anecdotally and in my personal experience. Disputants typically come to mediation either because they have been referred and have to attend, or because they cannot resolve their dispute themselves and they have chosen mediation. In either case they expect some "value-add" from the mediator – something they could not get without her or him, especially if they have been required to attend. Desiring "value-add" suggests some direction, concrete help or suggestions from the mediator. In other words, it may be that pragmatic disputants and lawyers want mediators who are more evaluative or directive, like popular culture mediators, despite the fact that dispute resolution professors and trainers teach the benefits of facilitative mediation.

In practice and definitely in popular culture many disputants appear to prefer evaluative processes as seen in *Fairly Legal* and *Amélie*. Certainly popular culture celebrates conflict intervener Amélie in her evaluative role; the film has viewers cheering when she is not neutral. Yet, if we held Amélie accountable to the European Code of Conduct for Mediators, she would fail Section 2.2 on impartiality. It states: "Mediators must at all times act, and endeavour to be seen to act, with impartiality towards the parties and be committed to serve all parties equally with respect to the process of mediation."[93] What Amélie does breaches the code. She

92 Bernard S. Mayer, *Beyond Neutrality: Confronting the Crisis in Conflict Resolution* (San Francisco, CA: Jossey-Bass, 2004) at 107.

93 http://ec.europa.eu/civiljustice/adr/adr_ec_code_conduct_en.pdf. To date, no mediator in Canada or the United States has successfully been sued. See Jennifer L. Schulz, "Mediator Liability in Canada: An Examination of Emerging American and Canadian Jurisprudence" (2001) 32 *Ottawa Law Review* 269.

circumvents voluntary disputant participation and thwarts party self-determination. She does not act with impartiality toward the parties, nor does she treat them equally. And, by making final decisions, Amélie is arbitrating, not mediating. However, we may still use *Amélie* as an illustrative popular culture text to interrogate our commitment to neutrality and to purely facilitative mediation. When we watch Amélie intervene in others' conflicts we can question whether there is anything about her directive, evaluative interventions that we might adopt in our mediation work. Amélie attunes us to the reality that we could practise mediation more evaluatively and still be good mediators. Or, as Jane Kidner points out, it does not need to be so binary, either facilitative or evaluative mediation. The mediator's style may move along a continuum or a sliding scale between both approaches.[94] Jeffrey H. Goldfien and Jennifer K. Robbennolt state "mediators can, and do, use techniques from both sets of behaviours and may be simultaneously highly elicitive and highly directive."[95] Dwight Golann notes that many mediators use a mix of styles in the same mediation.[96] E. Patrick McDermott and Ruth Obar[97] similarly refer to eclectic mediation, as does Jeffery Stempel,[98] and John Lande advocates for the integration of different approaches to mediation.[99] So it behoves us to be flexible and open-minded, two hallmarks of mediation. Plus, in the case of vulnerable disputants, "a good mediator will not remain completely facilitative, but instead use more evaluative techniques to prevent an unfair or unjust solution."[100] We see this all the time in mediation and we call it "balancing power." It means we are treating the parties differently or that we are not actually neutral.

Shapira takes what he calls a professional ethics perspective and "adopts a substantive, realist interpretation of impartiality that accommodates, within limits, different treatment of parties."[101] He places himself at the tension between mediator impartiality and ensuring disputant self-determination, and comes out in favour of

94 Jane Kidner, "Perspectives on ADR/Mediation: The Limits of Mediator 'Labels': False Debate between 'Facilitative' versus 'Evaluative' Mediator Styles" (2011) 30 *Windsor Review of Legal and Social Issues* 167 at 167.

95 Jeffrey H. Goldfien & Jennifer K. Robbennolt, "What if the Lawyers Have Their Way? An Empirical Assessment of Conflict Strategies and Attitudes Toward Mediation Styles" (2007) 22:2 *Ohio State Journal on Dispute Resolution* 277 at 305.

96 Dwight Golann, "Variations in Mediation: How and Why Legal Mediators Change Styles in the Course of a Case" (2000) *Journal of Dispute Resolution* 41.

97 E. Patrick McDermott & Ruth Obar, "What's Going On in Mediation: An Empirical Analysis of the Influence of a Mediator's Style on Party Satisfaction and Monetary Benefit" (2004) 9 *Harvard Negotiation Law Review* 75.

98 Jeffery W. Stempel, "The Inevitability of the Eclectic: Liberating ADR from Ideology" (2000) *Journal of Dispute Resolution* 247.

99 John Lande, "Toward More Sophisticated Mediation Theory" (2000) *Journal of Dispute Resolution* 321 at 327.

100 Jane Kidner, "Perspectives on ADR/Mediation: The Limits of Mediator 'Labels': False Debate between 'Facilitative' versus 'Evaluative' Mediator Styles" (2011) 30 *Windsor Review of Legal and Social Issues* 167.

101 Omer Shapira, *A Theory of Mediators' Ethics: Foundation, Rationale, and Application* (Cambridge: Cambridge University Press, 2016) at 228.

occasionally treating disputing parties differently. Shapira proposes the following standard of impartiality:

A mediator shall treat parties differently where:

a Same treatment would favour the interests of one party and disadvantage another; and
b The mediator's intervention is (i) required in order to give effect to an ethical right of a party (in particular self-determination), or (ii) necessary for the preservation of public trust in the profession and process of mediation.

Any such intervention shall be limited to one that is:

a The minimum necessary for the realization of the party's right; and
b Can be reconciled with other mediator obligations; and
c Would not be perceived as an act of partiality in the eyes of a reasonable person and thus would not result in a loss of public trust in the profession and process of mediation.[102]

Shapira thus decides that when balancing impartiality against self-determination, self-determination prevails. He advocates that mediators treat disputants differently where it is required to ensure a party is able to exercise self-determination. Similarly, Tony Bogdanoski advocates a postmodern rejection of the grand theory of mediator neutrality in favour of accepting a situated understanding of neutrality.[103] This is important to prevent one party from exploiting the other, and is, as mentioned, called "addressing power imbalances" in mediation training. We need to allow disputants on all sides of the dispute to maximize their control over the process. "The fact that mediators are more or less interventionist depending on the subject being negotiated does not mean that the mediators should be regarded as 'more' or 'less' neutral."[104] Rather, it means that neutrality is situated and nuanced, which allows for party self-determination, power balancing and mediator suggestions.

In 1989 Dean G. Pruitt el al. conducted studies at two American community mediation centres. They found that mediator interventions that were predictive of high quality mediation outcomes included posing substantive problems for the disputants to solve and requesting reactions to ideas suggested by the mediator or the other disputant.[105] In 2017 the American Bar Association (ABA) Section of

102 Ibid., at 230 and 400.
103 Tony Bogdanoski, "Beyond the Paradox of Neutral Intervention: Towards a Situated Theory of Mediator Neutrality" (July 2010) 10/64 Legal Studies Research Paper, http://ssrn.com/abstract=1639074
104 Ibid., at 11.
105 D. Pruitt, G. Welton, W. Fry, N. McGillicuddy, L. Castrianno, C. Ippolito & J. Zubeck, "The Process of Mediation: Caucusing, Control and Problem Solving," in Rahim M. Afzalur, ed., *Managing Conflict: An Interdisciplinary Approach* (Westport, CT: Praeger, 1989) at 205.

Dispute Resolution established a Task Force on Research on Mediator Techniques in order to learn what existing empirical evidence reveals about which mediator actions enhance mediation outcomes and which do not.[106] The ABA Task Force was unable to conclude with confidence that any particular mediation action *will* have a positive or negative effect, only that the action *can* have a positive or negative effect. It explicitly suggests the need for caution in the use of broad statements such as "the research shows" and articulates a need for a body of empirically derived knowledge about which mediator actions and approaches enhance mediation outcomes in order to improve mediation practice.[107] The Task Force found that when a mediator elicits disputants' suggestions or solutions, that has the potential to increase settlement and to enhance disputants' perceptions of mediation and relationships with the other side. This is not surprising. What is surprising is the Task Force's finding that when mediators offer recommendations, suggestions, evaluations or opinions, it either increases or has no effect on settlement. This is remarkable because mediator actions considered directive either increase settlement or have no effect, which is contrary to the typically accepted wisdom that facilitative approaches are better than directive approaches. The finding that mediators' suggestions increase the chance of settlement, or have no effect on settlement, means it is not actually problematic to offer suggestions. This is the opposite of the last two decades of mediation teaching in law schools, yet is exactly in line with what popular culture mediators are doing. So when Kate tells the disputants on *Fairly Legal* that they should listen to her suggestions, or when Amélie intervenes without the parties' full consent, that might be acceptable "mediator" behaviour, or at least something to canvass and discuss with our ADR students.

While the ABA Task Force found that when mediators offer suggestions it either increases or has no effect on settlement, it also found that when mediators offer suggestions it has mixed effects on disputants' relationships and perceptions of mediation – positive, negative and no effects. This means that providing suggestions can have negative effects on disputants' relationships and perceptions of mediation, and this is certainly worthy of further examination. While disputants' perceptions may be negatively impacted, the Task Force found, consistent with my personal experience, that providing suggestions only has positive effects on participating lawyers' views of mediation. So we may conclude, in line with popular culture mediators' practice, that providing suggestions is not nefarious. Suggestions are part of the "value-add" that mediators may bring to the process, and in many cases are why the mediator was hired in the first place. I have certainly found this in my own practice. When lawyers contact me directly to mediate cases for them they always prefer a more "interventionist" approach, going so far as to tell me, "that's why we're paying you. If we could've figured this out without your input, we would have negotiated it over the phone." Since lawyers are the ones

106 Task Force on Research on Mediation Techniques, commissioned by the ABA Section of Dispute Resolution (June 12, 2017), www.americanbar.org/groups/dispute_resolution.html

107 Ibid., at 4.

who typically select the mediator, and mediators are usually looking for work, it is not hard to imagine that some mediators will begin to mediate in ways more stylistically similar to popular culture mediators, offering suggestions, recommendations and even opinions and evaluations along the way.[108]

Mayer goes further than many in the mediation field, suggesting that "conflict resolution professionals have the potential to make a major difference if they can incorporate genuine advocacy into their work."[109] That is to say, Mayer advocates for mediators using their power much more overtly than most, but in the service of fairness. Incorporating advocacy into mediation work is obviously diametrically opposed to mediators' "stay neutral" mantra. However, it may fit with parties' hopes for mediation, especially if those hopes are based on popular culture portrayals. Debbie De Girolamo says:

> A mediator becomes much more than the non-aligned third party intervener throughout the course of a mediation. ... The mediator is *the* third party intervener and becomes *the* party as well as *the* party adviser. ... the mediation becomes *his* negotiation; the party becomes *his* client. His identity merges with party identity in the search for resolution.[110]

De Girolamo states that the mediator is not a distant third party intervener. The mediator is also an adviser, adversary and supporter, which puts the mediator in the epicentre of the mediation.[111] Similarly, Benjamin Lowndes and Sharon Press argue that mediators can serve as excellent allies by lending their specialized skills to advancing causes.[112] Richard Birke goes much further. Based on his research into neuroscience and its possible connections with settlement, Birke argues that mediators can give forceful suggestions and advocate. He states:

> resolution of conflicts is something that may be worth pushing to the edge of ethics, and lasting satisfaction can come from coercive environments. In short,

108 The International Academy of Mediators (IAM) and the Straus Institute for Dispute Resolution at Pepperdine University School of Law conducted a survey of 130 IAM mediators (IAM/Straus Institute Survey on Mediator Practices and Perceptions [Spring, 2014]). They found that 80% of respondents indicated that their reputation as a mediator who can offer useful assessments of parties' cases was a factor in attracting and maintaining clients (Thomas J. Stipanowich, "Insights on Mediator Practices and Perception" [Winter 2016] *Dispute Resolution Magazine* 4 at 7). California mediators were much more likely than mediators outside the United States to develop and propose potential agreements, give their predictions, and assess the legal strength of arguments. Mediators from other areas of the globe were more likely to help parties develop or communicate proposals, but not offer their opinion regarding the proposals.

109 Bernard S. Mayer, *Beyond Neutrality: Confronting the Crisis in Conflict Resolution* (San Francisco, CA: Jossey-Bass, 2004) at 118.

110 Debbie De Girolamo, "A View from Within: Reconceptualizing Mediator Interactions" (2012) 30 *Windsor Yearbook of Access to Justice* 103 at 127; emphasis in original.

111 Ibid.

112 Benjamin Lowndes & Sharon Press, "Ally-ship and Dispute Resolution Practitioners: A Continuum" (2016) 42:5 *Mitchell Hamline Law Review* 1572 at 1584.

> maybe a mediator's proposal, even if argued forcefully, produces the greater good if it generates forced concessions resulting in closure.[113]

For the many mediators in the middle of the spectrum between "never give suggestions" and "forcefully argue proposals" it is important to recognize that mediators' duties are not clear. And mediators like Kate Reed and conflict interveners like Amélie may not be as bad as we originally thought.

Fair outcomes

Mediators have mediated for millennia. The first cave people mediators may not have been neutral in all situations, but they were likely fair-minded or they would not have been chosen to mediate. Cheryl Picard et al. note that certain mediators – for example, social network mediators in small communities and authoritative mediators in certain organizations – are also not always neutral, but it is always expected that they "will be fair and trustworthy."[114] While Lela P. Love and Jonathan Hyman say "a mediator does not have the responsibility to determine an appropriate remedy or a just distribution,"[115] many mediators do not share that view. They believe they have a duty to ensure fair outcomes. The tension between balancing our duty to remain impartial with our duty to ensure party self-determination is exacerbated when the mediator also desires a fair outcome. As Ellen Waldman puts it, "there is an incontrovertible tension between the duty to remain impartial and the duty to encourage fair outcomes"[116] and "as soon as a mediator attempts to ensure a balanced process by helping a weak party, she has compromised her impartiality."[117] Impartiality, self-determination and fair outcomes are all compelling and all important, and how each is prioritized in any given mediation session is up to the mediator. Some mediators, especially those who mediate with disputants represented by counsel, argue that mediation disputants are like any other adults who contract with the benefit of independent legal advice – they are free to make their own agreements, as long as they are not unconscionable or illegal, and those agreements do not need to be fair per se. Other mediators believe they have a duty to ensure fair outcomes and that is precisely why they take training in and are concerned about "balancing power" or maximizing parties' relative control in relation to one another[118] in mediation sessions.

113 Richard Birke, "Neuroscience and Settlement: An Examination of Scientific Innovations and Practical Applications" (2010) 25 *Ohio State Journal on Dispute Resolution* 477 at 523.
114 C. Picard, P. Bishop, R. Ramkay & N. Sargent, *The Art and Science of Mediation* (Toronto: Emond Montgomery, 2004) at 106.
115 Lela P. Love & Jonathan M. Hyman, "If Portia Were A Mediator: An Inquiry into Justice in Mediation" (2002) 9 *Clinical Law Review* 157 at 158.
116 Ellen Waldman, ed., *Mediation Ethics: Cases and Commentaries* (San Francisco, CA: Jossey-Bass, 2011) at 303.
117 Ibid., at 300.
118 Tony Bogdanoski, "Beyond the Paradox of Neutral Intervention: Towards a Situated Theory of Mediator Neutrality" (July 2010) 10/64 Legal Studies Research Paper, http://ssrn.com/abstract=1639074 at 6.

There is no one correct answer as to how to prioritize the competing mediation values of impartiality, self-determination and fairness. Mediators have to examine each case individually. Hilary Astor and Christine Chinkin say:

> A nuanced analysis of neutrality does not invite us to wallow in a multiplicity of single instances without reference to any principles. It demands that we examine context and culture, identity and values and their impact on disputes and dispute settlement in order to distinguish appropriate from problematic mediator behaviour.[119]

Sara Cobb and Janet Rifkin have discussed neutrality as equidistance and say that mediators who are equidistant can do asymmetrical things in mediation in order to attempt to achieve symmetry.[120] It is possible to treat the disputants differently in order to bring about a fair settlement if that is a value prioritized by the mediator. So the mediator is engaged (not remote, distant and "impartial") equally with each party because she is equidistant from each party. Leah Wing argues that, in order to provide equal narrative opportunities, mediators may need to intervene asymmetrically.[121] Certainly, as mediators, when we take the self-determination of the parties seriously we must ensure *both* parties are experiencing self-determination in our mediation chambers. If one party is being disadvantaged by the other party and the mediator fails to intervene, that mediator participates in a process that not only does not privilege self-determination but is also exploitative. That cannot be right. It also suggests that treating the parties "the same" is less important than processual fairness.

A very persuasive type of mediator intervention is to suggest the parties consider reversing roles or positions. Stark and Frenkel call this counter-attitudinal advocacy and argue that it is acceptable to virtually all mediators, regardless of orientation. Further, they note it is effective as a self-persuasion method that research demonstrates can produce lasting attitudinal change.[122] Similarly, Bogdanoski calls for a situated theory of mediator neutrality.[123] It is important to have a situated sense of neutrality, or to understand neutrality as a value that can be prioritized more or less highly depending on the mediation circumstances, because, when it comes to ensuring fairness, strict neutrality is unlikely to achieve the fairness goal.

119 Hilary Astor & Christine Chinkin, *Dispute Resolution in Australia*, 2nd edn (Sydney: Butterworths, 2002) at 156.

120 Sara Cobb & Janet Rifkin, "Practice and Paradox: Deconstructing Neutrality in Mediation" (1991) 16:1 *Law and Social Inquiry* 35 at 43–45.

121 Leah Wing, "Whither Neutrality? Mediation in the twenty-first century," in M. Trujillo, S.Y. Bowland, L.J. Myers, P.M. Richard & B. Roy, eds, *Recentering Culture, Knowledge and Conflict Resolution* (New York: Syracuse University Press, 2008).

122 James H. Stark & Douglas N. Frenkel, "Changing Minds: The Work of Mediators and Empirical Studies of Persuasion" (2013) 28 *Ohio State Journal on Dispute Resolution* 263 at 280.

123 Tony Bogdanoski, "Beyond the Paradox of Neutral Intervention: Towards a Situated Theory of Mediator Neutrality" (July 2010) 10/64 Legal Studies Research Paper, http://ssrn.com/abstract=1639074

As Astor points out, "the requirement of mediator neutrality may act to disempower precisely the people it was designed to assist, allowing us to think of mediation as a process that is fair, when neutrality and the privacy of the process may conceal unfairness."[124]

Mediators can have fair outcomes, impartiality and party self-determination if impartiality is understood in a more fluid, postmodern fashion. Impartiality is situated, fluctuating and contextual, and sometimes, in order to ensure party self-determination and non-exploitative outcomes, mediators may have to treat the parties unequally in order to ensure fairness.[125] This can occur more than once and in different directions within the same mediation session. This is what Amélie does. Throughout the film she is guided by her sense of fairness (or even justice) and intervenes in the lives of her neighbours and co-workers to resolve conflict. It is clear that she does so without taking the parties' right to self-determination to heart, but she does succeed in crafting fair resolutions. Omer Shapira would say this is okay, because disputants are entitled to expect substantive fairness, not formal fairness.[126] He advocates for a substantive-realist approach to fairness rather than a formal-technical approach.[127] This means that mediators can intervene in the mediation process to prevent unfair agreements. For example, a mediator could intervene when a party is ignorant of relevant information in order to ensure a true, substantive, fair exercise of self-determination, not just a technical exercise of decision-making.

As I have mentioned, I prefer the word "impartiality" to "neutrality." Another helpful word is "even-handedness." If one practises mediation in an even-handed fashion it allows for substantive equality, rather than an "all or nothing" formal equality approach or "am I neutral or not" anxiety. Adrian Challis and Sandy Koop Harder advocate for a balanced partiality approach.[128] Instead of thinking about neutral/impartial, they think about fair/balanced. Their process begins with individual meetings, followed by a joint session where past events and misunderstandings are discussed, and then individual debriefings with each side plus coaching. Thereafter there is a second joint session that focuses on the future. What insights have the parties developed? What can they now acknowledge? What are their needs and can they generate options and make offers that address them? This is an effective, even-handed, fair way to mediate. Vicky Assegued uses the word "multi-partial" instead of balanced or even-handed. She says she prefers an all-inclusive approach of being allied with every participant in the mediation – multi-partial – to bring out the wonderful collaborative possibilities

124 Hilary Astor, "Mediator Neutrality: Making Sense of Theory and Practice" (July 2007) 07/46 Legal Studies Research Paper, http://ssrn.com/abstract=998202 at 5.

125 Tony Bogdanoski, "Beyond the Paradox of Neutral Intervention: Towards a Situated Theory of Mediator Neutrality" (July 2010) 10/64 Legal Studies Research Paper, http://ssrn.com/abstract=1639074

126 Omer Shapira, *A Theory of Mediators' Ethics: Foundation, Rationale, and Application* (Cambridge: Cambridge University Press, 2016) at 307.

127 Ibid., at 310.

128 As told to the author in conversation in 2012.

of mediation.[129] It may be that when mediators care about fairness and work to maximize party self-determination, emphasizing consensuality is more important than emphasizing impartiality. And, happily, with an emphasis on consensuality or even-handedness, fairness tends to flow.

Mediators seeking to maximize party control and fairness of course have an obligation to think about their own power, to ensure it is minimized and the parties' is maximized.[130] Kate Reed and Amélie do not do this. They blatantly use their power and do not worry if the disputants' power is curtailed. Mediative intervention that circumvents voluntary disputant participation, thereby thwarting party self-determination, is unethical. If we held Kate and Amélie accountable to mediator codes of conduct they would both fail miserably and would have to worry about mediator liability.[131] However, Kate and Amélie think they know what is best and feel that their disputants should trust them. Desmond Manderson has described the logic of the protagonists of law shows as "you're just gonna have to trust me."[132] This logic is shared by popular culture TV mediator Kate and filmic conflict intervener Amélie. Despite the fact that decision-making power rests with mediation disputants, pop culture mediators routinely enjoin disputants to "trust them" as they fashion resolutions for them, acting more like arbitrators than mediators. "Trust me" logic puts a premium on individual responsibility over institutional or legal accountability. Indeed, the solutions that Kate and Amélie devise are very helpful to individuals but do not relate to more generalized social problems.[133] Michelle Scatton-Tessier suggests that Amélie's "quickfixes," her repeated focus on "that which can be quickly rectified ... implies a diversion from the larger social and political issues."[134] Just like Kate, Amélie seems far less likely to move from the personal to the political; her various quests focus on the problems faced by particular individuals rather than those of broader social groups.[135] Nevertheless, when

129 Vicky Assegued, "I'm Not Neutral About Neutrality: I'm Partial to Multi-Partiality" (June 2018), www.mediate.com/articles/assegued-multi-partiality.cfm

130 Hilary Astor, "Mediator Neutrality: Making Sense of Theory and Practice" (July 2007) 07/46 Legal Studies Research Paper, http://ssrn.com/abstract=998202 at 15.

131 To date, no mediator in Canada or the United States has successfully been sued. See Jennifer L. Schulz, "Mediator Liability in Canada: An Examination of Emerging American and Canadian Jurisprudence" (2001) 32 *Ottawa Law Review* 269.

132 Desmond Manderson, "Trust US Justice: *24*, Popular Culture, and the Law," in Austin Sarat, ed., *Imagining Legality: Where Law Meets Popular Culture* (Tuscaloosa, AL: The University of Alabama Press, 2011) at 40.

133 Jim Morrissey, "Paris and voyages of self-discovery in Cléo de 5 à 7 and Le Fabuleux Destin d'Amélie Poulain" (2008) 8:2 *Studies in French Cinema* 99 at 103.

134 Michelle Scatton-Tessier, "Le Petisme: flirting with the sordid in Le Fabuleux destin d'Amélie Poulain" (2004) 4:3 *Studies in French Cinema* 197 at 197.

135 I have previously noted the same. See Jennifer L. Schulz, "Confectionery and Conflict Resolution? What *Chocolat* Reveals about Mediation" (2006) 22 *Negotiation Journal* 251 at 265:

> Although personal conflict transformations hold promise for systemic change, they often bring relief to only a few, neglecting the larger, systemic problems of many. Therefore it has been argued that mediation may be better equipped to address

we look to popular culture we see characters in mediative roles who assist in the resolution of others' conflict, privileging fairness over neutrality. Shapira says: "Since all norms are relative, party self-determination might have to give way to other ethical norms in appropriate circumstances."[136] One of these norms may well be fairness. Nadja Alexander has noted the significant discrepancy between evaluative mediation practice and mediation theory, describing it as one of the major challenges facing mediation.[137] Popular culture mediators such as Kate and Amélie suggest that privileging fairness may be the way to bridge the divide between mediation practice and theory. This might be necessary because, as Ellen Waldman notes, "Standards requiring mediator impartiality while simultaneously requiring the mediator to ensure informed decision-making, a balanced process, or some other type of fairness demand a high-wire act that often cannot be sustained."[138]

Real-life mediators must remember that lawyers can be of enormous assistance in mediations where fairness is a concern. Julie Macfarlane notes that it is the lawyer's job to ensure that any emerging consensus in mediation "upholds basic standards of equality and fairness, in relation to both fair procedures and just outcomes. These need not be identical to legal protections, but should not violate principles of equality, anti-discrimination, or non-oppression."[139] Thus lawyers, in the instances where they are present in mediation, can ensure fairness. Lawyers can work with their clients to ensure their rights are protected and fairness is pursued, leaving even-handedness and party self-determination to the mediator. Ultimately, of course, there is a real difference between characters who are involved in popular culture conflict resolution interventions and real people who are practising mediators, accountable to codes of conduct or court roster procedures. It is the former who tend to make a lot of suggestions, privileging fairness and ignoring impartiality and self-determination, and who, like Kate and Amélie, are celebrated for it.

We celebrate Kate and Amélie because they are engaging, fun and fair. Although they do not move from the personal to the political, we agree with their conflict resolution interventions because they seem just. *Fairly Legal* and *Amélie* remind us that, as mediators, we must care about good, fair agreements. And, when we do, we must decide how to best go about helping disputants achieve them. Will the facilitative approaches we teach our students be enough or will we need to emulate some aspects of the evaluative styles we see in popular culture? Or will we devise entirely new approaches? These popular culture examples open our eyes to the possibility that classic conflict resolution

individual disputes than societal injustices. Similarly, cinematic representations of conflict resolution favour individual approaches.

136 Omer Shapira, *A Theory of Mediators' Ethics: Foundation, Rationale, and Application* (Cambridge: Cambridge University Press, 2016).

137 Nadja Alexander, ed., *Global Trends in Mediation*, 2nd edn (Alphen aan den Rijn: Kluwer Law International, 2006) at 8.

138 Ellen Waldman, ed., *Mediation Ethics: Cases and Commentaries* (San Francisco, CA: Jossey-Bass, 2011) at 301.

139 Julie Macfarlane, *The New Lawyer: How Clients are Transforming the Practice of Law*, 2nd edn (Vancouver: University of British Columbia Press, 2017) at 172.

teachings may represent the ideal, but not necessarily the reality, of mediation practice. *Fairly Legal* and *Amélie* construct dispute resolution knowledge in new ways. They demonstrate that mediators can practise in unorthodox or anti-classic ways, and still help create fair agreements. Reel mediators are more directive and evaluative than the way dispute resolution professors teach mediation should be. If reel mediators are providing services closer to what real disputants actually desire, what should facilitative mediators do? Change their mediation practices? Try new things? When we watch popular culture mediators we challenge ourselves to widen what we include under the umbrella of positive dispute resolution interventions.

Conclusion

In this chapter I began the process of looking at mediation through the lens of popular culture. I used the character Kate Reed on the first American primetime mediation drama, the now off-the-air TV series *Fairly Legal*, as well as the protagonist in the eponymously titled French film *Amélie* as illustrative case studies. *Fairly Legal* and *Amélie* make us think about what mediation theory can borrow from popular culture. Close analyses of Kate and Amélie's mediations provide ideas about the usefulness of popular culture for thinking through the important mediation issues of impartiality, self-determination and fairness. Classic mediation stresses a facilitative orientation or approach wherein mediators facilitate disputants' negotiations, attempting to help them reach a settlement on their own terms, based on the parties' own sense of what works for them. The notion of party self-determination is universally accepted in the mediation field. However, neither Kate nor Amélie mediate in a facilitative fashion. Rather, they take explicitly evaluative approaches and do not worry about preserving impartiality or about party self-determination.

Evaluative mediation in and of itself is not unethical. If the mediator has the disputants' consent to proceed in an evaluative fashion, and if she individualizes her approach to the particular dispute,[140] an evaluative approach like Kate's or Amélie's can be effective. As Robert D. Benjamin writes, by cleverly reframing, mediators allow disputants to gain a new perspective on the conflict and to consider "pragmatic, alternative solutions that may not strictly follow established moral or legal precepts but work nonetheless."[141] Impartiality, party self-determination and fairness are all important mediation goals. Self-appointed popular culture dispute resolvers, such as Kate and Amélie, are not interested in neutrality or in party self-determination, but they do seem to care about fairness. Mediators, like their popular culture counterparts, should be allowed to intervene in the mediation process to prevent unfair agreements. This means that, sometimes, mediators will have to prioritize one or more of the goals – impartiality, party self-determination or fairness – over the others, depending on the particular dispute. So, for example, in

140 Jennifer L. Schulz, "Confectionery and Conflict Resolution? What *Chocolat* Reveals about Mediation" (2006) 22 *Negotiation Journal* 251 at 265.

141 Robert D. Benjamin, "The Mediator as Trickster: The Folkloric Figure as Professional Role Model" (1995) 13:2 *Conflict Resolution Quarterly* 131 at 143.

order to ensure non-exploitative outcomes, Kate and Amélie treat their disputing parties unequally in order to ensure fair outcomes, even doing so more than once and in different directions within the same session.

The American Bar Association's Task Force findings support the idea that mediators can give suggestions because doing so either increases or has no effect on settlement. Thus it is not hard to imagine that some mediators may move (or already have moved) away from facilitative mediation toward evaluative, directive approaches, more closely mirroring their popular culture counterparts. In practice and in popular culture, many disputants prefer more suggestive/evaluative processes because they want to know what to do. Today's mediators need to take this seriously and ensure that both parties are experiencing self-determination in mediation, or, if not that, then at least that the outcome is fair. Mediation trainers, teachers and professors may need to seriously reconsider how they teach mediation as there is a disconnect between mediation training, professional clients' expectations (i.e., lawyers) and disputants' expectations.[142] As mediators, how do we respond? Jean Poitras' empirical research demonstrates that a mediator's impartiality and empathy are strong factors in determining the disputants' trust in the mediator.[143] Poitras postulates that, by focusing on empathy, mediators gain access to important information and this can speed up the mediation process.[144] His results lead him to "suggest that empathy might ultimately be more important than impartiality in establishing mediators' trustworthiness."[145] If empathy brings mediators closer to important information and may be more important than impartiality, it suggests that disputants' feelings are very important. Empathy is directly related to a mediator's ability to work with disputants' emotions, bringing us to the importance of feelings and intuition, the topics of the next chapter.

142 Kenneth F. Dunham, "Practical Considerations in Mediation Training: Should Mediators be Trained to Adapt to the Circumstances of Each Case?" (2012) 11 *Appalachian Journal of Law* 185 at 187–188, referencing L. Randolph Lowry, "To Evaluate or Not: That Is Not the Question!" (2001) 38:1 *Family Court Review* 48 at 54, and John Lande, "Symposium, Toward More Sophisticated Mediation Theory" (2000) *Journal of Dispute Resolution* 321 at 323.

143 Jean Poitras, "The Strategic Use of Caucus to Facilitate Parties' Trust in Mediators" (2013) 24 *International Journal of Conflict Management* 23 at 32.

144 Ibid., at 36.

145 Ibid., at 36.

3 Feelings and expert intuition

Popular culture: *Orange is the New Black, The Good Wife, Star Trek: The Next Generation* (TV shows, USA) and *Face to Face* (film, Australia)
Research from: Australia, Canada, Denmark, Greece, Israel, New Zealand, UK and USA

Feelings

Feelings have long counted for more in mediation than in law. While the lawyer asks "what brings you to my office?" or "what is the problem?," the mediator adds "and how do you *feel* about it?" Mediators care about how disputants feel, how the dispute has impacted them, and what they need out of a mediation session to feel better, obtain closure or settle. The reason mediators care more about disputants' emotions than lawyers do is because mediators understand that it is each party's understanding of the facts and her or his feelings about those facts that result in the conflict situation. Mediators therefore attempt to privilege feelings in their interventions with disputants and virtually all mediation educators promote this. While lawyers typically think of emotions as conflict escalators, mediators usually attempt to harness emotions and transform them into conflict resolution motivators. (Unfortunately, not all mediators truly welcome the expression of feelings in mediation. Some mediators say they care about disputant emotions, but what they really mean is that they allow for the venting of unwanted emotions so that the "real" work of mediation can begin. For example, Laurence Boulle and Kathleen J. Kelly note that mediators "may also decide to allow one or both parties to vent their negative feelings, on the assumption that this cathartic release is a necessary prerequisite for rational discussions."[1]) These exceptions aside, most mediators know that when feelings are engaged it is easier to help people move out of intractable conflict patterns. Quite simply, most disputants cannot "separate the people from the problem"[2] so mediators have to be able to work with disputants' feelings. As Bernard S. Mayer says, if the disputants "feel better, the conflict must be resolved; if they do not, then no matter what else has occurred, the conflict is still as bad as ever."[3]

The American Bar Association's Section of Dispute Resolution formed a Task Force on Research on Mediator Techniques in order to learn what existing empirical

1 L. Boulle & K.J. Kelly, *Mediation: Principles, Process, Practice*, Canadian edn (Toronto: Butterworths, 1998) at 171.
2 R. Fisher & W. Ury, *Getting to Yes* (New York: Penguin Books, 1981).
3 Bernard S. Mayer, *The Dynamics of Conflict: A Guide to Engagement and Intervention*, 2nd edn (San Francisco, CA: Jossey-Bass, 2012) at 39.

evidence reveals about which mediator actions enhance mediation outcomes and which do not.[4] The Task Force found that addressing disputants' emotions, relationships and feelings either increased or had no effect on settlement, and either reduced or did not affect post-mediation court actions. So, dealing with disputants' emotions is a no-brainer for mediators. Doing so either improves the situation or does nothing – there is no downside to dealing with emotions. Similarly, working to build rapport and trust, expressing empathy, giving praise and structuring the agenda all have no downsides for mediators. Doing these things has the potential to increase settlement and enhance disputants' perceptions of and relationships with the other side. Mediators know they must engage with feelings, and research confirms this. In this chapter I want to push our engagement with feelings further and try to make mediation a more embodied process.

In order to surface disputants' feelings and engage with them, mediators typically begin their sessions asking each party to tell the conflict story from his or her perspective. In Season 4, Episode 6 of *Orange is the New Black*, a very popular, award-winning, original Netflix TV series featuring women in prison, a mediation is shown.[5] The mediator, an African American woman and fellow prisoner, lets the two female prisoners tell their stories and then they come up with a resolution. Cindy, one of the disputants, is black, and the other disputant, Alison, wears a headscarf and is brown. The mediator begins in a take-charge fashion, saying, "As I understand it, Cindy, you need a cellphone, and Alison, you have a cellphone. I'm sure we can reach some sort of an agreement." At that point the disputing prisoners burst into impassioned speeches, each explaining how the other has wronged her, indicating that their histories, conflict stories and feelings are extremely important, and may be more important than the cellphone. The mediator wisely lets the two women tell their stories; however, after the story-telling degenerates into insults, she says, "Ladies, ladies! Let's remember to use I statements please!" The mediator also says, "Digging up the past ain't gonna get us nowhere. We need to stay focused on moving forward." This leads Alison to make a proposal regarding the cellphone, whereupon the mediator says, "seems fair to me – Cindy?" Cindy accepts the proposal and the women have a deal.

Film and television are helpful for mediation education because they, like mediation, tell stories. Popular culture visual media, law and mediation are all committed to narrative as a central organizing principle. While lawyers tell stories to persuade, mediators facilitate disputant storytelling to clarify, summarize and pave the way toward resolution. Summary and paraphrase are crucial in mediations' and in films' narrative practices. David Bordwell notes that: "The narrative film is so made as to encourage the spectator to execute story-constructing activities. The film presents cues, patterns, and gaps that shape the viewer's application of

4 Task Force on Research on Mediation Techniques, commissioned by the ABA Section of Dispute Resolution (June 12, 2017), www.americanbar.org/groups/dispute_resolution.html

5 *Orange is the New Black*, Season 4, Episode 6, at 49 minutes.

schemata and the testing of hypotheses."[6] Similarly, mediators, more actively than popular culture viewers, help illuminate the patterns, fill in the gaps and test the hypotheses in disputants' conflict stories.

The stories told in law tend to have a linear narrative order or progression, and are not often focused on emotions. In order to be able to mediate, however, students need to develop comfort with emotions; and with exposure to different approaches to storytelling they will develop that comfort. Conflict resolution storytelling, like filmic storytelling, is often done in a back and forth, emotional fashion. Flashbacks are utilized, and spiral ways of telling stories are common. Exposure to different storytelling approaches leads to fresh perspectives, which are more likely to engender the understanding and sensitivity necessary to eventually fully engage in processes of conflict resolution with real-life disputants. Effective settlement and satisfactory resolution are what movies are after, which parallels mediators' search for settlement and resolution. Both film and mediation are processes in which obstacles are overcome and goals are attained. Perhaps ideally, in both film and mediation, we seek closure, the resolution of ambiguity and even happy endings.

As a mediator and a consumer of popular culture I am struck by the similarities between mediation and popular culture. The similar foci on narrative, summarizing and moving toward resolution intrigue me, as the parallels between trials and film intrigue Law & Film scholars.[7] Television shows and films are narrative and representational spaces with substantive and stylistic components that blend dialogue, music, scenery and action in a cohesive way, engaging multiple senses. Mediators do the same thing. They reorient the parties toward one another through dialogue, setting, ambience and actions – in other words, in a way that engages each disputant in the story and in the feelings of the other. John Winslade and Gerald Monk developed a theory of mediation called narrative mediation which is based on this very idea, stressing the importance of disputants attempting to jointly author a new story.[8] In stories, TV shows and mediation sessions there are often important moments that are crucial to the plot. Scholars at Harvard have written about critical moments in mediation – the "a-ha" moment when suddenly resolution seems possible.[9] Scholars at Carleton University in Canada have developed an approach to mediation called insight mediation.[10] Insight mediation focuses on lessening the threats to disputants'

6 D. Bordwell, *Narration in the Fiction Film* (Madison, WI: University of Wisconsin Press, 1985) at 33.

7 Carol Clover highlights the similarities between film and trials and states that: "Film metaphors permeate descriptions of trials." (C. Clover, "Law and the Order of Popular Culture," in A. Sarat & T.R. Kearns, eds, *Law in the Domains of Culture* [Ann Arbor, MI: The University of Michigan Press, 1998] at 104, note 15).

8 John Winslade & Gerald Monk, *Narrative Mediation: A New Approach to Conflict Resolution* (San Francisco, CA: Jossey-Bass, 2001).

9 Linda L. Putnam, "Transformations and Critical Moments in Negotiations" (2004) 20 *Negotiation Journal* 275; Kimberlyn Leary, "Critical moments as relational moments" (2004) 20 *Negotiation Journal* 311.

10 Cheryl A. Picard & Kenneth R. Melchin, "Insight Mediation: A Learning-Centered Mediation Model" (2007) 23 *Negotiation Journal* 35; Cheryl A. Picard & Kenneth R. Melchin. *Transforming Conflict Through Insight* (Toronto: University of Toronto Press, 2008).

cares so that disputants reach insight – the moment when they understand enough about the other that they stop perceiving the other as a threat and begin to believe they can resolve their differences. The mediator in narrative mediation, critical moment and insight mediation maintains a curious, non-judgmental posture, trying to enhance the parties' communication and improve their conflict story. Film and television stories can help mediators build those skills.

In mediation, mediators typically validate disputants' stories. However, Howard Gadlin, Andrea Kupfer Schneider and Christopher Honeyman state that "we know that we cannot take literally the stories disputants tell us about their conflicts."[11] I do not begin my mediation sessions distrusting the disputants. Instead I take my cue from popular culture mediators. As I will explain later in this chapter, popular culture mediators have expert intuition and they prioritize feelings, recognize emotions and value stories. Disputants' stories need to be validated because sometimes their stories involve real blame. Sometimes, contrary to Roger Fisher and William Ury,[12] the people really are the problem. Mediators typically do not focus on the past, preferring instead to be forward-looking. However, if the past is taken out of the equation in favour of focusing on agreements for the future, an important part of the disputants' stories can be lost. Without the past, without context and without blame, disputants operate without their true stories, something feminist analyses warn us to avoid. Often for women, people of colour, minorities and other marginalized people, non-contextual analysis and intervention is not helpful. Therefore it is important for mediators to hear and validate disputants' stories and push our engagement with their feelings further.

Mediators should honour disputants' expression of their feelings, and, as Peter Eastwood enjoins us, not rewrite disputants' conflicts; we should allow parties to make their own determinations of what their stories mean.[13] In so doing we honour the expression of disputant feelings and try to make mediation a more embodied process. Developing our feelings literacy is a first step. Nonverbal cues lend useful insights into disputant emotions. Face-to-face negotiations tend to be more successful than telephone or online mediation for exactly this reason. Tim Hicks recommends taking a neurological perspective,[14] wherein we attend more deliberately to neuro-biological reactions in mediation. From Gestalt psychologists we know about the Cycle of Experience. This cycle highlights that we naturally begin with sensation, go to awareness, experience the building of energy, and only then do we act. It is important to remember that we begin with sensation or

11 Howard Gadlin, Andrea Kupfer Schneider & Chris Honeyman, "The Road to Hell is Paved with Metaphors," in Chris Honeyman & Andrea Kupfer Schneider, eds, *The Negotiator's Desk Reference*, Vol. 2 (St. Paul, MN: Dispute Resolution Institute Press, 2017) at 9; emphasis in original.

12 R. Fisher & W. Ury, *Getting to Yes* (New York: Penguin Books, 1981).

13 Peter Eastwood, "Great Expectations: Popular Culture and the Narration of Conflict in Litigation and Mediation" (2012) 2 *Masks: The Online Journal of Law and Theatre* 26, www.masksjournal.com

14 Tim Hicks, *Embodied Conflict: The Neural Roots of Conflict and Communication* (Abingdon: Routledge, 2018).

feeling – an embodied response – and that we should continue to work with feelings. Mediators need to maintain involvement with sensations, feelings and embodied responses throughout the mediation session. We can be more aware of physical sensations in the mediation room and include the tactile environment in our preparations. Joshua M. Ackerman, Christopher C. Nocera and John A. Bargh, of MIT, Harvard and Yale respectively, conducted a series of experiments that demonstrate just how embodied negotiations are.[15] They explored how the feel of physical objects can influence our decisions, without us even being aware of it. Their results show that mediators need to be more attuned to somatic awareness than we have been.

Ackerman, Nocera and Bargh asked passers-by to evaluate a job candidate by reviewing résumés of identical candidates on either light or heavy clipboards. Those who were given heavy clipboards rated the candidate as better overall and more interested in the position than those who were given light clipboards. The results suggest that the physical heft of the clipboards affected how "weighty" participants viewed the job applicant to be. In another experiment, participants sat on either a wooden chair or a cushioned chair while reading the same scenario. Those who sat on hard chairs judged the protagonist in the scenario to be significantly more stable and less emotional than those who sat on soft chairs. Hardness, as manifested through the sense of touch, produced perceptions of strictness, rigidity and stability, even when the touch experience was passive; i.e., merely sitting. "Hard objects made others seem both more negative (strict and rigid) and more positive (stable), with corresponding effects on decision-making."[16] Next, the same participants were asked to negotiate for a new car. Chair hardness affected participants' willingness to raise their offers in a second round of negotiations. Those who sat on soft chairs raised their offers by an average of $1,243.60; those who sat on hard chairs raised their offers significantly less: $869.50. The experience of sitting on a hard chair appeared to unconsciously translate into a more hardline approach to negotiation.

We need to take results like these seriously. Impressions can be influenced by one's tactile environment, and mediators have control over the tactile environment of the mediation. Questions about seating and chairs take on new import. What if we replace hard boardroom chairs with upholstered couches? What if we hand disputants mediation agendas or proposals on clipboards? Chairs and clipboards can have ethical implications because mediators can use these things to influence disputants in particular directions. If a piece of furniture can have ethical import, then thinking about how mediation seating feels is not a waste of time. What about the mediation table? Michelle LeBaron and Carrie MacLeod state: "Folk wisdom confirms that physical movement and rituals help people shift out of destructive patterns, yet conflict transformation processes are frequently designed

15 Joshua M. Ackerman, Christopher C. Nocera & John A. Bargh, "Incidental Haptic Sensations Influence Social Judgments and Decisions" (June 25, 2010) 38 *Science* 1712, www.sciencemag.org

16 Ibid., at 1713.

with a table as the reflexive, static centre."[17] Why are mediators, like lawyers, literally stuck around tables? Why don't we move around? LeBaron and MacLeod advocate jostling disputants into awareness by harnessing somatic realization,[18] which can best be accomplished through movement and the sense of touch. Mediators should consider less static approaches. For example, a mediator could physically move the disputants or take the mediation outdoors. Any process adaptation that moves away from legal linearity will likely increase the possibility of more embodied, more creative conflict resolution.

While mediators definitely engage with disputants' feelings to a greater extent than lawyers do, we can do more. We can work harder to include a fuller range of sensory experiences when we consider disputants' feelings. We can really contemplate how the tactile mediation environment feels. We can focus more on the atmosphere in the room. For example, Richard Birke notes it is well-documented that by the time a person becomes conscious s/he is afraid, the body has increased the blood supply to the legs in preparation for freeze, fight or flight responses, which are common across the entire human species.[19] He infers that the effects of troubling information that surface in mediation may similarly activate primitive parts of the brain during the session, so mediators need to be aware that threatening information can foreclose the possibility of creative thinking. Effective option generation simply does not happen when disputants are too worried to think imaginatively. So, for example, if mediators create a loss frame of mind in disputants by saying "if you don't settle, think of all the bad things that will happen," disputants may be less likely to brainstorm effectively. Mediators can enhance the likelihood of creative option generation and positive resolution if they refrain from inducing fear and, instead, work to calm fearful disputants. David Paul argues for canine-assisted mediation for just this reason.[20] He enumerates the many physical and psychological benefits of human-dog interactions, such as decreased blood pressure and heart rate, and decreased stress and anxiety. "Numerous studies and considerable experience from other disciplines have provided convincing evidence of a dog's ability to bring stability to one's affective and cognitive disposition."[21] Therefore Paul recommends canine-assisted mediation and LeBaron and MacLeod suggest arts approaches.[22]

17 Michelle LeBaron & Carrie MacLeod, "Inviting Persephone to Dance: Arts & Movement-Based Approaches to Peacemaking," in Susan Nan, Zachariah Mampilly & Andrea Bartoli, eds, *Peacemaking: From Practice to Theory*, Vol. 1 (Santa Barbara, CA: Praeger, 2012) at 313.

18 Ibid., at 316.

19 Richard Birke, "Neuroscience and Settlement: An Examination of Scientific Innovations and Practical Applications" (2010) 25 *Ohio State Journal on Dispute Resolution* 477 at 526.

20 David A. Paul, "Canine-Assisted Mediation" (2017) 23 *Harvard Negotiation Law Review* 123, www.hnlr.org/wp-content/uploads/HNLR-Paul-Final.pdf

21 Ibid., at 174.

22 Michelle LeBaron & Carrie MacLeod, "Inviting Persephone to Dance: Arts & Movement-Based Approaches to Peacemaking," in Susan Nan, Zachariah Mampilly &

Art, music and movement use different feelings and different parts of our brain and are therefore helpful for creative conflict resolution.

Looking toward art leads to popular culture. One of the reasons I find movies and TV so helpful for mediation study is because they assist with multi-sensory awareness – we see, we hear and we feel differently than when we merely read manuals and attend classes. A now off-the-air primetime American television show, *The Good Wife*, features a mediation episode that highlights the importance of feelings. *The Good Wife* is an Emmy Award-winning legal drama series that can be watched in its entirety on Netflix. In Season 7, Episode 5, entitled "Payback," there is an in-firm mediation between three law partners. It shows that the moment feelings are appreciated is the moment that resolution becomes possible.

Diane Lockhart, the named partner and senior woman at the firm, acts as mediator in a dispute between the youngest male partner, Cary Agos, and the oldest, Howard Lyman. Howard has threatened to sue the law firm for its alleged ageism, which he argues is predominantly perpetrated by Cary. The partners want to avoid a lawsuit so they attempt mediation. Diane is an excellent, powerful lawyer who is always portrayed as strong and in control yet does not wear pant suits or try to be like a man. *The Good Wife*'s "wardrobe designer has successfully created a new aesthetic for working women, one that celebrates the fusion of femininity and unapologetic power,"[23] and we see that in Diane. She dresses in a very powerful, feminine style and stares imperiously at anyone who does not recognize her authority (see Figure 3.1).

Diane is not a classic third party neutral. As Cary and Howard's law partner, Diane is heavily invested in the success of the mediation; she is not impartial. She does not want a lawsuit, and she has the power to personally "make things better" as she is the senior partner. Also, Diane, unbeknownst to Howard, has participated with Cary in making ageist jokes at the firm. Therefore Diane is absolutely not a neutral mediator, but she is agreed upon by both Cary and Howard and ultimately proves to be an effective conflict resolver. At the start of their session, held in the firm's boardroom, Diane explains that mediation does not replace litigation and that they will try to "amicably resolve the dispute in the best interests of the firm." The three partners work together and, after several false starts, reach a meaningful moment outside the mediation room, in Howard's office. This moment is meaningful because, for the first time, empathetic feelings are raised and expressed. It is perhaps no coincidence that the moment is reached after the parties have gotten up and walked to Howard's office.

During the mediation session in the boardroom, Cary expresses incredulity that Howard is actually experiencing any harm. Diane also wonders if Howard is

Andrea Bartoli, eds, *Peacemaking: From Practice to Theory*, Vol. 1 (Santa Barbara, CA: Praeger, 2012) at 314.

23 Ernest Macias, "*The Good Fight* costume designer on dressing Christine Baranski's powerful Diane Lockhart" (April 4, 2018), https://ew.com/tv/2018/04/04/the-good-fight-christine-baranski-wardrobe/

Figure 3.1 Christine Baranski as Diane Lockhart in *The Good Wife*

not exaggerating the extent of ageist jokes in their workplace. Howard motions them to follow him and he leads them to his office. The parties move. They stand up from the table, leave the boardroom and go to Howard's office, where he shows them an adult diaper with the words "property of Howard Lyman" written on it in marker pen. Someone in the firm has also left a bib and catheter for Howard. The music changes and Diane and Cary's faces also change. The auditory and the visual signal the emotional change. Diane and Cary feel badly for Howard. They feel remorse and it shows on their faces. This is the critical moment, or moment of insight, for all three parties. Diane immediately apologizes to Howard, saying, "I am sorry for the ageist culture we may have unwittingly fostered at the firm and we will take meaningful steps to rectify the situation." By physically moving the parties, having them get up and walk to a different office, and showing them examples of the hurt he has experienced, the disputant Howard is able to engage the sympathy and emotions of the other disputant, Cary, and the mediator, Diane.

The next scene shows the entire law firm participating in sensitivity training with an outside facilitator. The facilitator has all the lawyers put cotton into one nostril (to make breathing more difficult), wear diffusing glasses (to impair vision) and walk around the firm with raw kernels of corn in their shoes (to simulate daily pain). The facilitator explains that this should help the lawyers "feel what it is like to be eighty." Many of the lawyers, especially the young associates, are visibly moved. Although Cary wonders if Howard placed the diaper, bib and catheter in his office himself, Diane reminds him that sensitivity training does not hurt, and the scene ends with Howard smiling. This episode of *The Good Wife* shows viewers the importance of movement and how settlement becomes possible once empathic feelings are engaged. It allows viewers to *feel* how successful movement and empathy can be.

The importance of feelings literacy, empathy, movement and even furniture is also wonderfully demonstrated on *Star Trek: The Next Generation*, a long-running, Emmy award-winning, American science fiction television series. "Loud as a Whisper," the fifth episode of the second season of *Star Trek: The Next Generation*, first aired on January 9, 1989. This is noteworthy because it is not easy to find mediation in popular culture now, more than 30 years later, and yet this old episode features excellent mediation insights. It too can be found on Netflix. The crew of the USS Enterprise bring a mediator to Solais V to negotiate the end of a bloody civil war. The mediator, Riva, has been mutually selected by both sides and has a reputation as being the best. Captain Jean Luc Picard and Counsellor Deanna Troi go to meet Riva at what is described as a ceremonial greeting but is actually a pre-mediation session of sorts. Captain Picard tells his crew, "I think we should do everything to assist him," thereby demonstrating that mediation should be taken seriously. When they meet Riva they discover something incredible: the mediator is deaf. However, he is also telepathic.

Riva has a team of two men and one woman who accompany him everywhere. They are dressed all in white (the "good guys") in a Grecian style of dress, reminiscent of the three Muses, important to Greek (and, later, Roman) mythology for their knowledge of literature, science and the arts (see Figure 3.2). Riva was born deaf and he telepathically conveys his thoughts and emotions to his team, or chorus. Riva tells the Star Trek crew, "my chorus is so attuned they can hear my thoughts and translate to you." One of Riva's men speaks for Riva's intellect and logic and translates Riva's dreams. The other man in white describes Riva's passion, romance and libido and is also a warrior. The woman binds all three together and is Riva's voice of harmony and wisdom. The chorus and their individuated roles clearly demonstrate how many skills one good mediator must have. There are so many aspects to mediation that three chorus members are necessary – all of the skills required cannot be embodied in one person. Riva and his chorus are an excellent popular culture example of the depth of skill, nuance, feeling and experience a mediator must have. The work of mediation is so multi-faceted that a team is required to do it justice.

Riva, his chorus, Counsellor Troi and Captain Picard all meet again for a briefing, or official pre-mediation session. Captain Picard is prepared to brief Riva on

Figure 3.2 Riva, far left in a grey robe, and his chorus, dressed all in white

the details of the situation on Solais V. The factions have been at war for 15 centuries. There are so many dead on each side that both societies are on the verge of extinction. However, Riva declares that the specifics of the conflict are of no relevance to him. He suggests that the background portfolio they have prepared will say that the conflict is over a tangible asset such as money or property. However, he and everyone present knows the factions have been in conflict for so long that it has become personal for them. As such, Riva declares, "the basis for peace must also become personal." Riva will have to determine what has changed between the factions that they now seek peace, as they have indicated they will only speak to Riva. Riva haughtily states, "To date, I have never failed." He ends the pre-mediation session abruptly, without reading the background portfolio, leading the crew to wonder aloud if he can deliver, and suggesting that his mediation expertise is more relevant than content expertise.

Although Riva does not read the mediation brief, he does prepare the physical mediation setting. He uses a topographical map to choose the proper location for the meeting. He does not want the security that Captain Picard offers, because he wants to go in with as few people as possible. Writers have noted the importance of parties' spatial position in mediation[24] and Riva knows this too. When Riva, his chorus, Captain Picard and Counsellor Troi are beamed to the high, cliff platform

24 Barbara G. Madonik, *I Hear What You Say, But What Are You Telling Me?: The Strategic Use of Nonverbal Communication in Dispute Resolution* (San Francisco, CA: Jossey-Bass, 2001), and Desislavia Kamenova, "Meaning of Space and its Use in the Mediation Procedure" (May 2018), www.mediate.com/articles/krasinovad1.cfm

that Riva chooses as the location of the mediation, Riva says, "It is important that we set this up properly." He declares he needs a three-sided mediation table made out of material "resembling indigenous rock." This is incredibly forward-thinking for 1989 television mediation. A table with three sides would be interesting to try today. Even more important is the mediator's insight to fashion it from something resembling indigenous rock. Here Riva demonstrates his respect for the disputants. Not only does he want to give them each a seat equivalent to his at the mediation table, he also wants to create the table out of something that will be comfortable and familiar to them. He chooses to honour the place and the people of the mediation by making the table out of material that resembles what the disputants themselves use for building. Riva's first words to the emissaries of the warring factions are also excellent: "You coming here proves not only your courage, but your wisdom." Unfortunately, the mediation session then goes terribly wrong. One warrior shoots and kills Riva's entire chorus, and his comrade-in-arms kills the shooter. Riva, Captain Picard and Counsellor Troi are all immediately beamed back to the ship.

On the USS Enterprise no one can communicate with Riva because his chorus has been killed. Fortunately Lieutenant Commander Data, a non-human, android member of the crew, learns five different gestural languages in a few moments via computer and is then able to communicate with Riva. Riva is despondent, saying the death of his chorus is his fault. In his arrogance he thought no one would harm him. Counsellor Troi asks Riva: "When dealing with two factions, so diametrically opposed, so entrenched in their positions, where do you start?" Riva answers:

> My technique was to look for some thing, no matter how small, that was common to both groups and then to begin a process where one person or one group expresses themselves to each other. Getting each to really listen to each other is even harder. And then to understand. The real secret is turning disadvantage into advantage.

Counsellor Troi then implores Riva to turn his disadvantage – his lack of chorus – into an advantage, and he agrees. Riva declares that he and the disputants will have to learn how to sign in order to communicate with each another. Riva and his custom mediation table are beamed back onto the cliff ledge. Learning sign language together will be part of the warring factions' process of learning how to live together in peace. Riva's plan to have them perform a joint task of communication is wise and turns his disadvantage – an inability to speak – into an advantage because the parties and the mediator will together learn how to communicate with one another. Lieutenant Commander Data notes that it took him only moments to learn sign language but that it will take the Solais people months. Counsellor Troi counters that it will be time well spent. This highlights how crucial communication and patience is for conflict resolution. The mediator knows he cannot change the disputants' attitudes in a day. Riva recognizes the time it will take after generations of hostility to establish peace. However, he is prepared to put in the time, alone, without weapons and without backup, to do the work, and the episode ends with Riva waiting to begin working with both sides.

Expert intuition

New and old television episodes from *The Good Wife* and *Star Trek: The Next Generation* respectively provide interesting examples of mediation. They demonstrate the importance of movement, emotion, physical set-up and communication. *The Good Wife* mediation lets us experience the moment when feelings between the disputants shift and resolution becomes possible. The *Star Trek* episode graphically demonstrates just how multi-layered, nuanced and difficult the job of mediation is. TV mediators like Diane and Riva use feelings to create empathic mediation experiences. They are expert mediators, as are real mediators who create embodied mediation experiences for their disputants. Expert mediators have so much experience that they have developed expert intuition – they know just when and how to intercede. According to the Concise Oxford Dictionary, intuition is immediate apprehension by a sense or immediate insight. Synonyms include: instinct, insight, perception, sensitivity, sixth sense, hunch and feeling. Other words for intuitive are: instinctive, innate, inborn, perceptive, spontaneous, insightful, sensitive and shrewd. Excellent mediators may appear to intervene intuitively. The reality, however, is that mediators who know just when, and just how, to intercede only know this due to years of experience. Their combination of knowledge, experience and artistry leads to interventions that appear intuitive but are actually expert.

The reason it may appear that mediators intervene intuitively is because how mediators make decisions about what to do in mediation is not really understood.[25] Kenneth Kressel and Dean G. Pruitt state:

> Mediators appear to be influenced by an immediate stimulus (such as rising hostility) and perhaps by a generalized preference for a particular style of mediation, but not by any integrated perspective about the proper response to various underlying dysfunctional dynamics.[26]

That was true in 1989 when Kressel and Pruitt wrote it, and now in 2020 it is still true; it is not clear we understand mediator intervention much better today. Greg Rooney correctly points out that "the decision by the mediator to do something in the mediation session is the point at which theory meets practice."[27] Academics tend to be much more interested in theory than practitioners. We wonder: is an articulated mediation theory informing what the mediator does? Is it training? Or is it something more personal to the mediator? If popular culture depictions of the mediative role are anything to go by, it may well be something more personal to the mediator. In the same way that viewers cheer for the lawyer who thinks outside the box to solve the problem, viewers applaud TV and film conflict resolvers who just "intuitively" know what to do – like Riva, who does not

25 K. Kressel & D. Pruitt, eds, *Mediation Research: The Process and Effectiveness of Third Party Intervention* (San Francisco, CA: Jossey-Bass, 1989) at 235.

26 Ibid., at 425.

27 Greg Rooney, "The Use of Intuition in Mediation" (2007) 25:2 *Conflict Resolution Quarterly*.

even need to read the mediation brief. Practising mediators say that their decisions to intervene in a certain way "just came to them."[28] Michael D. Lang and Alison Taylor describe it as intuition.[29] Robert D. Benjamin calls it systematic intuition, "an intentional oxymoron designed to convey the ability and necessity to work with subjective and objective information simultaneously."[30] I call it expert intuition.

Peter J.D. Carnevale, Rodney G. Lim and Mary E. McLaughlin note how formal training works together with trial and error, inductive reasoning and experience to lead mediators to do what they do.[31] This means that, as in any field, more experienced practitioners are better at intervening than beginners, and those who prepare extensively perform better than those who do not. Lang and Taylor assert that intuition is really artistry, or a highly developed capacity to synthesize theory and technique into decisions and actions.[32] It is not a gut or knee-jerk reaction. It is not a quick, intuitive guess. Expert intuition is knowing what to do and when to do it, based on long experience synthesizing theory and practice.

The current proliferation of privately offered mediation training courses across North America suggests that "anyone can learn to be a mediator." While anyone can take a 40-hour mediation training course, 40 hours of mediation training is not nearly enough to reach the level of expertise that makes one's mediation work look effortless. According to Malcolm Gladwell it requires 10,000 hours to become expert at something.[33] It is those mediators who have thousands of hours of experience who appear to be intervening on intuition. However, what they actually have is expertise. They have done so much work and spent so much time mediating that they have reached a state of conscious competence or conscious expertise[34] or expert intuition. Barbara Wilson notes that mediation experts operate from a deep understanding of the total situation they confront.[35] Elaine Newman says that mediators must appreciate how they perform – "not at an

28 Ibid.

29 M.D. Lang & A. Taylor, *The Making of a Mediator: Developing Artistry in Practice* (San Francisco, CA: Jossey-Bass, 2000) at 111.

30 Robert D. Benjamin, "The Mediator as Trickster: The Folkloric Figure as Professional Role Model" (1995) 13:2 *Conflict Resolution Quarterly* 131 at 134.

31 P.J.D. Carnevale, R.G. Lim & M.E. McLaughlin, "Contingent Mediator Behaviour and its Effectiveness," in K. Kressel & D. Pruitt, eds, *Mediation Research: The Process and Effectiveness of Third Party Intervention* (San Francisco, CA: Jossey-Bass, 1989).

32 M.D. Lang & A. Taylor, *The Making of a Mediator: Developing Artistry in Practice* (San Francisco, CA: Jossey-Bass, 2000) at 7.

33 Malcolm Gladwell, *Outliers: The Story of Success* (New York: Little, Brown & Co, 2008).

34 Initially known as the "four stages for learning any new skill," Noel Burch promulgated the four states of competence in the 1970s: unconscious incompetence, conscious incompetence, conscious competence and unconscious competence. Unconscious competence is akin to intuitive intervention and outright mastery.

35 Barbara Wilson, "(Naughty) Departures: Expertise, Orthodoxy and the Role of Theory in the Practice of Mediation," in Pia Deleuran, ed., *Conflict Management in the Family Field and in Other Close Relationships – Mediation as a Way Forward* (Copenhagen: DJØF Publishing, 2011).

intuitive, 'gut' level, but with the consciousness and intentionality that the role demands."[36] In other words, at the level of artistry or expertise.

Intuition born of expertise can help a mediator make sense of an event or decide on her next intervention, and, according to Greg Rooney, it comes from the in-the-moment experience in the mediation chamber.[37] Rooney, however, argues that the intuitive thought will not emerge unless the mediator relinquishes her attachment to the need to be in control.[38] This comports with Robert A. Baruch Bush and Joseph P. Folger's views, who argue that mediators must move away from the culture of expert problem-solving.[39] If they are correct it means that mediators must move away from any needs they have to be treated as experts, even though it is their very expertise that accounts for their thoughtful, empathic mediation interventions. An example from *The Good Wife* highlights this point. "Dear God" (Season 6, Episode 3) features plaintiff Ed Pratt, who patented a seed for a development cost of $400 million. He is having a dispute with his neighbour, the defendant Wendell Keller, who does not buy his seed yet grows it on his land. Wendell argues that a bit of seed blew onto his land and that he did not fraudulently procure it. Both men have hired lawyers, but the lawyers are fighting so much in court that both clients feel unheard. During one particularly heated exchange between counsel that results in the judge yelling "shut up!" to all the lawyers, the two clients look at each other, nod and walk out of the courtroom, whereupon they proceed to discuss their case alone in the hallway. Lawyer Cary Agos follows them out and Ed says, "Cary, this trial isn't working for us." Cary responds that they should be talking to their lawyers. Ed says, "That's just the problem. It's about the lawyers, not us. Wendell is my neighbour. I should be talking to him." Wendell notes that his wife has found an arbitrator. Cary cautions that arbitration is just as binding as court, but Wendell promises this will be different. Why? Because it is binding Christian arbitration. Christian arbitrator Dell Paul explains that it is a better way than the adversarial approach and it is called the Matthew Process. It is real and based on Chapter 18 of the Book of Matthew in the Bible.

Dell opens the session with prayer; unconventional to be sure, but permissible in this context where both parties have willingly chosen to participate in Christian arbitration. Interestingly, Dell's process of arbitration does not feel like arbitration. Dell does not care about the formalities typically associated with arbitration. He is very down to earth and encourages a conversational-style process that is very informal. Dell also does not care about the rules of evidence that normally apply in arbitration. For example, when one of the lawyers objects to hearsay evidence, Dell says he does not care. "The witness is a good Christian widow and the lawyers will just have to trust the process and what

36 Elaine Newman, "Who Are We When We Mediate?" (2012) 21 *Canadian Arbitration and Mediation Journal* 42 at 42.

37 Greg Rooney, "The Use of Intuition in Mediation" (2007) 25 *Conflict Resolution Quarterly* 239 at 248.

38 Ibid., at 252.

39 Robert A. Baruch Bush & Joseph P. Folger, "Reclaiming Mediation's Future: Re-Focusing on Party Self-Determination" (2015) 16 *Cardozo Journal of Conflict Resolution* 741 at 751.

she says." As a result, Dell's process feels like mediation. He deliberately moves away from the usual position of arbitrator as expert. He proceeds informally, as he likes, according to his own process, without any evidentiary rules. He trusts each party present, even though none is sworn in, just as mediators hope that all parties participate in good faith. Dell intervenes based on his expertise in the Matthew Process and asks the parties to "Just answer the question. Tell the truth," and they do. At the end of the first day of the process, Dell indicates that he thinks intention to sin is necessary in the case. The next day Dell says he may have been too hasty, saying he would "like to reflect on this, pray on it, and return with my decision." Dell returns and says, "Thank you all. After much reflection and prayer, and returning to scripture with an open heart, I realize I was wrong. Knowledge of sin is to some extent irrelevant." Dell clearly takes himself out of the expert role and admits to making a mistake.

Bush and Folger argue that mediation, as most commonly practised today, does not provide the experience of empowerment to disputants.[40] Because many mediators have settlement or problem-solving goals, mediation has changed. Solving the problem has become more important than empowering the parties. Mediators think of themselves as the experts, when in reality the parties are the ones most capable of coming up with resolutions to their own problems. Bush and Folger convincingly argue that taking a central mediator role is attractive to mediators because of how it feels for them – being looked to as an expert feels good. However, Bush and Folger argue that when mediators see themselves as experts they move away from their central mandate, which is supporting party self-determination. Letting go of control and following the parties is not only harder than being the in-control problem solver, it also feels far less glamorous because supporting self-determination is self-effacing as compared to being the star of the process. Bush and Folger point out that the parties need to be the stars of the mediation process. Dell knows this. He is capable of admitting his mistake and not taking a central role. His disputants come up with their own resolution, even in an "arbitration" process, where normally Dell should decide. Only when mediators are truly grounded in the present moment can they help the parties improve their understanding of the past or enhance their future. Dell is present and grounded.

Dell's next step is to call a forensic botanist to speak. This opens the path for the parties to address their future. The botanist indicates that it is his expert conclusion that Wendell has been saving and replanting seeds. The lawyers get excited and begin to speak over one another, just as they did earlier in court. And again, just as they did before, the disputants speak directly to one another. Ed says to Wendell, "you know you've been doing it and it's unfair." Wendell says, "Yes, I've been replanting your seeds. I know it's against the law, but it is a rotten law. I lied before God and I'm sorry." The disputants reach a transformative moment on their own, in a process where the neutral was able to admit he made a mistake. The lawyers continue to argue vociferously so the disputants look at each other, nod and leave the session. Just like last time, Cary also leaves to see what the disputants come up with. Wendell says, "I will pay your fees for the seeds I used but that will make me a customer, and then I'd like a discount." Ed replies, "I think that's a good idea." The disputants shake

40 Ibid., at 744.

hands and leave; they have settled their dispute themselves. Their lawyers are still shouting, and the arbitrator's "ruling," if there ever really was one, is not adhered to. It was the disputants' process, which is just what good mediation should be. Later Cary's law partner, Alicia Florrick, describes it from a lawyer's perspective, saying "so, no money." However, the partner to whom she speaks replies, "at least they are friends." This popular culture example reminds us that the success of mediation needs to be measured from the perspective of the disputants, not the lawyers.

Another popular culture example of a mediator who does not seek the limelight and is able to let go of some control comes from Australia. *Face to Face* is a 2011 Australian film directed by Michael Rymer, based on David Williamson's play of the same name. *Face to Face* won Best Dramatic Feature at the 2012 Byron Bay International Film Festival and the Golden Palm Award at the 2011 Mexico International Film Festival. It is available on YouTube and follows a victim–offender mediation from start to finish.[41] The mediation involves a first-time offender, is based on actual case notes and takes place in a community centre, using a community conference or community circle process. The offender, Wayne, is accused and admits to deliberately rear-ending his boss Greg's car multiple times in Greg's driveway. Mediator Jack informs Wayne that he does not have to participate in mediation, but if he leaves he faces court instead. Wayne wants to participate because he loves his job and wants it back. It becomes clear that workplace harassment suffered by Wayne is what drove him to damage his boss' car, and, had his boss Greg better managed the workplace, Wayne would likely not be in mediation. Wayne's co-workers set him up and made a fool of him through a long-standing, cruel joke. Boss Greg knew about the joke/harassment and did nothing about it. In fact Greg told Wayne it was all done at his expense. Wayne got so angry he beat up his foreman, Richard, and Greg fired Wayne for beating up Richard. Wayne damaged Greg's car because he was upset that he got fired.

In the mediation session Wayne apologizes to Richard and actually gets up out of his seat, walks across the circle and hugs Richard. Richard accepts Wayne's apology, saying, "I was the foreman. I should have stopped it. Wayne was the best of the lot of them." Throughout this transformative process, mediator Jack intervenes very little. He is in the background, delicately directing, but not commanding, the process. Jack is just one of many important people in this community mediation. His stature is never elevated above the parties nor the other participants. The movie's poster illustrates this well (see Figure 3.3). It is not clear from viewing the poster who the mediator is, nor who the most important characters in the film are. The mediator is just one of many faces pictured. The interplay of faces on the poster – victim, offender, mediator, support people, co-workers and family members – does not lead to any obvious conclusions. This suggests that all participants in the mediation session are important and that the mediator, unlike Kate Reed for example (see Chapter 2, Figure 2.1), does not have a starring role.

Mediator Jack asks Wayne's remorseless mates, "you guys want to say anything?" It is a small intervention and it is perfect because the answer is: "I should have stopped it. I used to laugh along with them." Greg says it's a tragedy that

41 www.youtube.com/watch?v=1ehWP7X9HTs

Figure 3.3 Movie poster for *Face to Face* – the mediator is just one of many faces pictured (second from the top right-hand corner)

Wayne has to leave. Wayne says he'll come back and work even harder. The mediator might have stopped there and the parties would likely have felt better and an agreement would have been reached. However, mediator Jack stays involved in the process. He is expert and intuitive enough to know there is more. Jack does what Greg Rooney recommends. Rooney describes mediation as "a moment to moment exercise involving a partnership between the mediator and the parties."[42] Jack "partners" with Wayne and asks the question that improves everything for the circle participants. Jack asks if Greg is actually paying the lowest wages in the industry to his employees. Greg confirms that he is. The mediator then concludes that low workplace morale may have more to do with the present conflict than Greg thinks. This leads to the last phase of the mediation and the film, where the parties are able to tackle the underlying workplace problems that

42 Greg Rooney, "Rebooting Mediation by Detaching from the Illusions of Neutrality, Just Outcomes, and Balanced Power" (February 2015), www.mediate.com//articles/RooneyFutures.cfm

led to the mediation in the first place. Jack is pretty hard on Wayne, saying to him, "Come on mate, make an effort. Are you thick, Wayne?" Jack also says to the boss, "Greg, there seems to be a consensus forming: if you took a normal CEO package then there would be money to pay staff properly." Jack tells both Wayne and Greg that they must apologize. The film ends when the mediation concludes. Wayne is happy and tells the mediator, "this is one of the best days of my life." The mediator, self-effacing as Bush and Folger would recommend, and like Dell in *The Good Wife*, replies, "It's not me, it's the process."

We must look at mediative interventions from the perspective of the disputants, not the mediators, and certainly not the lawyers. The process is meant to serve the disputants who have chosen it. It is not meant to make money for lawyers (though it does). It is meant to provide resolution of conflicts (which it also does). Mediator Jack and "arbitrator" Dell moved away from any need they had to be seen as experts or in total control, and as a result the parties settled their disputes and, even more incredibly, retained their jobs in *Face to Face* and remained friends in *The Good Wife*. It is Dell and Jack's expertise and confidence that provide the setting for thoughtful, empathic results. They are expert conflict resolvers; they just do not need to proclaim themselves as such. The best mediators, like Dell, have something extra, something that cannot be taught, that makes them great at facilitating the dispute resolution processes of others. Donald Schön describes these mediators as having more wisdom, intuition or artistry.[43] Michael Moffitt says that "mediation is – and likely will forever remain – an art, at least in part."[44] Michelle LeBaron and Carrie MacLeod argue that artistry, the capacity to create with fluidity and flexibility, is key to effective conflict transformation practice, training and process design.[45] Embracing the idea that some of what mediators do may be unteachable and intuitive suggests that the best mediators are more like artists than scientists.

Is mediation artistry feminine? Feminist work has taught us that gender is the socially constructed notion of what is male and what is female, and litigation is gendered male and mediation is often gendered female.[46] Despite the great skill, nuance and expertise that is required to mediate effectively, mediation is often understood as softer, easier and more relationship-focused than litigation and therefore better suited to women. Mediation is not, however, "law-lite." The art of mediation includes expertise, feelings literacy and understanding how much of the entire person – mind, body and spirit – is involved in the dispute being mediated. The mediators I have described in this chapter in *The Good Wife*, *Star*

43 Donald A. Schön, *Educating the Reflective Practitioner* (San Francisco, CA: Jossey-Bass, 1987) at 13.
44 Michael Moffitt, "Suing Mediators" (2003) 83 *Boston University Law Review* 147 at 188.
45 Michelle LeBaron & Carrie MacLeod, "Inviting Persephone to Dance: Arts & Movement-Based Approaches to Peacemaking," in Susan Nan, Zachariah Mampilly & Andrea Bartoli, eds, *Peacemaking: From Practice to Theory*, Vol. 1 (Santa Barbara, CA: Praeger, 2012) at 308.
46 Jennifer L. Schulz & Jocelyn Turnbull, "Mediation: The 'Girly' Litigation?" (2012) *Journal of Arbitration and Mediation* 43.

Trek: The Next Generation and *Face to Face*, whether men or women, privilege disputants' feelings and have expert intuition. Their skills and artistry, feminine or otherwise, should be celebrated. If we de-emphasize them, precisely the attributes that set mediation apart from litigation – such as its focus on feelings and entire personhood, making it one of the best options for addressing disputing parties' needs and wants – will be devalued.[47]

Stereotypes about men and women and mediation styles persist. These stereotypes include: women are more collaborative than men and care more about preserving relationships; men are more adversarial than women; and women are more accommodating, focusing on people more than men do. Stereotypes lead to expectations about how women and men will behave. It is these expectations that are the real problem. For example, research demonstrates that women tend to be more egalitarian and more fair than men in negotiations,[48] but these differences between women and men are actually small in comparison to differences in stereotypical *expectations* about what women and men will do. Our expectations about differences have more impact upon negotiation and mediation than any actual differences.[49] This means that differences in behaviour actually have less weight than differences in expectations about behaviour.

While stereotypical expectations are not likely to vanish soon, I am encouraged to see that my law students hold fewer stereotypical expectations about women and men's negotiation behaviours than students held when I was in law school. One of my ADR students put it thus:

> It seems to me that most of the studies approach success from a binary perspective (deal or no deal?) or from a monetary perspective (who got the highest total?). The reality of negotiations and mediations is that there are a number of factors that define success.

One of those factors is the longevity of the agreement. There is at least one mediation study that found female mediators achieve more stable mediation agreements than male mediators,[50] possibly because the women mediators are more sensitive to the contexts of negotiations, especially when they involve a relationship, than the male mediators are.[51]

47 Ibid., at 73.

48 C. Eckel, A. de Oliveira & P. Grossman, "Gender and Negotiation in the Small: Are Women (Perceived to Be) More Cooperative than Men?" (2008) *Negotiation Journal* 429.

49 Ibid. Similarly, Deborah Kolb, "Too Bad for the Women or Does it Have to Be? Gender and Negotiation Research over the Past Twenty-Five Years" (2009) 25 *Negotiation Journal* 515 at 521 notes: "Gender schemas are implicit sets of hypotheses or assumptions about sex differences. Such schemas, although not wholly inaccurate, can inject bias into evaluations of professional women's behaviour."

50 K. Payne, P. Kohler, J.P. Cangemi & H. Fuqua, Jr, "Communication and strategies in the mediation of disputes" (2000) 29 *Journal of Collective Negotiations in the Public Sector* 29.

51 C. Eckel, A. de Oliveira & P. Grossman, "Gender and Negotiation in the Small: Are Women (Perceived to Be) More Cooperative than Men?" (2008) *Negotiation Journal* 429.

I am aware that it is gendered to be discussing gender in a chapter on feelings and intuition, and I am not trying to further replicate the gender binary. I am merely pointing out that mediation and ideas about mediators are gendered and stereotyped, and we need to address those ideas. For example, a male scholar has suggested that: "A good mediator should understand the importance of having an aura of peace about her."[52] What does he mean by that? Should male mediators strive for an aura of peace as well? Are women better at creating such auras? An Israeli study found that women mediators were more transformative than men mediators, but no less problem-solving.[53] The Israeli study notes that female mediators ascribe more importance to parties' emotions and that women mediators endorse goals of transformation more than men mediators, and endorse facilitative practices more than male mediators.[54] According to the study, overall both women and men mediators share the same primary mediation goal, which is problem-solving to help parties reach agreement. They just go about it differently. Carrie Menkel-Meadow has noticed the same about women lawyers, saying: "Female lawyers are more likely to engage in problem solving and collaborative behaviour in mediation settings, suggesting that the role that gender plays in dispute resolution is strongly tied to role (professional) as well as to place or site of dispute resolution."[55]

Tamara Relis conducted a study based on 131 interviews in the USA which demonstrates the many variables that impact upon the influence of gender in a mediation setting.[56] For example, disputants, lawyers and mediators may all have different goals, mediators can use a variety of techniques and different styles, and these tend to vary based on site and case type. As a result it is very difficult to opine on "the" influence of gender. One's gender is not a consistent predictor of negotiating behaviour or mediation performance in any event. Iris Bohnet and Hannah Riley Bowles have found that it is situational factors that make gender more or less relevant,[57] and the Israeli study found that status and situational power can interact to affect negotiation performance, sometimes rendering gender insignificant.[58] As researchers are increasingly concluding,

52 Richard Calkins, "Caucus Mediation – Putting Conciliation Back into the Process" (2005–2006) 54 *Drake Law Review* 259 at 300.

53 Noa Nelson, Adi Zarankin & Rachel Ben-Ari, "Transformative Women, Problem-Solving Men? Not Quite: Gender and Mediators' Perceptions of Mediation" (2010) 26 *Negotiation Journal* 287.

54 Ibid.

55 Carrie Menkel-Meadow, "Women in Dispute Resolution: Parties, Lawyers and Dispute Resolvers: What Difference Does 'Gender Difference' Make?" (2012) *Dispute Resolution Magazine* 4 at 6; emphasis in original and referencing the work of Tamara Relis, *Perceptions in Litigation and Mediation: Lawyers, Defendants, Plaintiffs, and Gendered Parties* (Cambridge: Cambridge University Press, 2009) at 26.

56 Tamara Relis, *Perceptions in Litigation and Mediation: Lawyers, Defendants, Plaintiffs, and Gendered Parties* (Cambridge: Cambridge University Press, 2009).

57 I. Bohnet & H. Riley Bowles, "Introduction: Gender in Negotiation" (2008) 24 *Negotiation Journal* 389.

58 Noa Nelson, Adi Zarankin & Rachel Ben-Ari, "Transformative Women, Problem-Solving Men? Not Quite: Gender and Mediators' Perceptions of Mediation" (2010) 26 *Negotiation Journal* 287 at 291.

context and personality may actually matter more than gender in mediation.[59] Research conducted in Greece supports the view that female and male lawyers are equally competitive negotiators, likely because the shared norms and values of their competitive professional culture play a critical role in how all lawyers negotiate.[60] My students tend to agree. One student in my ADR class said to his Canadian classmates:

> I do not perceive any of my female classmates to be disinclined towards competitiveness. My experience in 2nd year negotiations put me up against women far more voraciously competitive than me, a man. Does the fact that we all attend the same program help to negate some of the so-called gender differences?

I think the answer is "yes." Jennie Huang and Corinne Low conducted an experiment that further establishes the importance of context. Their research shows that the election of Donald Trump in 2016 had a profound impact on negotiations conducted in lab settings.[61] Huang and Low found that when they repeated one of their previous experiments after the 2016 USA presidential election there were important differences from their previous findings. Now Americans are less cooperative in general, more likely to use adversarial strategies, and less likely to reach an agreement; and this, according to the researchers, is particularly driven by men acting more aggressively toward women. Thus, socio-political context is significant for mediation.

Mediation context is highly relevant to the relative importance of gender and all other aspects of identity, such as age, race, ethnicity, class, ability and sexual orientation. As Deborah Kolb notes, gender is a shifting dimension of individual identity that is shaped by the contexts in which negotiation and mediation occur.[62] Another word for context is culture. Culture comprises the enduring norms, values, customs and behavioural patterns common to a group of people. Cultures are dynamic and contain subcultures, so it is impossible to definitively say what a culture does or believes or how it deals with feelings. Yet culture will suggest appropriate emotions, behaviours and thoughts to its members. Our cultural backgrounds act as standards against which we judge the actions and ideas of others, and, as such, culture is clearly implicated in conflict and its resolution. While certain cultures can be categorized as, for example, more individualistic in

59 Carrie Menkel-Meadow, "Women in Dispute Resolution: Parties, Lawyers and Dispute Resolvers: What Difference Does 'Gender Difference' Make?" (2012) *Dispute Resolution Magazine* 4.

60 Andreas Feidakis & Aspasia Tsaoussi, "Competitiveness, Gender and Ethics in Legal Negotiations: Some Empirical Evidence," http://ssrn.com/abstract=1336282

61 Jennie Huang & Corinne Low, "Trumping Norms: Lab evidence on aggressive communication before and after the 2016 US presidential election" (2017) Wharton Business School, experimental protocol in authors' working paper, "Men Don't Ask (Women): Benevolent Sexism in a Negotiation Experiment."

62 D. Kolb, "Too Bad for the Women or Does it Have to Be? Gender and Negotiation Research over the Past Twenty-Five Years" (2009) 25 *Negotiation Journal* 515 at 517.

orientation than collectivist, no culture is characterized by one specific conflict style that all its members exhibit. As Bernard S. Mayer points out, the same range of styles is found in all cultures, but the distribution of the styles varies.[63] Cultures, like women and men, may be described in terms of predominant approaches to conflict; for example, tendencies to avoid conflict or engage with it head-on. But obviously the predominant approach is not shared by all members of a gender nor all members of a culture. Indeed, cross-cultural mediation work that highlights differences "may, in the long term, serve more to uphold divisive stereotypes than undermine them."[64]

Mayer argues that it is not the differences that are most important, but rather the commonalities or similarities between cultures and people. "The most basic constant is that everyone fundamentally wants to be understood and will usually respond well to others who are making genuine, respectful efforts to grasp what is being said."[65] This is what expert mediators know and do. In turn, disputants will usually try to clarify, explain or simplify in order to facilitate better communication when they see the mediator's attitude is one of curiosity, not judgment. The best mediators are those who encourage the expression of feelings, create more embodied sessions and base interventions on their expert intuition. They are flexible and can holistically integrate their great mediation skills with intuitive people skills. They know that gender, culture, context, personality, ethnicity, ability, sexual orientation, class and age all work together to influence how mediation plays out. For these expert mediators their role may even be experienced akin to a calling.[66] They pursue mediation because of a desire to help others while promoting healing and reconciliation,[67] as do expert popular culture mediators such as Riva in *Star Trek: The Next Generation* and Dell in *The Good Wife*. Mediation is thus an art and a social science, both in the real and in the reel world.

Conclusion

Mediators care about how disputants feel and expert mediators know just when and how to intervene in order to make the most of disputants' feelings. One of

63 Bernard S. Mayer, *The Dynamics of Conflict Resolution: A Practitioner's Guide* (San Francisco, CA: Jossey-Bass, 2000) at 73.

64 Howard Gadlin, "Conflict Resolution, Cultural Differences and the Culture of Racism" (1994) 10 *Negotiation Journal* 33.

65 Bernard S. Mayer, *The Dynamics of Conflict Resolution: A Practitioner's Guide* (San Francisco, CA: Jossey-Bass, 2000) at 81.

66 Cheryl A. Picard, "The Emergence of Mediation as a Profession," in C. Morris & A. Pirie, eds, *Qualifications for Dispute Resolution: Perspectives on the Debate* (Victoria: University of Victoria, 1994) at 141–163; Cheryl A. Picard, "Why Mediators Mediate," in *Alternative Dispute Resolution Practice Manual*, Vol. 1 (Toronto: CCH Canadian Limited, June 2003) at 1501–1584.

67 Susan S. Raines, "Becoming the Change We Wish to See: The Unexpected Benefits of Conflict Resolution Work" (January 24, 2018) 35 *Conflict Resolution Quarterly* 319, https://ssrn.com/abstract=3134802

the ways they do that is by privileging their stories, which parallel mediation stories in television and film. TV and movies blend dialogue, music, scenery and action in a cohesive way, engaging multiple senses, and mediators can do the same thing. In this chapter I advocated that mediators push engagement with feelings further to make mediation a truly embodied process. Mediators can go beyond honouring the expression of disputant feelings to including the tactile environment and disputants' physical and neurological responses. Movie and TV mediators, such as those in *Face to Face, The Good Wife* and *Star Trek: The Next Generation*, create positive spaces for conflict resolution, embrace disputant emotions, and are celebrated for it. Popular culture visions of mediators and mediation are interesting, fun and different from how we teach mediation in law school. They broaden our understanding of mediation and suggest new ways mediators might create more embodied, multi-sensory dispute resolution processes. The idea that mediation as seen on TV or in practice could be quite different than as taught in theory, and yet still be good, is an idea worth exploring.

Creative, experienced popular culture mediators and real mediators who use feelings and their intuition to create the most embodied and empathic mediation experiences for disputants are experts worthy of emulation. Ideas about who is most expert at handling feelings can be gendered. There are many personal, cultural, religious and other reasons, in addition to gender, why some mediators are more or less comfortable intervening in legal disputes in more deliberately embodied ways. While stereotypes persist, both women and men mediators excel in the art of mediation and they share the same primary mediation goal, which is problem-solving to help parties reach agreement. Mediators need to engage all aspects of disputants' identities in deliberately embodied ways, just as all aspects of mediators' identities, such as age, culture, ethnicity, gender, ability, class and sexual orientation, are engaged in the task of mediating. As researchers are increasingly concluding, context, culture and personality probably matter the most. Indeed, in the current political context of Donald Trump, Noam Ebner notes that we may need to teach negotiation differently.[68] Now that fake news, alternative facts and non-existent truths are realities, negotiation and mediation teachers will need to teach more empathy.[69]

To be empathic and honour feelings requires us to engage our bodies, something that the law typically avoids. I encourage all of us – professors, trainers, mediators, law students and aspiring mediators – to engage our senses, work more deliberately with feelings, and privilege disputants' stories. To sense, as a verb, relates to grasping, feeling and understanding – central verbs in the mediation

68 Noam Ebner, "Begun, the Trust War Has: Teaching Negotiation When Truth Isn't Truth" (2019) 35:1 *Negotiation Journal* 207.

69 See also (2019) 35:1 *Negotiation Journal*, a special issue in which over 30 negotiation scholars and practitioners write about various aspects of negotiation theory and practice in the Trump era.

lexicon. To sense, to feel, to put ourselves back in touch with our emotions and our bodies makes us more complete, empathic humans. Then we can ask what remains unheard, unseen or unfelt? Whose feelings count? Which lines of critique become possible, or are foreclosed, once we consider the way the parties' dispute looks, sounds, feels, smells or tastes? How can we become experts? What new ways of practising mediation will further develop our expert intuition? Popular culture depictions of mediation can suggest things to try, or teach us and our students what to avoid. When we put disputants more in touch with their feelings and bodies, only good will come.

4 Conflicts of interest and repeat business

Popular culture: *The Office*, *Fairly Legal* (TV shows, USA) and *Wedding Crashers*, *The Break-Up* (films, USA)
Research from: Australia, Canada, Singapore, UK and USA

Conflicts of interest

Mediators, no matter how expertly intuitive, must ensure the self-determination of disputants. In order to do so, mediation theory, educators, trainers, manuals and codes of conduct all agree that mediators must mediate free from bias, and also free from the appearance of bias. Conflicts of interest are simply not allowed. Inappropriate connections cannot exist between mediators and disputants or mediators and the subject matter of the dispute. As such, mediators must be careful when pre-existing personal, professional or financial relationships exist between them and one or more of the disputants, or when they have an emotional or financial involvement in the content or outcome of the dispute. Scholars note that even social connections can be problematic. For example, social outings with one side and not the other or volunteer work in the subject matter area in dispute can lead to conflicts of interest. Richard Calkins even cautions against mediators riding the elevator to the mediation room with only one side because that may create the appearance of a conflict of interest.[1] If a mediator finds herself in a situation where she has a pre-existing relationship or an interest in the outcome, she must either withdraw or disclose her interest to all parties and let the parties decide how to proceed.

The American Model Standards of Conduct for Mediators state: if a mediator's conflict of interest might reasonably be viewed as undermining the integrity of the mediation, the mediator shall withdraw from or decline to proceed with the mediation regardless of the expressed desire or agreement of the parties to the contrary.[2] The ADR Institute of Canada's Code of Conduct for Mediators states that, before accepting an appointment as mediator and at all times after accepting such an appointment, a mediator shall disclose in writing any circumstance that could

1 Richard Calkins, "Caucus Mediation – Putting Conciliation Back into the Process" (2005–2006) 54 *Drake Law Review* 259 at 308.
2 Model Standards of Conduct for Mediators, Standard III, Conflicts of Interest (E), www.americanbar.org/content/dam/aba/migrated/2011_build/dispute_resolution/model_standards_conduct_april2007.pdf

potentially give rise to a reasonable apprehension of a lack of independence or impartiality in the mediation of a dispute. Any mediator who makes such a disclosure shall continue to serve as mediator if all parties to the dispute waive, in writing, the right to object to any reasonable apprehension of a lack of independence, impartiality or conflict of interest.[3] The European Code of Conduct for mediators states that if there are any circumstances that may, or may be seen to, affect a mediator's independence or give rise to a conflict of interest, the mediator must disclose those circumstances to the parties before acting or continuing to act.[4] The duty to disclose is a continuing obligation throughout the process of mediation. For mediators who are also lawyers, they cannot mediate if they currently represent or have previously represented one of the parties in a same or substantially related matter. Also, "a lawyer shall not mediate a dispute involving a party concurrently represented by a member of the lawyer's firm on a same or substantially related matter."[5] In general, disclosure of all conflicts, even if they seem small, is the rule. This makes sense because party self-determination is paramount; disputants need to be able to choose their mediators and decide whether to participate in mediation. If the mediator reveals a conflict of interest and, despite it, the parties provide their written consent for the mediator to proceed, she may proceed. Even then, Ellen Waldman explains, mediators should still ask themselves whether the possibility of bias seems real and pressing.[6] If the possibility for bias is real, the mediator should withdraw, even if she obtained the parties' consent.

It is not only pre-mediation activities and alliances that can cause conflict of interest concerns. Mediators should also be aware of their post-mediation interactions. This is because mediators should avoid any conduct that jeopardizes public faith in them or in mediation. The British College of Mediators' Code of Conduct states that mediators must be aware of the potential risks of developing personal relationships through social media with mediation participants and must not "friend" or communicate with mediation participants or their families through any personal social media platform.[7] The American Model Standards note that, subsequent to a mediation, a mediator shall not establish another relationship with any of the participants in any matter that would raise questions about the integrity of the mediation.[8]

When thinking about how best to teach the importance of avoiding conflicts of interest to our mediation students, there are several popular culture examples that

3 http://adric.ca/rules-codes/code-of-conduct/ at 5.1 and 5.2.
4 http://ec.europa.eu/civiljustice/adr/adr_ec_code_conduct_en.pdf at section 2.1.
5 Michelle D Gaines, "A Proposed Conflict of Interest Rule for Attorney-Mediators" (1998) 73:3 *Washington Law Review* 699 at 720.
6 Ellen Waldman, ed., *Mediation Ethics: Cases and Commentaries* (San Francisco, CA: Jossey-Bass, 2011) at 279.
7 www.collegeofmediators.co.uk/sites/default/files/CoM%20Code%20of%20Practice%20V2a.pdf at 4.4.5.
8 Model Standards of Conduct for Mediators, Standard III, Conflicts of Interest (F): www.americanbar.org/content/dam/aba/migrated/2011_build/dispute_resolution/model_standards_conduct_april2007.pdf

can be used as pedagogical tools. A popular 2005 American film, *Wedding Crashers*, demonstrates the difficulties conflicts of interest can cause in mediation.[9] *Wedding Crashers* won Best Movie at the MTV Movie Awards and Best On-Screen Team for its lead actors, Vince Vaughn and Owen Wilson, playing divorce mediators Jeremy Grey and John Beckwith respectively (see Figure 4.1). The film opens in a family mediation session. Jeremy and John are co-mediating[10] the divorce agreement between a husband and wife, who attend the mediation with their lawyers (normally in North America parties attend family or divorce mediation without counsel). Jeremy and John do many things in this mediation session that real mediators would never do – for example, they interrupt the parties, start singing a song, swear and use crass language – clearly falling

Figure 4.1 Vince Vaughn as Jeremy and Owen Wilson as John, co-mediators in *Wedding Crashers*

9 For readers interested in another American popular culture portrayal of divorce mediation, see *Untying the Knot*, a Bravo television series, available at www.bravotv.com/untying-the-knot. The website describes the show:

> Celebrity divorce attorney and expert mediator Vikki Ziegler travels the country using her distinct brand of honest, empathetic, and to-the-point communication to help couples divorce with dignity through mediation. Expert appraisers Michael and Mark Millea evaluate the items in contention so Vikki can determine a fair, equitable division of assets. Why let a judge decide your fate when this divorce diva can cut through all the drama?

10 See Jennifer L. Schulz, "Using Film to Teach ADR," in Christine Corcos, ed., *The Media Method: Teaching Law With Popular Culture* (Durham, NC: Carolina Academic Press, 2019) at 388–392 for a discussion of co-mediation as illustrated in *Wedding Crashers*.

afoul of the ADR Institute of Canada's Code of Conduct, which requires mediators to avoid impropriety or the appearance of impropriety.[11] When the divorcing couple attempts to decide how their air miles will be shared, Jeremy suggests they might wish to "throw a couple of miles at us." This conflict of interest can be discussed and examined in the classroom. Are the co-mediators allowed to ask for some of the couple's air miles? Is this unethical? Family Mediation Canada, Canada's largest national institute of family and divorce mediators, mandates that its mediators never suggest receiving or accept any part of the parties' assets for their service as mediators[12] unless such an arrangement has been explicitly agreed to in advance by both parties. So, what if the former spouses agree at the mediation session? Can Jeremy and John leave with air miles as payment for their mediation services?

Another popular American film, also starring Vince Vaughn, is 2006's *The Break-Up*. Vaughn plays Gary Grobowski and Jennifer Aniston plays Brooke Meyers. Aniston won the People's Choice Award for Favourite Movie Star for *The Break-Up*, and together she and Vaughn won the Teen Choice Award for Best Movie Chemistry. They play a heterosexual Chicago couple living in a beautiful condo. Their relationship ends and they are in dispute over the condo because each wants to be the one who keeps it. After unsuccessfully trying to live in the condo together after their break-up, Gary and Brooke meet with their mutual friend, Mark Riggleman, who is a real-estate agent. In the film's mediation scene, Brooke and Gary are seated far apart from one another on the living room sofa. Mark sits directly across from them, perched on their coffee table. Once Mark establishes that the couple definitely will not reconcile, he says, "As your friend and as your realtor, I'm not going to leave here tonight until we decide what to do about this condo, as this living situation is obviously not working out." Gary thinks Brooke should move out and Brooke thinks Gary should be the one to leave. The two begin to fight about what each has done to depreciate the value of the condominium. Their complaints escalate, becoming louder and louder. Finally, Mark, the mediator, interrupts them by saying "you guys are gonna kill each other." Mark continues:

> Realistically speaking, neither one of you can afford this mortgage on your own. That's a shame because this building will continue to increase in value. I get nothing but phone calls about it, waiting for a unit to open up. So, as your realtor, the *last* thing I would suggest is selling. But, as your friend, I don't see any other solution. You take your halves, you go your separate ways, and you get on with your lives. I know that selling is not the easiest thing, but I do think that it's the best. And, to be honest, this is a situation where I would just as soon not take a commission.

11 ADR Institute of Canada, rule 7, http://adric.ca/rules-codes/code-of-conduct/

12 Family Mediation Canada, *Members Code of Professional Conduct*, article 15: "It is inappropriate for a mediator to base fees on the outcome of the mediation process." See http://fmc.ca/sites/default/files/sites/all/themes/fmc/images-user/Members%20Code%20of%20Professional%20Conduct_0.pdf

"That's great," says Brooke; "thank you for that," says Gary. But Mark Riggleman "wriggles out," saying:

> I wish I didn't have to, but company policy says I cannot waive that. But I'm saying, in theory, in this situation, because we're friends, I *wish* I could waive it. No can do though. As soon as you can, I'd love a set of keys and then I'll be bringing people by all weekend. Is it okay to leave you two alone now?

The scene ends with Mark leaving and Brooke and Gary sitting silently and forlornly on the sofa (see Figure 4.2).

Brooke wants the condo, Gary wants the condo, and Mark, their friend and mediator, wants to make money from listing and selling the condo. This scene in *The Break-Up* clearly demonstrates the conflict of interest that arises when the mediator has an interest in the subject matter of the dispute. The American Model Standards of Conduct would require Mark to withdraw from mediation because his conflict of interest – his desire to obtain the condo listing – undermines the integrity of the mediation. The ADR Institute of Canada's Code of Conduct and the European Code of Conduct for mediators would both require Mark to disclose, in writing, his interest in the condo listing. If Brooke and Gary both agreed, in writing, to Mark continuing to mediate, despite his conflict, Mark could then continue.

Figure 4.2 Vince Vaughn as Gary and Jennifer Aniston as Brooke in *The Break-Up*, right after Mark the mediator leaves

Repeat business

Brooke and Gary choose Mark as their mediator because he is their friend. Personal networks and lawyers are the source of many mediators' work referrals. Nadja Alexander writes:

> Anecdotal evidence suggests that in most cases gatekeepers within the legal system will tend to refer matters to lawyer-mediators; gatekeepers outside the legal system are likely to refer to other mediators with whose work and disciplinary background they are familiar.[13]

Waldman notes that a lawyer's power of referral could lead a mediator, consciously or unconsciously, to lean toward that lawyer's client's side.[14] Similarly, Diane Mainville states that "mediators in private practice may not want to offend the lawyer who was responsible for getting them appointed."[15] Thus the lure or hope of repeat business from a lawyer may lead a mediator to favour that lawyer's client, as a happy lawyer is a more likely source of future work for the mediator.

My own mediation experience bears out the possibility that the lure of repeat mediation business may have motivational force for mediators. I am fortunate to mediate for a provincial mediation programme in my home city. It provides steady, interesting mediation work and handles all the administrative details. I have found myself, on more than one occasion, going into the mediation programme manager's office after a successful mediation to announce how well it went. Upon reflection, I must admit this is either an exercise in ego on my part or a desire for more referrals. We see this in popular culture as well. A popular American TV show, *The Office*, based on the successful British series of the same name, stars Steve Carell as Michael Scott, the regional manager of a paper company. Michael's character is based on the character David Brent, played by Ricky Gervais in the British original. Season 2, Episode 21, entitled "Conflict Resolution," features Michael as a mediator of sorts. The episode begins with a dispute between Caucasian Angela, the owner of a poster featuring a white baby and a black baby playing miniature saxophones, and Latino Oscar, a co-worker who hates the poster and wants it removed from their workplace. Despite the fact that Toby is charged with managing office conflict, Michael decides to step in. He sits in a conference room with Angela, Oscar and other office staff, "training" them from a manual entitled *A Mediator's Tool Chest*. The manual describes five different styles of conflict. After a funny sequence wherein Michael determines that none of the staff wishes to choose the lose-lose method, he notes that, while method number four is win-win, they will employ method number five, win-win-win. In this

13 Nadja Alexander, ed., *Global Trends in Mediation*, 2nd edn (Alphen aan den Rijn: Kluwer Law International, 2006) at 33.

14 Ellen Waldman, ed., *Mediation Ethics: Cases and Commentaries* (San Francisco, CA: Jossey-Bass, 2011) at 282.

15 Diane Mainville, "What is Good Faith Negotiation and Mediation?" (2018) 27:1 *Canadian Arbitration and Mediation Journal* 10 at 15.

method, not only do the disputants win but so does the mediator, and Michael is very interested in winning. Michael is interested in winning, or settling disputes, because it looks good upon him, the mediator. He wants the ego boost of a win, the accolades of his colleagues for being a better mediator than Toby, and all future work as the office mediator.

Research demonstrates that lawyers prefer mediators who settle, and often choose mediators based on their settlement records.[16] Therefore a good reputation for achieving settlement helps the mediator's reputation, leading to more work. Julie Macfarlane states that "Mediators have an incentive to develop positive relationships with 'repeat-player' lawyers (and, less often, 'repeat-player' clients) since their livelihood usually depends on the market's assessment of their work."[17] Referring lawyers, rosters and other case-referrers, such as judges, look to mediators' records because records of agreements are viewed as synonymous with success. So, for example, in the TV show *Fairly Legal*, Judge Nicastro assigns mediator Kate to work with a high-school football coach whom the judge feels indebted to for the coach's previous life-changing work with the judge's son. Kate says to the judge, "Sir, mediators aren't partial, so …" Here we see that Kate knows mediators are supposed to be impartial. The judge responds, "just be fair." Kate replies, "I can do that sir." The judge says, "I'll be watching, closely."[18] Kate knows the judge wants her to facilitate an agreement that will work well for his friend, the coach. In other words, despite her explanation that mediators should be impartial, she goes into this mediation session knowing that the judge will be watching closely to ensure the result is fair for his friend. Judge Nicastro, due to his position as a judge, and by virtue of the fact that he is the member of the bench that most often assigns Kate the mediation cases that comprise her livelihood, has compromised Kate's independence as a mediator. This episode clearly depicts how conflicts of interest and repeat business are linked.

If the lure of repeat business does not lead to an actual conflict of interest in mediation practice, it could lead to what John Wade describes as "predictable pressure" on dispute resolution professionals to recommend "splitting the difference" so as to remain marketable.[19] This obviously implicates mediation style. If compromising maintains marketability, will other mediation styles that are not about compromising, such as transformative or insight mediation, fall out of favour? The American Bar Association Task Force on Improving Mediation Quality found that 95% of lawyer consumers of mediation want mediators to give an analysis of the

16 Julie Macfarlane, *The New Lawyer: How Clients are Transforming the Practice of Law*, 2nd edn (Vancouver: University of British Columbia Press, 2017) at 207; B. McAdoo, "A Report to the Minnesota Supreme Court: The Impact of Rule 114 on Civil Litigation in Minnesota" (2002) 25 *Hamline Law Review* 401 at 428–429.

17 Julie Macfarlane, *The New Lawyer: How Clients are Transforming the Practice of Law*, 2nd edn (Vancouver: University of British Columbia Press, 2017) at 207.

18 Episode 103, "Benched."

19 John Wade, "Evaluative Mediation – Elephants in the Room?" (February 20, 2019), www.mediate.com/pfriendly.cfm?id=14034 at 13.

case, including strengths and weaknesses.[20] In other words, 95% of American lawyers who participate in mediation prefer an evaluative mediation style, and Robert A. Baruch Bush describes a preponderance of coercive and evaluative practices amongst court-connected and other institutionally based mediators.[21]

An evaluative approach to mediation appeals to lawyers who want quick answers, and who are often evaluative in style themselves. As Stephen B. Goldberg and Margaret L. Shaw state, "there was a general sense among the mediators we interviewed that lawyers, including retired judges, now dominate the mediator market" and they are evaluative in style.[22] The International Academy of Mediators (IAM) and the Straus Institute for Dispute Resolution at Pepperdine University School of Law conducted a survey of 130 IAM mediators.[23] They found that 80% of respondents indicated that their reputation as a mediator who could offer useful assessments of parties' cases was a factor in attracting and maintaining clients.[24] California mediators were much more likely than mediators outside the United States to develop and propose potential agreements, give their predictions, and assess the legal strength of arguments. Mediators from other areas of the globe were more likely to help parties develop or communicate proposals, but not offer their opinion regarding the proposals.[25] This evaluative approach, as discussed in Chapter 2, is the style we see in popular culture mediations but is quite opposite the facilitative style of mediation we teach in our law schools. If mediators are moving toward settlement and agreements precipitously, just to enhance their settlement records, that is both a mediation style problem and a conflict of interest problem. One of my ADR students put it this way in his written comments for class:

> I would assume that there have been many instances where the mediator was suspicious that one or more parties were not acting in good faith, but in an effort to avoid slowing down the process, or for other reasons, such as keeping the business, continued on with mediation.

This is worrisome indeed.

Due to a desire to garner repeat business, mediators may be mediating when conflict of interest rules would suggest they should not; which is connected to the

20 American Bar Association Task Force on Improving Mediation Quality, Final Report (2008) and James H. Stark & Douglas N. Frenkel, "Changing Minds: The Work of Mediators and Empirical Studies of Persuasion" (2013) 28 *Ohio State Journal on Dispute Resolution* 263 at 311.

21 Robert A. Baruch Bush, "Staying in Orbit or Breaking Free: The Relationship of Mediation to the Courts over Four Decades" (2008) 84 *North Dakota Law Review* 705 at 732–739.

22 Stephen B. Goldberg & Margaret L. Shaw, "The Past, Present, and Future of Mediation as Seen through the Eyes of Some of Its Founders" (April 2010) 26:2 *Negotiation Journal* 237 at 244.

23 IAM/Straus Institute Survey on Mediator Practices and Perceptions (Spring 2014).

24 Thomas J. Stipanowich, "Insights on Mediator Practices and Perception" (Winter 2016) *Dispute Resolution Magazine* 4 at 7.

25 IAM/Straus Institute Survey on Mediator Practices and Perceptions (Spring 2014).

problem of repeat players in the litigation system, identified by Marc Galanter decades ago.[26] As compared to those who are involved in the system on only a one-shot basis, such as most clients, repeat players, such as lawyers, data-rich insurance companies, judges and some mediators, have more experience and expertise. They have advance information, access to experts, relationships with others in the system and greater credibility.[27] Defendant insurance companies, data-rich repeat players in mediation, typically have more information than one-shot claimants do, including settlement amounts of similar cases and mediator predispositions.[28] If a repeat player insurance company feels the final resolutions with a particular mediator are insufficiently in its favour, it is not fanciful to imagine that, in the future, it may choose a different mediator. This, in turn, may affect how that mediator mediates in future cases. It is also reasonable to conclude that repeat players such as lawyers and insurance company representatives may work together to ensure efficient mediation outcomes. This may mean that repeat players will see mediation as their process and not the claimants' process, which could negatively impact mediation creativity. Mediation might become what we are seeing in many large commercial centres: fixing a monetary value through shuttle "mediation."[29]

A leading Canadian mediator, Rick Russell, notes: "The practice of mediation, particularly commercial mediation, has moved a long way from the interest-based ideal that many mediators were taught."[30] Two mediation staples – a facilitative approach and using joint sessions – may be on the wane. In Ontario, Canada, for example, commercial mediators are expected to give substantive feedback. The lawyers who expect this do not seem to mind if the line between offering legal advice and legal information is blurred. Commercial mediators are often hired for their substantive knowledge and then, as Russell notes, expected to use their knowledge to convince parties to move away from unrealistic positions. In other words, an evaluative approach is greatly preferred to facilitative mediation. Indeed, Kenneth Roberts says that purely facilitative mediation no longer exists in complex

26 Marc Galanter, "Why the 'Haves' Come Out Ahead: Speculations on the Limits of Legal Change" (1974) 9 *Law & Society Review* 95 (suggesting that the basic structure of litigation is such that the "haves" [wealthy, professional, repeat-players] will consistently enjoy more favourable norms, rules, institutions, and outcomes). See also Carrie Menkel-Meadow, "Do the 'Haves' Come Out Ahead in Alternative Judicial Systems? Repeat Players in ADR" (1999) 15 *Ohio State Journal on Dispute Resolution* 38.

27 Marc S. Galanter, "Why the 'Haves' Come Out Ahead: Speculations on the Limits of Legal Change" (1974) 9 *Law & Society Review* 95 at 98–104.

28 Edward Brunet, "Reevaluating Complex Mediation Generalizations" (2011) 18:1 *Connecticut Insurance Law Journal* 279 at 293.

29 Nancy A. Welsh, "The Thinning Vision of Self-Determination in Court-Connected Mediation: The Inevitable Price of Institutionalization?" (2001) 6 *Harvard Negotiation Law Review* 1. Mediators in the UK report significant resistance from lawyers to joint sessions in mediation; see A Survey of Commercial Mediator Attitudes and Experience in the United Kingdom, www.cedr.com/docslib/The_Eighth_Mediation_Audit_2018.pdf

30 Rick Russell, "The Principle of Impartiality: Is it relevant to dispute resolution practitioners?" (2019) 27:2 *Canadian Arbitration and Mediation Journal* 9–12.

commercial mediation. Evaluative methods, used in a facilitative process, are essential for successful commercial mediation, according to Roberts.[31] He says that mediators do not make final determinations, but that in complex commercial mediations they should provide information and advice to parties, predict outcomes and provide possible solutions.[32] This is because, in his view, the goal of mediation is not settlement but, rather, information and enhanced understanding of the dispute in order to be prepared for litigation should mediation fail.[33] This is very different from what we typically teach our mediation students.

Lawyers tend to prefer mediators with substantive area expertise, backgrounds in law, and evaluative approaches. Jeffrey H. Goldfien and Jennifer K. Robbennolt's research supports this observation. They found that those who prefer to handle their conflicts competitively, such as lawyers, also prefer directive mediator behaviours and mediators who give their own opinions. They do not desire creative mediators or joint sessions.[34] Lela P. Love and Ellen Waldman argue that the process offered by commercial mediators lacks many of the distinguishing characteristics of traditional mediation, such as party self-determination, communication exchange and creative problem-solving; "the busiest mediators veer sharply toward more traditional evaluative practices."[35] This approach gives the lawyers a lot of power, power that more rightly belongs in the hands of the disputants, and limits opportunities for mutual brainstorming. The evaluative approaches of many commercial mediators are more in line with lawyerly adversarial behaviour and competition than with the facilitative mediation training received by most mediators, or the relational needs of many disputants; research shows that disputants do want creative and elicitive mediation approaches.[36] This is directly related to repeat business because lawyers will select mediators whom they believe will complement their preferred mediation strategies.[37] As Goldfien and Robbennolt note, "mediators may seek to define themselves in terms of mediation style as a response to market pressures resulting from attorneys' influence over the selection of mediators."[38] The concern is that this may lead to a reduction in the use of facilitative mediation approaches and joint sessions. When I mediate for a

31 Kenneth M. Roberts, "Mediating the Evaluative-Facilitative Debate: Why Both Parties are Wrong and a Proposal for Settlement" (2007) 39:1 *Loyola University Chicago Law Journal* 187 at 188.
32 Ibid., at 210.
33 Ibid., at 211.
34 Jeffrey H. Goldfien & Jennifer K. Robbennolt, "What if the Lawyers Have Their Way? An Empirical Assessment of Conflict Strategies and Attitudes Toward Mediation Styles" (2007) 22:2 *Ohio State Journal on Dispute Resolution* 277 at 308.
35 Lela Love & Ellen Waldman, "Hopes and Fears of All the Years: 30 Years Behind and the Road Ahead for the Widespread Use of Mediation" (2016) 31 *Ohio State Journal on Dispute Resolution* 123 at 149.
36 Jeffrey H. Goldfien & Jennifer K. Robbennolt, "What if the Lawyers Have Their Way? An Empirical Assessment of Conflict Strategies and Attitudes Toward Mediation Styles" (2007) 22:2 *Ohio State Journal on Dispute Resolution* 277 at 318.
37 Ibid., at 312–313.
38 Ibid., at 313.

provincial mandatory mediation programme in Ontario I occasionally have the feeling that I am not really mediating, but rather engaging in a settlement conference, shuttling between break-out rooms, as the desire for private sessions is much higher than for joint session mediation. Repeat players such as myself are able to work with lawyers and mediation administrators to ensure that cases are handled in an efficient manner. This may be beneficial for the system as a whole but it can hinder more creative mediation outcomes and can hamper disputant input and party self-determination. John Lande posits that mediators may even come to see the lawyers as their clients, rather than the disputing parties.[39]

The IAM and Straus Institute survey of 130 IAM mediators[40] found that experienced mediators highly value preliminary preparation,[41] a good thing, but that almost 40% of them begin mediation in caucus.[42] Caucus is a private meeting within the mediation session, wherein the mediator meets with only one side. Then the mediator leaves that party and meets with the other side, also in private. (For a more detailed treatment of caucusing, see Chapter 5.) The IAM study found that mediators practising in California are the most likely to begin mediation with the parties in caucus, while mediators practising outside the United States, including Canada, Europe, Australia and Latin America, are much less likely to do so. Surprisingly, one quarter (24.6%) of all mediators always keep parties in caucus during the entire mediation; this means the parties are not together in joint session at all. According to the IAM study, California mediators were the most likely to keep parties in caucus throughout, and mediators practising outside the USA were much less likely to do so. American mediators outside of California fall somewhere in between.[43] California mediators laid the blame for this at the feet of lawyers, whom they report do not want joint sessions in mediation. Eric Galton notes:

> In various parts of the United States, mediations are regularly conducted without joint or general sessions. … Mediators, fearing market reprisal if they refuse, either acquiesce or even promote "I don't do joint sessions" as a marketing tool. Before our very eyes, we are seeing a structural dismantling of the mediation process that was held so dear.[44]

Galton explains this is because mediators need to follow the business, and lawyers are the ones who provide the business by choosing the mediators. Commercial lawyers are comfortable in mediations without joint sessions. Lawyers often do not

39 John Lande, "How Will Lawyering and Mediation Practices Transform Each Other?" (1997) 24 *Florida State University Law Review* 839 at 882.
40 IAM/Straus Institute Survey on Mediator Practices and Perceptions (Spring 2014).
41 Thomas J. Stipanowich, "Insights on Mediator Practices and Perception" (Winter 2016) *Dispute Resolution Magazine* 4 at 8.
42 Ibid., at 5. The precise figure is 39.7%, according to Stipanowich.
43 Ibid., at 6.
44 Eric R. Galton, "The Mediation Witches" (2015) 16 *Cardozo Journal of Conflict Resolution* 825 at 826.

want joint sessions because, in joint sessions, lawyers are not in control and clients participate "too much." The lawyer thinks, "what if my client says something I don't expect, don't like, or can't control?" and so the lawyer chooses a mediator who favours caucusing, where clients' comments will not be heard by the other side. Wade describes it this way: "Standardly lawyers ask the mediator to 'leave the room,' so that they can have the allegedly 'real' and confidential conversations with their clients about their actual goals and risks."[45] Other lawyers do not like joint sessions because they think they are a waste of time; the parties merely rehash what "everyone already knows." These lawyers also choose mediators who are prepared to dispense with joint sessions. Since lawyers function as the gatekeepers for mediator selection, if mediators want continued paid work they begin to increase the amount of caucusing they do. Over time this erodes the mediation process as we understand it and teach it in law schools. Scholars are reporting the decline of joint sessions in mediations.[46] Galton states that the mediation process, thousands of years in the making, is being dismantled for two simple reasons – money and fear.[47] Mediators want to make money and they are afraid of losing business. Instead of resisting the movement toward no joint sessions, some mediators are aligning themselves with lawyers and are offering shuttle "mediation," or mediation with no joint sessions.

Mediators' desire for repeat business is connected to repeat player concerns. Donna Erez-Navot asks what happens when everyone in the court-connected mediation chamber knows each other, except for the plaintiff.[48] Can the plaintiff get justice, as the only outsider in the session? Will the lawyers have more allegiance to the system that they have to participate in every day than to their one-shot clients? Even more distressingly, Erez-Navot argues that mediation may be a more favourable venue than court for a repeat player seeking an advantage over a marginalized party.[49] Her fear is that one-shot players will receive second-class justice in mediation. This may be a legitimate fear. Nancy Welsh notes the trend toward less party control and less self-determination in court-connected mediation.[50] Lisa Bingham

45 John Wade, "Evaluative Mediation – Elephants in the Room?" (February 20, 2019), www.mediate.com/pfriendly.cfm?id=14034 at 12.

46 James R. Coben, "Barnacles, Aristocracy and Truth Denial: Three Not So Beautiful Aspects of Contemporary Mediation" (2015) 16 *Cardozo Journal of Conflict Resolution* 779 at 779–80; and Jay Folberg, "The Shrinking Joint Session: Survey Results" (Winter 2016) *Dispute Resolution Magazine* 14 at 15 (showing that mediators in east/central parts of the United States use an initial joint session 68.5% of the time, in the northwest 34% of the time, and in the southwest 23.6% of the time).

47 Eric R. Galton, "The Mediation Witches" (2015) 16 *Cardozo Journal of Conflict Resolution* 825 at 827.

48 Donna Erez-Navot, "The Repeat Player Effect in Child Protection Mediation: Dangers of and Protections Against Second-Class Justice for Marginalized Parties" (2015) 16 *Cardozo Journal of Conflict Resolution* 831.

49 Ibid., at 832.

50 Nancy A. Welsh, "The Thinning Vision of Self-Determination in Court-Connected Mediation: The Inevitable Price of Institutionalization?" (2001) 6 *Harvard Negotiation Law Review* 1 at 25–26.

finds that employee success rates in labour arbitration are only 11% when the employer is a repeat player, as compared to 48% when the employer is a non-repeat player.[51] Erez-Navot notes that the repeat player effect is especially likely to rear its head in court-connected mediation programmes where the plaintiffs are often one-shot users of the system, whereas the lawyers, mediators and insurance company representatives are repeat players.[52] This means that a system designed to help the one-shot user, mediation, is actually being co-opted for the benefit of the repeat players.

I have encountered this in my own practice. In the Manitoba mediation programme in which I mediate, cases typically consist of a claimant on one side and a representative of the insurance company on the other. Lawyers may attend, but they seldom do. Claimants are either unrepresented or they attend with a claimant advisor to assist them. In the spring of 2019 I conducted two different mediations for the programme, one day after the other. They were two separate claims and two different claimants, but the insurance company representative was the same person in both mediations, and I mediated both disputes. Thus the defendant insurance representative and the mediator were repeat players, and the claimants were one-shot players. The insurance representative and I talked about both cases, compared the two, and noted that the claimant in one case was quite unsophisticated. We discussed how best to proceed. In this particular instance I believe my established relationship with the insurance representative enabled me to coach her as to how best to proceed with the unsophisticated claimant who needed much reassurance. This helped the claimant and made the mediation proceed more smoothly. I also suspect that the insurance representative's knowledge about me, the mediator, helped her in ways that I am unaware of. Although it did not happen in our case, it is easy to imagine a situation where a mediator's relationship with a repeat player insurance company representative could lead the mediator and representative to conduct "trade-offs" when they have two or more mediations together, or to conduct themselves in ways where conflict of interest provisions might be called into question. A relationship between repeat players or a mediation programme manager's power of referral could lead a mediator, consciously or unconsciously, to develop a conflict of interest in favour of the defendant's or programme's future mediation business.

Do mediators have to disclose their referral relationships to their disputants? Josh Stulberg says, "The widespread reported practice was 'it's none of that party's damn business that 70 percent of my income comes from the other party'."[53] Stulberg found that response "stunning."[54] We could ask our students if they agree. Do

51 Lisa B. Bingham, "Employment Arbitration: The Repeat Player Effect" (1997) 1 *Employment Rights and Employment Policy Journal* 189 at 213.

52 Donna Erez-Navot, "The Repeat Player Effect in Child Protection Mediation: Dangers of and Protections Against Second-Class Justice for Marginalized Parties" (2015) 16 *Cardozo Journal of Conflict Resolution* 831 at 842.

53 As quoted in Stephen B. Goldberg & Margaret L. Shaw, "The Past, Present, and Future of Mediation as Seen through the Eyes of Some of Its Founders" (April 2010) 26:2 *Negotiation Journal* 237 at 244.

54 Ibid.

mediators have an ethical obligation to let all parties know the source of their work referrals? This is at the crux of the tension between repeat business and conflicts of interest. In the Manitoba mediation programme I mediate for, on one side there is a Crown corporation insurance company, a repeat player. On the other side are many one-off mediation claimants. While I am an independent contractor mediator, I too am a repeat player in that programme and 100% of my income from that mediation programme comes from the Crown corporation, albeit a different branch. Is this a conflict of interest? Is it ethical? Do I need to disclose this information to all disputants? Do your answers change if you know that this programme is well respected, consistently reports good success/settlement rates, has been in existence for years and has been positively reviewed by disputant users? With current growing interest from law students in practising as mediators, we cannot only address the problem of where they will obtain work once they are trained. We must also surface the ethical issues inherent in mediation referrals and openly tackle conflict of interest questions around garnering work, especially from repeat players.

The repeat player effect is also important when it comes to systems design. Repeat players tend to have the most input in designing court-connected mediation programmes, again leaving out the one-shot players – the disputants, whom the programmes should actually be for. The same "Conflict Resolution" episode of *The Office* previously discussed provides an example. Netflix summarizes the episode as follows: "When Michael takes over Toby's conflict resolution duties, his approach of encouraging 'cooperation through confrontation' may ruin office morale." In the episode Michael takes the file of office complaints and confronts the staff. Michael notes they need to get "all of the festering negativity out in the open," so he reads their complaints out loud, thereby breaching the confidentiality they presumed they had when they made the complaints and embarrassing them all in front of one another. The episode ends with Michael "mediating" a series of conflicts in the same boardroom he mediated Angela and Oscar's dispute (see Figure 4.3) in front of a sign that reads, "Communicate: Working Together to Resolve Conflict."

Figure 4.3 Steve Carell as Michael, holding up "The Mediator's Tool Chest" in *The Office*. Angela is on the left and Oscar is on the right. The sign in the background says "Communicate: Working Together to Resolve Conflict."

Nadja Alexander notes, "organizations representing 'repeat player' businesses may use mediation to promote their own interests without the influence of external social, moral, cultural and legal norms, and public scrutiny."[55] This is exactly what Michael does. He is a repeat player with power in the office and he uses his power to tailor the mediation system to his needs, not to the employees'/disputants' needs. He "mediates" a parking space dispute and calls it solved, despite the fact that it is not. In a sexual harassment dispute between two employees regarding sexually suggestive remarks, Michael "resolves" it by telling the woman she can retaliate by making sexually suggestive remarks to the man that will make him uncomfortable. Michael is clearly not helping; he is hindering workplace relationships and condoning actionable behaviour. In real life we need to ensure that one-shot mediation disputants receive excellent mediation services wherein they are able to exercise self-determination, and that mediators mediate for the disputants, not for the lawyers or for any future business that may ensue.

In her research on repeat arbitrators, Natalia Giraldo-Carrillo found that European courts have held that arbitrators must have received more than three appointments by the same counsel or law firm within the past three years in order for their independence to be compromised.[56] I am not suggesting that the formula of "not more than three in three years" should be applied to mediators, but it is interesting to think about whether there should be a formula or a cap, and what it might be. Giraldo-Carrillo also notes that for "factual repeat arbitrators," those who have previously worked on the same set of facts or transaction, European courts tend to favour the repeat appointments.[57] This parallels what I have seen in my own mediation practice; that once I mediate for parties and we reach a resolution, if they run into difficulty a few years later they contact me to mediate again due to my familiarity with the case. Most arbitrators and mediators care deeply about their reputations and would be unlikely to risk them by taking on cases that could jeopardize how their independence was perceived by their colleagues.[58] However, it is equally true that most arbitrators and mediators are desirous of more business and must be careful to always practise ethically, free from conflicts of interest.

The final, very important, problem with repeat users of mediation services is the fact that repeat business does not favour women or other marginalized mediators. Lawyers and personal networks are still the primary source of mediators' work referrals, and referrers usually refer people who look like, or are like, them. Thus women and members from equity-seeking groups are less often referred. In an American study conducted by Andrea Kupfer Schneider and Gina Viola Brown, the authors found that when mediators are selected by lawyers, or clients choose

55 Nadja Alexander, ed., *Global Trends in Mediation*, 2nd edn (Alphen aan den Rijn: Kluwer Law International, 2006) at 12.

56 Natalia Giraldo-Carrillo, "The 'Repeat Arbitrators' Issue: A Subjective Concept" (2011) 19 *International Law* 75 at 90, referencing Swedish case law and the International Bar Association's *Guidelines on Conflicts of Interest in International Arbitration*, available at www.ibanet.org

57 Ibid., at 96.

58 Ibid., at 92.

from their personal networks, few women are selected to mediate.[59] When parties or their lawyers choose from rosters created by ADR providers or courts, the percentage of women selected as mediators goes up significantly. Kupfer Schneider and Brown sent their survey to lawyer-members of the American Bar Association's Dispute Resolution Section. Ninety percent of the respondents had been involved, either as a neutral or as an advocate, in at least one dispute within the past year. A significant majority, 70%, were born between 1940 and 1959, and of that group the vast majority were men. In the cohort born in 1970 or later, there were more female respondents than male respondents, and, overall, respondents were younger in mediation than in arbitration. The overall baseline of survey respondents was 66% men and 34% women, which compares to the composition of ADR Section members in the American Bar Association. For mediators, 63% were men and 37% were women, but for arbitration, 80% were men. Sixty-six percent of panel arbitrations had three male arbitrators and none of the reported cases had all-women panels. Women did sometimes serve as arbitrators alone, or with two other men on a panel. Only 8% of cases had one man and two women on the arbitration panel. Of the 294 arbitrators who served on panels in the survey, only 14% were women. Kupfer Schneider and Brown also found that corporate, construction, insurance and intellectual property disputes are significantly dominated by male ADR practitioners, while women serve as mediators in more than half the cases dealing with family, elder and consumer law, as well as small claims. Women serve as mediators much more often in disputes involving claims under $100,000. Of the cases worth more than $100,000, women mediated only 25% of them. The International Academy of Mediators and the Straus Institute for Dispute Resolution survey also demonstrates the lack of diversity of mediators who conduct high-value mediations.[60] Their typical survey respondent was a white man in his early 60s who mediates more than 50 cases a year, and has mediated more than 1,000 disputes in a 20–25 year career.[61]

These are not encouraging results for women mediators and arbitrators. Kupfer Schneider and Brown postulated that since fewer women than men have many decades of experience, this could explain why women are selected less often than men. However, their hypothesis was not borne out in their survey results, so they conclude that "experience does not appear to be a satisfactory answer"[62] to why women are chosen less. The authors instead point to the way mediators are selected

59 Andrea Kupfer Schneider & Gina Viola Brown, "Gender Differences in Dispute Resolution Practice: Report on the ABA Section of Dispute Resolution Practice Snapshot Survey" (2014) 14–04 Marquette Law School Legal Studies Paper, http://papers.ssrn.com/sol3/papers.cfm?abstract_id=2390278

60 IAM/Straus Institute Survey on Mediator Practices and Perceptions (Spring 2014).

61 Thomas J. Stipanowich, "Insights on Mediator Practices and Perception" (Winter 2016) *Dispute Resolution Magazine* 4 at 4.

62 Andrea Kupfer Schneider & Gina Viola Brown, "Gender Differences in Dispute Resolution Practice: Report on the ABA Section of Dispute Resolution Practice Snapshot Survey" (2014) 14–04 Marquette Law School Legal Studies Paper, http://papers.ssrn.com/sol3/papers.cfm?abstract_id=2390278

as the problem. Kupfer Schneider and Brown note that when the mediators are selected by lawyers or clients who choose from their personal networks, only 29% of mediators are women.[63] When parties or their lawyers choose from rosters created by ADR providers or courts, the percentage of women selected as mediators went up to 47%.[64] Also, unsurprisingly, the gender of the lawyers in the mediation sessions has an impact. Male lawyers choose male mediators 84% of the time, and even female lawyers choose male mediators 63% of the time. Finally, mediation and arbitration are not the same; women are less integrated into arbitration than they are into mediation, which means there are even fewer practising women arbitrators than women mediators. Kupfer Schneider and Brown found that: "The percentage of women serving as arbitrators seems to hold steady at 20% regardless of selection process and decreased even further in panel arbitrations."[65]

Obviously there is a long way to go before mediators and arbitrators will be representative of the diverse disputant communities they serve. We must care about this and work toward it, just as we care about the composition of the bench. Empirical research out of the United States of America demonstrates that judges' gender makes a difference in sex discrimination and sexual harassment cases because female judges are more likely than male judges to decide in the plaintiffs' favour.[66] So when Pat K. Chew conducted a study of sex discrimination and sexual harassment cases arbitrated by members of the American Arbitration Association between 2010 and 2014 I suspected she would obtain similar findings. Chew did not. She found that there is no significant difference in the decisions made by female as compared to male arbitrators. Female arbitrators are more likely than female judges to hold against the plaintiff and for the defendant employers. What could explain this and why is it relevant in this chapter on conflicts of interest and repeat mediator business? Because Chew hypothesizes that the employers' advantages as repeat arbitration players, competitive pressures on arbitrators, and arbitrators' total discretion in decision-making all work together and explain the difference in gender effect. In other words, repeat business was highly implicated in Chew's arbitration findings and is therefore also likely relevant in mediation settings. Chew found that employers have more control than employees over who is selected as an arbitrator, just like employers have more control than employees over who is selected as a mediator. Employers, not employees, are repeat players, and arbitrators and mediators need to be continually selected in order to make money. Counsel for employers choose arbitrators whom they believe will best serve the employer's position.

63 Ibid.

64 For arbitrators, the percentage of women arbitrators chosen from networks was 20% and the percentage from rosters or lists was 19%.

65 Andrea Kupfer Schneider & Gina Viola Brown, "Gender Differences in Dispute Resolution Practice: Report on the ABA Section of Dispute Resolution Practice Snapshot Survey" (2014) 14–04 Marquette Law School Legal Studies Paper, http://papers.ssrn.com/sol3/papers.cfm?abstract_id=2390278

66 Pat K. Chew, "Comparing the Effects of Judges' Gender and Arbitrators' Gender in Sex Discrimination Cases and Why it Matters" (2017) 32 *Ohio State Journal on Dispute Resolution* 195.

Having a good reputation amongst corporate counsel is essential for arbitrators who are interested in repeat business, and so it is in arbitrators' interest to reach decisions favourable to employers. The combination of employers having control over who arbitrates and arbitrators wanting the employers' business can result in more pro-management arbitrators than pro-management judges, according to Chew. The situation is exacerbated for female arbitrators who are already so seldom hired that, if they manage to crack into the business (currently at a rate of 20%, compared to 80% for men[67]), there are even more pressures to toe the employers' line with pro-management decisions. Chew's evidence suggests that women arbitrators may have a higher propensity in close cases to go with management, given the strong normative and business pressures upon them.[68] We do not know if mediators are similarly impacted.

Homogeneous groups of lawyers tend to be the primary source of mediators' work referrals. This leads to certain types of mediators receiving more referrals than others. The lack of diversity in the legal profession means that an already unrepresentative profession is choosing the practitioners in another unrepresentative profession. When lawyers select and refer mediators, they typically choose known mediators who look like them. This means that white, male, heterosexual, able-bodied mediators get most of the work. By putting more mediators from equity-seeking groups on rosters and requiring random selection, more women and other diverse mediators will be able to mediate. We must also make additional efforts in male-dominated practice areas[69] so that male mediators do not mediate all the commercial disputes while women mediators mediate all the family disputes. Another potentially interesting idea would be limiting repeat players in the number of times they can use the same mediator.

Conclusion

I began this chapter indicating that conflicts of interest are simply not allowed in mediation. Inappropriate connections cannot exist between mediators and disputants or mediators and the subject matter of the dispute. It is contrary to mediator codes of conduct for mediators to mediate with an undisclosed conflict of interest. Once cleared of any conflicts of interest and enabled to proceed, mediators try to help the parties reach agreement. Facilitating agreements is not only in the mediator's interest

67 Andrea Kupfer Schneider & Gina Viola Brown, "Gender Differences in Dispute Resolution Practice: Report on the ABA Section of Dispute Resolution Practice Snapshot Survey" (2014) 14–04 Marquette Law School Legal Studies Paper, at 9, Chart 9, https://papers.ssrn.com/sol3/papers.cfm?abstract_id=2390278

68 Pat K. Chew, "Comparing the Effects of Judges' Gender and Arbitrators' Gender in Sex Discrimination Cases and Why it Matters" (2017) 32 *Ohio State Journal on Dispute Resolution* 195 at 213.

69 Andrea Kupfer Schneider & Gina Viola Brown, "Gender Differences in Dispute Resolution Practice: Report on the ABA Section of Dispute Resolution Practice Snapshot Survey" (2014) 14–04 Marquette Law School Legal Studies Paper, http://papers.ssrn.com/sol3/papers.cfm?abstract_id=2390278

because doing so will make the disputants happy; it will also make the mediator's referral source – lawyer, judge or mediation roster – happy. The power of referral could lead a mediator, consciously or unconsciously, to lean toward or favour the referring body's side. Lawyers are frequent sources of mediation referrals and mediators want to preserve those referral relationships in order to secure future work for themselves by facilitating agreements that lawyers like. The combination of lawyers having control over who mediates their files and mediators wanting the lawyers' repeat business could result in conflicts of interest. Popular culture texts such as *Wedding Crashers*, *The Break-Up*, *The Office* and *Fairly Legal* overtly depict the worrisome link between repeat business and conflicts of interest. Personal mediation experience further bolsters it.

While we know that a good reputation for achieving settlement helps the mediator's reputation and leads to more work, we also know that, in an effort to obtain that work, mediators may change how they mediate, especially in response to repeat players' wishes. We cannot prematurely narrow the creativity in our field or the ways in which we practise in order to accede to others' wishes. It simply may not be the case that commercial mediation is always best done without joint sessions, shuttling between rooms, using an evaluative style. We must ensure that repeat players do not use mediation to promote their own interests at the expense of disputants' interests[70] and we must work to promote the selection of women mediators and other marginalized mediators for cases worth more than $100,000. One-shot mediation disputants, just like repeat player insurance companies, deserve excellent mediation services wherein they are able to exercise self-determination and express their feelings in processes leading to fair outcomes. Mediators must mediate for the disputants. And, when they do, they need to do so without deception. Or so we say, teach and think. The next chapter reveals that mediators in reel and real life may not always mediate how they have been taught to mediate.

70 Nadja Alexander, ed., *Global Trends in Mediation*, 2nd edn (Alphen aan den Rijn: Kluwer Law International, 2006) at 12.

5 Deception and caucusing

Popular culture: *The Good Wife* (TV show, USA) and *Bajrangi Bhaijaan* (film, India)
Research from: Canada, India, Israel, Netherlands, UK and USA

Introduction

Looking at mediation through a popular culture lens, as I am doing in this book, makes sense because both mediation and popular TV and movies are deeply concerned with stories. However, as Catherine MacKinnon has pointed out, "Lies are the ultimate risk of storytelling as method."[1] Because mediation is so heavily dependent on storytelling, disputants and lawyers often fear lies: "What if the other side lies?," "What if they don't reveal all of their assets?" and "What if we are taken advantage of?" We are accustomed to worrying about deception on the part of the other disputant and that disputant's lawyer because professional conduct rules for lawyers allow for bluffing and puffery, two euphemisms for lying, in negotiations. So it is not unusual to be concerned that disputants might conceal their bottom lines, fail to disclose relevant facts or not actually be willing to settle. We know that disputants might inflate demands, exaggerate strengths or weaknesses, feign anger to manipulate us, hide their true intentions, intentionally obfuscate and falsely claim lack of settlement authority. We do not typically call these behaviours deception; nor do we use the word "lying." We expect them as part of the other side's potential behaviour in mediation. What we do not expect, however, are deceptive mediators. Yet puffery, exaggeration, bluffing, omissions, white lies and chicanery can also be committed by mediators, as is often demonstrated in popular culture.

As we have seen, most popular culture mediators are not bothered about impartiality or party self-determination, and they favour an evaluative style. They are very concerned about disputants' feelings and employ their own intuition frequently and expertly. Reel mediators are less concerned about conflicts of interest than real mediators, and most employ deceptive techniques in their work, especially when meeting with one side alone or in private caucus. In previous work I noted that the character Vianne Rocher, played by Juliette Binoche in the 2000 British-American film *Chocolat*, demonstrates that to "fudge" in conflict resolution

1 Catherine A. MacKinnon, "Law's Stories as Reality and Politics," in Peter Brooks & Paul Gewitz, eds, *Law's Stories: Narrative and Rhetoric in the Law* (New Haven, CT: Yale University Press, 1996) at 232.

can be fruitful.[2] I have also noted that Kate Reed, the mediator protagonist in the American TV series *Fairly Legal*, uses deceptive techniques in her mediation work and viewers applaud her for it.[3] In Chapter 2 I noted that Amélie, the eponymous character in *Amélie*, breaks and enters and lies in order to facilitate the resolution of conflict. Indeed, the use of deceptive techniques, especially when working with only one party to the dispute, is the most common ethical infraction demonstrated by all popular culture mediators I have studied.

The reader may think such deception only occurs in popular culture. That is false. Deception amongst real lawyers and mediators is evidenced by research. Peter Reilly reports that lawyers lie, especially in negotiations.[4] Joseph P. Gaspar and Maurice E. Schweitzer argue that deception is pervasive in negotiations and they define it as the use of statements and/or behaviours, including acts of omission, that intentionally mislead a counterpart.[5] Jeffrey Krivis states that: "As long as the negotiation moves are not fraudulent, deceptive techniques tend to be the engine that drives the motor of litigated negotiations."[6] For those disputants and lawyers who understand conflict with a war metaphor, deception is not even understood as unethical; in war, deception is accepted practice and both sides should know that.[7] Scholars report that real mediators also deceive. Robert D. Benjamin says: "All human beings, and especially mediators, deceive, manipulate, and even sometimes lie. That is a given."[8] James R. Coben concurs, stating: "mediators themselves routinely and unabashedly engage in manipulation and deception to foster settlements."[9] In fact, Coben calls mediator manipulation "Mediation's Dirty Little Secret."[10]

2 Jennifer L. Schulz, "The Mediator as Cook: Mediation Metaphors at the Movies" (2007) 2 *Journal of Dispute Resolution* 455; and Jennifer L. Schulz, "Confectionery and Conflict Resolution? What Chocolat Reveals about Mediation" (2006) 22 *Negotiation Journal* 251.

3 Jennifer L. Schulz (2014) "*Fairly Legal*: A Canadian Perspective on the Creation of a Primetime Mediator," in M. Asimow, K. Brown & D.R. Papke, eds, *Law & Popular Culture: International Perspectives* (Newcastle upon Tyne: Cambridge Scholars Press, 2014) at 43–56.

4 Peter Reilly, "Was Machiavelli Right? Lying in Negotiation and the Art of Defensive Self-Help" (2009) 24 *Ohio State Journal on Dispute Resolution* 481, http://ssrn.com/abstract=1280465

5 Joseph P. Gaspar & Maurice E. Schweitzer, "The Negotiator's Challenge: Anticipating, Detecting, and Contending with Deception in Negotiations" (September 13, 2012), http://ssrn.com/abstract=2056885

6 Jeffrey Krivis, "The Truth About Deception in Mediation" (2004) 4:2 *Pepperdine Dispute Resolution Law Journal* 251 at 252.

7 Howard Gadlin, Andrea Kupfer Schneider & Chris Honeyman, "The Road to Hell is Paved with Metaphors," in Chris Honeyman & Andrea Kupfer Schneider, eds, *The Negotiator's Desk Reference*, Vol. 2 (St. Paul, MN: Dispute Resolution Institute Press, 2017) at 6–7.

8 Robert D. Benjamin, "The Constructive Uses of Deception: Skills, Strategies, and Techniques of the Folkloric Trickster Figure and their Application by Mediators" (1995) 13 *Mediation Quarterly* 3 at 17.

9 James R. Coben, "Mediation's Dirty Little Secret: Straight Talk About Mediator Manipulation and Deception" (2000) 2 *Journal of Alternative Dispute Resolution in Employment* 4.

10 Ibid., at 4.

While mediators certainly do not typically admit to using deceptive tactics, the most likely place for these to surface is in private caucus. The mediation caucus is a private meeting between the mediator and only one party to the conflict. The extra confidentiality and privacy of the caucus in an already confidential mediation process is a concern because no one really knows what goes on behind the closed caucus door. Mediators vary in their use of the caucus, but mediators who caucus typically employ it as an opportunity to speak confidentially with one side. In the caucus the mediator might wish to probe the party's interests more deeply, ask pointed questions, coach the party to help her communicate with the other side more productively, or conduct a process of reality testing to ensure the party understands the ramifications of her position or behaviour. Caucusing is increasingly employed as a matter of routine, especially in mediations where disputants are represented by counsel and in mandatory mediation settings, yet it is rarely taught in law school nor examined in the literature. Many mediators use private caucuses in their mediation sessions, but we know very little about what goes on in these confidential meetings within mediations. A course can describe mediation ethics and caucusing, but watching deceptive mediators on screen actually lets students feel and react to breaches of mediation ethics. This can be a powerful pedagogical experience (and may also create a safe confessional space for mediators to admit to deception). Popular culture mediators make room for us to question whether a mediator must be completely honest and transparent at all times, or whether some deceptive moves are permissible.

Deception

So what is deception? Geoffrey Peters defines "lie" as a false statement made by one who knows its falsity and has the intent to deceive another as to the truth. Deception, in his view, is any method of concealing the truth, including silence.[11] Lying by omission is more prevalent as people tend to perceive lies of commission to be more serious. Lawrence Solan defines a lie as an assertion of some kind that the speaker knows to be false, and that the speaker intends to deceive.[12] He states that people generally consider lying to be morally worse than deceiving by misdirection.[13] Michael S. Pardo says that lying involves an intent to deceive, and therefore not all falsehoods are lies.[14] Don Fallis emphasizes the normative component of an assertion that is necessary for a statement to be a lie.[15] So while something might be a lie in conversation, where norms require truthfulness, the same statement may not

11 Geoffrey M. Peters, "The Use of Lies in Negotiation" (1987) 48 *Ohio State Law Journal* 1 at 11.
12 Lawrence M. Solan, "Lies, Deceit, and Bullshit in Law" (2018) 56 *Duquesne Law Review* 73 at 76.
13 Ibid., at 93.
14 Michael S. Pardo, "Lying, Deception, and fMRI: A Critical Update," in Bebhinn Donnelly-Lazarov, ed., *Neurolaw and Responsibility for Action* (Cambridge: Cambridge University Press, 2018).
15 Don Fallis, "What is Lying" (2009) 106 *Journal of Philosophy* 29 at 35.

be a lie when delivered on stage. Pardo says that "Lying takes place when the speaker communicates something believed to be false in a context where there is a norm against doing so."[16] Dwight Golann states that: "Where a client has made a representation that later proves false, failing to correct the record and inform opposing counsel of the misrepresentation constitutes fraud."[17] Solan notes that lying and deception in business and legal transactions are fraud if the party lied to or deceived reasonably relies on the lie or misrepresentation to his or her detriment.[18]

Disputants and lawyers have incentive to deceive due to their fears of being exploited if they reveal too much information in mediation. Yet mediation is most successful when communications are frank and forthright. Schweitzer et al. found that negotiators with a "win" frame of mind were more likely to use deception than negotiators with a "cooperate" frame of mind.[19] Wolfgang Steinel and Carsten K. W. De Dreu found that negotiators who perceived their counterparts as competitive misrepresented more information than those who perceived the other side to be cooperative.[20] Gaspar and Schweitzer remind us that norms regarding the appropriate use of deception and related constructs, such as the loss of face surrounding accusations of deception, are likely to vary dramatically across different cultures.[21]

T. Bradford Bitterly and Maurice E. Schweitzer note that answering direct questions can pose problems for disputants.[22] For example, the question "do you have another offer and for how much?" is tricky. If a disputant answers honestly and says "I have no other offers," the disputant may incur economic costs because the other disputant may then be willing to pay less. If the disputant is dishonest, saying he has another offer when he does not, he may incur reputational costs for engaging in deception. If the disputant says "I would rather not answer that question," he may suffer interpersonal costs, such as harms to likability or to the relationship. Bitterly and Schweitzer conducted experiments to explore the consequences of deflection instead, that is answering the direct question about another offer with a question. They conclude that deflection can mitigate the economic costs of honest answers, the reputational costs of engaging in deception and the interpersonal costs of

16 Michael S. Pardo, "Lying, Deception, and fMRI: A Critical Update," in Bebhinn Donnelly Lazarov, ed., *Neurolaw and Responsibility for Action* (Cambridge: Cambridge University Press, 2018) at 16.

17 Dwight Golann, "Mediating with Lies in the Room," in Ellen Waldman, ed., *Mediation Ethics: Cases and Commentaries* (San Francisco, CA: Jossey-Bass, 2011) 199 at 200.

18 Lawrence M. Solan, "Lies, Deceit, and Bullshit in Law" (2018) 56 *Duquesne Law Review* 73 at 76.

19 M.E. Schweitzer, L. DeChurch & D.E. Gibson, "Conflict Frames and the Use of Deception: Are Competitive Negotiators Less Ethical?" (2005) 35 *Journal of Applied Social Psychology* 2123.

20 W. Steinel & C.K.W. De Dreu, "Social Motives and Strategic Misrepresentation in Social Decision Making" (2004) 86 *Journal of Personality and Social Psychology* 419.

21 Joseph P. Gaspar & Maurice E. Schweitzer, "The Negotiator's Challenge: Anticipating, Detecting, and Contending with Deception in Negotiations" (September 13, 2012), http://ssrn.com/abstract=2056885

22 T. Bradford Bitterly & Maurice E. Schweitzer, "The Economic and Interpersonal Consequences of Deflecting Direct Questions" (November 2, 2017), https://ssrn.com/abstract=3063840

directly declining to answer a question.[23] This of course means that mediators must be alive to the presence of deflection in mediation and question what the speaker is avoiding saying by the deflection. Mediators should ask many direct, specific questions to help surface any omissions and get past any deflections. We must keep asking questions until we receive answers. Reilly encourages us to "drill deeper."[24] We must ask for documents to substantiate other bids a disputant claims to have received. Katie Shonk recommends pointing out the disputants' shared social identities and connections.[25] Parties are less likely to act unethically or attempt to deceive if their actions could get back to their friends or colleagues, or if they might lose valued social or business connections. Reminding disputants that they are accountable to industry standards or to their professional organizations should also promote honesty.

Despite our desire to promote honest, open communications, deception in mediation continues. Don Peters conducted an informal survey of 23 lawyers, five of whom were also practising mediators. When asked to estimate the frequency with which disputants or their lawyers lied in mediation, the average estimates ranged from 19% to 43%.[26] The average estimate of the prevalence of material misrepresentations in joint session was 25%.[27] The average estimate of the prevalence of lies concerning the value of disputed items and claims was 35%.[28] The average estimate of the prevalence of lies concerning reservation price or bottom line was 43%,[29] and the average estimate of the prevalence of lies regarding bargaining authority was 36%.[30] Art Hinshaw, Peter Reilly and Andrea Kupfer Schneider conducted a study and found that a significant minority of their lawyer respondents, at times approaching one third of them, engaged in unethical and sometimes fraudulent negotiation behaviour.[31] The authors suspect that under the pressure of real-life negotiation settings the lawyers might perform even more poorly.[32] I worry that mediators might too.

23 T. Bradford Bitterly & Maurice E. Schweitzer, "The Economic and Interpersonal Consequences of Deflecting Direct Questions" (November 2, 2017), https://ssrn.com/abstract=3063840
24 Peter Reilly, "Was Machiavelli Right? Lying in Negotiation and the Art of Defensive Self-Help" (2009) 24 *Ohio State Journal on Dispute Resolution* 481, http://ssrn.com/abstract=1280465
25 Katie Shonk, "Deceptive Tactics in Negotiation: How to Ward Them Off" (November 26, 2018), Negotiation Skills, Program on Negotiation, Harvard Law School, www.pon.harvard.edu/daily/negotiation-skills-daily/deceptive-tactics-in-negotiation-how-to-ward-them-off/?utm_source=WhatCountsEmail&utm_medium=daily&utm_date=2018-11-26-13-30-00&mqsc=E4008493
26 Don Peters, "When Lawyers Move Their Lips: Attorney Truthfulness in Mediation and a Modest Proposal" (2007) *Journal of Dispute Resolution* 119.
27 Ibid., at 124.
28 Ibid., at 130.
29 Ibid., at 130.
30 Ibid., at 133.
31 Art Hinshaw, Peter Reilly & Andrea Kupfer Schneider, "Attorneys and Negotiation Ethics: A Material Misunderstanding?" (July 2013) *Negotiation Journal* 265 at 265 and 284.
32 Ibid., at 285.

In the United States of America, standard VI(4) of the Model Standards of Conduct for Mediators imposes two duties on mediators: (i) abstain from knowingly misrepresenting any material fact or circumstance in the course of mediation; and (ii) promote honesty and candour amongst all participants.[33] A statement is material if the other side would attach importance to it in deciding whether to settle or not. "The definition of 'material' is crucial to any analysis because only 'material' facts fall under the requirement of truthfulness."[34] It is understood that estimates of price or value and a party's intentions are not ordinarily understood as material fact statements, which means that parties and mediators do not have to be honest about them in mediation. Lawyers also do not need to be honest about them.[35] Lawyers are allowed to distort their clients' bottom lines, value estimates, and whether they have settlement authority.

Given that parties, their lawyers and even mediators can distort non-material aspects of mediation, mediators cannot therefore easily police participants for honesty in the mediation session. Interests, goals and priorities are in the disputants' minds and can change throughout the mediation process. Mediators cannot realistically police whether interests and goals are being truthfully described; we are not fact checkers or mind-readers. Omer Shapira says that a mediator cannot ensure participants' honesty or good faith, but he or she should encourage it.[36] Dwight Golann says mediators must be truth cheerleaders.[37] Mediators can always discontinue the mediation session or withdraw if they believe the integrity of the mediation process has been destroyed. As Michael Dallaire correctly points out:

> The semi-cooperative nature of the mediation environment is most productive and equitable to both parties when disputants and their attorneys are open and forthright. The allowance for some deception under Model Rule 4.1 is incompatible with the goals and characteristics of the mediation format.[38]

33 www.mediate.com/articles/model_standards_of_conflict.cfm#LinkTarget_237

34 Art Hinshaw, Peter Reilly & Andrea Kupfer Schneider, "Attorneys and Negotiation Ethics: A Material Misunderstanding?" (July 2013) *Negotiation Journal* 265 at 269.

35 American Bar Association, Model Code of Professional Responsibility, rule 4.12: a lawyer shall not knowingly (a) make a false statement of material fact or law to a third person; or (b) fail to disclose a material fact to a third person when disclosure is necessary to avoid assisting a criminal or fraudulent act by a client, unless disclosure is prohibited by confidentiality requirements.

36 Omer Shapira, *A Theory of Mediators' Ethics: Foundation, Rationale, and Application* (Cambridge: Cambridge University Press, 2016) at 266 and 267.

37 Dwight Golann, "Mediating with Lies in the Room," in Ellen Waldman, ed., *Mediation Ethics: Cases and Commentaries* (San Francisco, CA: Jossey-Bass, 2011) 199 at 202.

38 Michael Dallaire, "Clarifying Candor: Why the model rules should draw bright lines for attorneys' truth-telling duties in arbitration, mediation and unassisted negotiation" (2014) 12:2 *Mayhew-Hite Report on Dispute Resolution and the Courts*, Moritz College of Law, Ohio State University at 3. Dallaire argues that "The longer the Model Rules go without forum-based rules of candor, the more engrained deceptive tactics will become in processes in which they will only be counterproductive" (at 5).

The ADR Institute of Canada's Code of Conduct for Mediators stipulates that a mediator who thinks ethical concerns are raised in a mediation in which he or she is involved, including deliberate deception, may terminate the process.[39] However, what if it is the mediator who has engaged in deception? *Bhasin v. Hrynew*,[40] a 2014 unanimous decision from the Supreme Court of Canada, recognizes that good faith contractual performance is a general organizing principle of Canadian common law. Parties to a contract are under a duty to act honestly in the performance of their contractual obligations; there is a duty of good faith or honest contractual performance. The Supreme Court of Canada says "it is a simple requirement not to lie or mislead the other party about one's contractual performance."[41] We do not yet know exactly what honest performance entails, but one would hope it includes candour in dealings with contractual partners, such as mediation partners. Tamara Buckwold argues that the Supreme Court's decision in *Bhasin* suggests that an agreement to negotiate in good faith is a contract if the parties intend it to have legal consequences.[42] This is interesting because it could mean that where disputants have agreed to negotiate in good faith under an express or implied term, as is common in mediation, that agreement is enforceable. *Bhasin v. Hrynew* recognizes a new common law duty that applies to all Canadian contracts, namely a duty of honest performance. Thus, if an agreement to negotiate in good faith is a contract, a party to that contract is required by *Bhasin* to act honestly in negotiations. The duty requires the parties to be honest with each other in relation to the performance of their contractual obligations.[43] The duty of honesty is not a duty of disclosure, however, which means that active dishonesty is distinguishable from merely not disclosing.[44] The Court says "parties must not lie or otherwise knowingly mislead each other about matters directly linked to performance of the contract."[45]

The Supreme Court of Canada notes that the organizing principle of good faith can be developed into new situations and that context is important, which suggests that mediation could be one such new situation wherein dishonesty could be actionable.[46] The Court also said that parties may put their own self-interest before

39 http://adric.ca/pdf/ADRMEDIATIONRULES2014.pdf at section 7.5
40 *Bhasin v. Hrynew* 2014 SCC 71.
41 Ibid., at para 73.
42 Tamara Buckwold, "The Enforceability of Agreements to Negotiate in Good Faith: The Impact of *Bhasin v. Hrynew* and the Organizing Principle of Good Faith in Common Law Canada" (2016) 58 *Canadian Business Law Journal.*
43 *Bhasin v. Hrynew* 2014 SCC 71 at para 93.
44 Ibid., at paras 73 and 86.
45 Ibid., at para 73.
46 *0856464 BC Ltd. v. TimberWest Forest Corp.* 2014 BCSC 2433 is authority for the view that *Bhasin v. Hrynew* supports the contractual enforcement of an agreement to negotiate in good faith. *Wastech Services Ltd. v. Greater Vancouver Sewerage and Drainage District* 2019 BCCA 66 (38601) is going to the Supreme Court of Canada and will be heard with *C.M. Callow Inc. v. Tammy Zollinger et al* (38463), which has facts similar to *Bhasin*, having to do with good faith in the termination of contracts, so

the interests of the opposite party, but they must have a degree of regard for the interest of the other that is appropriate in the circumstances.[47] Mediation is an example of a circumstance that requires regard for the other side's interests. The Supreme Court notes that "commercial parties reasonably expect a basic level of honesty and good faith in contractual dealings,"[48] and Shannon O'Byrne and Ronnie Cohen say the Court "seems to have suggested that equivocating can count as a form of dishonesty."[49] Parties are expected to act honestly as an aspect of the duty of good faith. When asked something directly, they must answer honestly. Parties who voluntarily assume an obligation to negotiate in good faith must be taken to have meant something by it.[50] This needs to be true in mediation and for mediators as well. Shapira says: "A professional must be honest in order to be worthy of his or her clients' trust. Mediation parties, therefore, legitimately expect mediators to be truthful in their communications with them and refrain from deception and lying."[51] Richard Calkins agrees, stating that mediators "must be principled, trustworthy, dependable, and act with integrity."[52] Honesty is connected to the important right of party self-determination. If mediators withhold information, the party cannot make informed decisions or exercise self-determination. Shapira describes this as honesty toward all the participants: disputants, lawyers, support people and co-mediators, as well as non-participants, such as courts and the media.[53]

Mediators certainly were taught that deception is not part of their role, and most mediators have made personal and often organizational commitments to mediate as ethically as possible. Nonetheless, mediators are still required to discern acceptable puffery from illegal fraudulent statements, and to ensure they are blameless as well. Are mediators maintaining their ethical obligations? How about when they privately caucus with each side? In caucus mediators might hide their true feelings about an issue, make themselves appear neutral when they are not, lead parties to believe they are unaware of information that they are aware of, reframe statements in ways that are not completely true to the original message, shuttle only some information between the parties, and present offers as their own that are not actually their own. Is this deception? Are these mediators breaching

it is likely that the Supreme Court of Canada will say more about the obligation to negotiate in good faith in Canada in the near future.

47 *Bhasin v. Hrynew* 2014 SCC 71 at para 65.
48 Ibid., at para 60.
49 Shannon O'Byrne & Ronnie Cohen, "The Contractual Principle of Good Faith and the Duty of Honesty in *Bhasin v. Hrynew*" (2015) 53 *Alberta Law Review* 1 at 11.
50 Tamara Buckwold, "The Enforceability of Agreements to Negotiate in Good Faith: The Impact of *Bhasin v. Hrynew* and the Organizing Principle of Good Faith in Common Law Canada" (2016) 58 *Canadian Business Law Journal.*
51 Omer Shapira, *A Theory of Mediators' Ethics: Foundation, Rationale, and Application* (Cambridge: Cambridge University Press, 2016) at 264.
52 Richard M. Calkins, "Caucus Mediation – Putting Conciliation Back into the Process: The Peacemaking Approach to Resolution, Peace and Healing" (2005–2006) 54 *Drake Law Review* 259 at 311.
53 Omer Shapira, *A Theory of Mediators' Ethics: Foundation, Rationale, and Application* (Cambridge: Cambridge University Press, 2016) at 265.

mediator ethics? "Anecdotal evidence suggests that many mediators have, from time to time, exaggerated disputants' positions, focused on some facts to the exclusion of other relevant facts, and played upon parties' desires to resolve the matter at hand."[54] When we examine popular culture mediations we see many depictions of deceptive mediators.

One such example comes from Season 3 of *The Good Wife*. Episode 3 of that season, entitled "Get a Room," begins with the African American, male mediator telling lead Caucasian characters Will Gardner and Alicia Florrick, "This is court-ordered mediation. This is not opt-out mediation or 'I don't feel like it' mediation." The mediator needs to "lay down the law" because the lawyers on both sides of the fraud case are extremely adversarial and continuously suggest going to court. The mediator reminds them, "the judge doesn't want to clutter up his docket. That's why he empowered me to keep you here as long as I want to until you can compromise, so show me some movement." The two sides of the dispute are in separate hotel suites, hence the episode's title, "Get a Room." The mediator shuttles across the hotel hallway whenever necessary to go speak to the other side. When mediators keep the parties in separate rooms throughout the mediation, moving between the rooms carrying messages, offers and counter-offers, the mediator becomes less the mediator and more the shuttle diplomat. The disputants do not really see each other and therefore do not learn how to work together to resolve their disputes. Debbie De Girolamo argues that, in cases of commercial mediation conducted entirely by shuttling between rooms, the mediator actually sheds the mediator cloak and steps into the fray as an advisor, or even as the opposing party, negotiating on the merits.[55] "The mediator engages in direct negotiation with the party against the party."[56] De Girolamo acknowledges the shuttle diplomat/mediator's active engagement with and between the parties, which is exactly what we see in *The Good Wife*.[57]

In the episode, Will and Alicia and their two junior associates are representing the plaintiff. The plaintiff's doctor, the defendant, implanted a non-federally approved device in her back to help with her pain but it did not work, so the young woman plaintiff is suing for fraud. Her debilitating back pain means she cannot work. Her husband has left her and she has three very young children. The first time the mediator caucuses with Will and Alicia he tells them, "You can lower your ask. Given the set of facts I am looking at, it's way too high, and the law is

54 Jennifer L. Schulz "The Mediator as Cook: Mediation Metaphors at the Movies" (2007) 2 *Journal of Dispute Resolution* 455 at 469.

55 Debbie De Girolamo, "A View from Within: Reconceptualizing Mediator Interactions" (2012) 30:2 *Windsor Yearbook of Access to Justice* 103 at 121–123.

56 Ibid., at 126.

57 According to J.G. Merrills, mediation in the international sphere also involves "the mediator as an active participant, authorized, and indeed expected, to advance fresh proposals and to interpret, as well as to transmit, each party's proposals to the other." (J.G. Merrills, *International Dispute Settlement*, 5th edn [Cambridge: Cambridge University Press, 2011] at 26). Merrills also notes that the mediator's task "is to devise or promote a solution from which both [parties] can devise a measure of satisfaction" (at 33).

far from clear." Alicia responds that they got their client to move from $30 million down to $14 million – "that's movement, where is the other side's?" The mediator walks across the hall to the other hotel suite and tells the other side, led by Caucasian lawyer Celeste and her five associates, that they need to raise their offer. The mediator justifies his comment by saying the exact same thing about the facts and the legal issues that he said to Will and Alicia. This shows viewers that mediators might be disingenuous; they will say the same thing to both sides, hoping for opposite results. Worse, when the mediator goes back to Will and Alicia he lies. The mediator tells them that the other side has agreed to increase their offer, which the other side absolutely did not do. The mediator tells a lie and is very directive, telling both sides that they have to meet in the middle or "I keep you here." Will tells Alicia and their two junior associates, "The mediator is threatening to keep us here through the weekend and I think he means it, so make arrangements." The vast majority of law professors would agree that mediators should not lie nor make threats, yet this is what we see on *The Good Wife*.

In a subsequent scene in the hotel's elevator, Celeste says to Will, "I think the mediator is lying to us." Will agrees. Neither lawyer is upset; it is as if mediator deception is normal. Celeste suggests that the two of them can settle the case on their own over a bottle of wine. She gives Will her cellphone number for "when you're ready to negotiate." This implies that mediation is not real negotiation and that mediators are not necessary or are even impediments to lawyers' work. I have noticed this characterization of mediation in Canadian television as well, where mediation is not considered as important or weighty as "real" law.[58] When Will and Alicia find out that the defendant doctor may not be found liable, they say "we have a gun to our heads and now we need to make a good deal in mediation – damn!" This highlights popular culture's tendency to reify the trial and litigation. Only when a trial is no longer an option do the lawyers take mediation more seriously and, even then, with disappointment. Again, this tendency is also observable in Canadian television, where settlement is depicted as the thing lawyers do when they feel they cannot win.[59]

When the parties are back in their respective hotel suites the mediator comes to Will and Alicia and suggests that the plaintiff accept $8 million from the doctor. The lawyers reply, "We can't give you our bottom line. You'll use it against us." The lawyers do not trust the mediator at all. They suspect him of lying and believe he will use their confidential information against them. Later, in the same spirit of deception, Will and Alicia decide to feign feelings they do not actually feel, to help their case with the mediator (despite the fact that the mediator does not decide anything), and Alicia is shown secretly smiling after she has deceived the mediator as to her true feelings. When the mediator finally brings all the parties together in the same room (see Figure 5.1), Will and Celeste merely shout at one another. The mediator says that "the point of bringing you two together is to talk," but the opposing lawyers cannot do so and negotiations break down again.

58 Jennifer L. Schulz, "Settlement and Mediation in Canadian Legal Television" (2011) 1 *Journal of Arbitration and Mediation* 77 at 89.

59 Ibid.

Figure 5.1 Lisa Edelstein as Celeste, Isiah Whitlock Jr. as the mediator, and Josh Charles as Will Gardner in mediation in "Get a Room," *The Good Wife*

The parties finally reach a settlement of $8 million and the mediator and Alicia talk about how "tough" mediations are. This is in direct contrast to the episode's earlier message, that mediation is easy or not real law. The show tells its viewers that mediation is harder than they think. Earlier the mediator was seen in the hotel hallway taking prescription medication. When asked if he is all right, the mediator replies "no." Again, this highlights that mediation and the toll it can take should be taken seriously. At the episode's conclusion we discover that the mediator knew Will and Alicia manipulated him. The mediator says to Alicia, "You got your client rich because you played them." The mediator openly acknowledges the efficacy of deception. *The Good Wife* makes the point that there was a settlement not because of the benefits of mediation as a dispute resolution process, but because the mediator and the lawyers successfully employed deceptive moves. This popular culture example of mediation enjoins us to consider the possibility that real mediators may occasionally employ some moves that are contrary to mediation theory's stipulation of transparency. Concerns about deceptive moves are especially salient in the mediation caucus.

Caucusing

The caucus is a confidential, separate, private meeting held by the mediator with one of the parties to a mediation. Caucusing is a matter of style or strategy in mediation; it is not essential to the mediation process. Caucusing is also to be distinguished from pre-mediation meetings, which are held separately with each side before the actual mediation takes place. Pre-mediation meetings are very helpful and, I would argue, essential for good mediation. If the mediator meets privately with each disputant before mediation she can provide disputants with the opportunity to vent and express their real needs and goals for the upcoming mediation session. Each side can also plan for the mediation session. In pre-mediation meetings it is important to ask, "what do you think the other side wants, and why?" Gregorio Billikopf-Encina also recommends asking: what do you value in the other?[60] The mediator learns the history of the dispute, the personality of the parties, the level of conflict and can make some preliminary agenda and mediation plans. If a disputant feels that the mediator has understood him, that lifts a burden, making listening to the other side and thinking about creative brainstorming more possible. Later, in joint session, things often go more smoothly between the disputants, and the mediator is better prepared to help the parties move toward resolution. The American Bar Association Section of Dispute Resolution formed a Task Force on Research on Mediator Techniques in order to learn what existing empirical evidence reveals about which mediator actions enhance mediation outcomes and which do not.[61] Regarding pre-mediation meetings, the Task Force found that, when they are used to establish trust and build a relationship with the disputants, pre-mediation meetings increase settlement and reduce disputants' post-mediation conflict. However, when used to "push an agenda," pre-mediation meetings have a negative effect or no effect on settlement and post-mediation conflict. "Pre-mediation caucuses with a trust focus have the potential for positive effects, and those with a substantive focus have the potential for negative effects."[62]

Kenneth Kressel has commented on the sometimes destructive approach of having each side tell its story at the outset of the joint mediation session. While it might be cathartic for the plaintiff to vent, it will be hard for the defendant to listen to venting and then move seamlessly toward conflict resolution.[63] Billikopf-Encina argues that this is where the pre-mediation session can be very beneficial.[64] If all the harshness has already been vented in front of the mediator in the pre-mediation session, there will be less of a need to do so in the mediation session or, at least, less vociferously. Also, if a disputant feels as if she has established her reasonableness to the mediator in the pre-mediation session, she is less likely to want to disrupt that reasonable perception during the mediation session. Where each disputant has prepared with the mediator in advance, each disputant will feel

60 Gregorio Billikopf-Encina, "Contributions of Caucusing and Pre-Caucusing to Mediation" (Spring 2002) 4 *Group Facilitation: A Research and Applications Journal* 3 at 6.

61 Task Force on Research on Mediation Techniques, commissioned by the ABA Section of Dispute Resolution (June 12, 2017), www.americanbar.org/groups/dispute_resolution.html

62 Ibid., at 3.

63 Kenneth Kressel, "Frances Butler: Questions that lead to answers in child custody mediation," in Deborah M. Kolb, ed., *When Talk Works: Profiles of Mediators* (San Francisco, CA: Jossey-Bass, 2001) at 25–26.

64 Gregorio Billikopf-Encina, "Contributions of Caucusing and Pre-Caucusing to Mediation" (Spring 2002) 4 *Group Facilitation: A Research and Applications Journal* 3 at 6.

more confident about the process of mediation generally and his or her goals for it specifically. The mediator too will feel more confident about leading the mediation session.

Caucusing is different from pre-mediation meetings. Christopher W. Moore states that "Caucuses are initiated in response to events, external or internal to the negotiations, that block or hinder productive bargaining in joint session,"[65] or to plan strategy. If the mediator or a disputant wants a private, confidential meeting, the caucus is held in a room separate from the joint session. A caucus can be initiated by the mediator or by a disputant and typically lasts for no more than 30 minutes. Then good mediators caucus with the other side, even if just briefly, in order to preserve the appearance of impartiality. It is best to offer the same number of caucuses and the same amount of time in caucus to all parties in the mediation. While the mediator meets with one side, it can be useful to offer the other side a real break – coffee or a chance to go outside – or an opportunity to work on the dispute by assigning tasks such as coming up with a workable settlement or considering compromises one might be willing to make.

Moore notes that mediators should not hold private caucus prematurely when people are still capable of working productively in joint session, or too late after unproductive exchanges have hardened positions.[66] Robert A. Baruch Bush and Joseph P. Folger echo this idea, saying that caucusing too early may interrupt any transformative momentum that is building.[67] In 1989 Dean G. Pruitt el al. conducted studies at two New York State community mediation centres. Their results led them to conclude that caucusing has many benefits and few costs.[68] The benefits of caucus primarily relate to reducing tension and increasing rapport. Research by Gary L. Welton, Dean G. Pruitt and Neil B. McGillicuddy found that direct hostility – such as yelling, swearing and hitting the table – decreases in caucus.[69] Tension is reduced and rapport can be built because the other side is not present. Most of the benefits of caucus stem from the fact that the disputant is alone with the mediator in a confidential session within an already confidential mediation process. This is why the mediator on *The Good Wife* employed caucusing throughout. He felt he would be able to make better headway with two very adversarial parties by keeping them separated. What is said in caucus remains confidential, unless the parties explicitly authorize the mediator to share it with the

65 Christopher W. Moore, "The Caucus: Private Meetings That Promote Settlement" (Summer 1987) 16 *Mediation Quarterly* 87 at 88.

66 Ibid., at 90–91; and Christopher W. Moore, *The Mediation Process: Practical Strategies for Resolving Conflict*, 2nd edn (San Francisco, CA: Jossey-Bass, 1996) at 320.

67 Robert Baruch Bush & Joseph P. Folger, *The Promise of Mediation: Responding to Conflict Through Empowerment and Recognition* (San Francisco, CA: Jossey-Bass, 1994) at 271.

68 D. Pruitt, G. Welton, W. Fry, N. McGillicuddy, L. Castrianno, C. Ippolito & J. Zubeck, "The Process of Mediation: Caucusing, Control and Problem Solving," in Rahim M. Afzalur, ed., *Managing Conflict: An Interdisciplinary Approach* (Westport, CT: Praeger, 1989) at 208.

69 G. Welton, D. Pruitt & N. McGillicuddy, "The Role of Caucusing in Community Mediation" (1988) 32:1 *The Journal of Conflict Resolution* 181 at 192.

other side. On *The Good Wife*, however, Will and Celeste specifically state that they do not trust the mediator to maintain this confidentiality.

While *The Good Wife* mediator conducted his mediation almost entirely via caucus, mediators typically call caucuses when there is a lack of forward movement in the mediation process. Once in private, the mediator is usually able to identify with the party, build or re-establish rapport and encourage the party to reveal more. Or, if one party is too tense or about to cry, breaking into caucus not only relieves tension but saves face, allowing for private expression of strong emotions. The disputant can weigh and discuss options and offers in private and conduct cost-benefit analyses. In caucus, mediators can coach disputants, helping them move past whatever tension or impasse arose in the joint session, and encourage them to speak in more productive ways to improve joint session communication. Unfortunately, *The Good Wife* mediator did not use his caucuses for this purpose. He did, however, try to engage in reality-testing with Will and Celeste, hoping to stimulate them to think more realistically about the situation, encouraging them to troubleshoot, see the conflict from another perspective, test out scenarios and think about what would happen if they did not settle in mediation. Parties can be challenged to try harder to make a deal or to think of new alternatives. Welton et al.'s research found that mediators are more likely to ask the disputants to suggest new alternatives in caucus than in joint session,[70] and that disputants offer more new settlement alternatives or suggestions during caucus than during joint sessions.[71] This is probably because defensiveness is reduced in caucus due to the absence of the other party, and the courage to suggest something new increases when the other side is not there to immediately critique it. Mediators can also typically speak positively about the other side and its proposals in a way that the disputant is able to hear. Will, Alicia and Celeste were unfortunately too entrenched in their positions to be able to hear anything positive about each other. Typically, however, without the opposing party in the room, disputants are less tense and therefore better able to creatively brainstorm[72] and reveal true bottom lines. Simply being alone with the mediator will often inspire disputants to be more forthcoming, revealing more about underlying interests, admitting weaknesses in their positions, and allowing for the strengths of the other side. Caucusing also allows mediators to do things they simply cannot do in joint session. Mediators can show more empathy, because in private caucus they will not be accused of bias. Welton et al. describe it as providing "unequal sympathetic attention."[73] "Caucusing allows mediators to take sides with one party in order to move the process along. Thus it appears that caucusing somewhat relieves the third party of the requirement of being strictly

70 Ibid., at 200.
71 Ibid., at 194.
72 D. Pruitt, G. Welton, W. Fry, N. McGillicuddy, L. Castrianno, C. Ippolito & J. Zubeck, "The Process of Mediation: Caucusing, Control and Problem Solving," in Rahim M. Afzalur, ed., *Managing Conflict: An Interdisciplinary Approach* (Westport, CT: Praeger, 1989) at 207.
73 Gary L. Welton, Dean G. Pruitt & Neil B. McGillicuddy, "The Role of Caucusing in Community Mediation" (1988) 32:1 *The Journal of Conflict Resolution* 181 at 185.

neutral between the two parties."[74] Mediators can pass proposals along, sometimes not saying whether they come from the other side or are the mediator's idea, and mediators can remind the party in caucus to "remember to share that when we get to joint session." Finally, the caucus provides an excellent opportunity for mediators to work in private to empower weaker parties.

Calkins is of the view that caucus mediation is the process which "is the most conducive to conciliation and peacemaking."[75] Jean Poitras argues that if the mediator demonstrates impartiality in joint sessions and empathy in caucus, the time required to reach an agreement is decreased.[76] However, the use of caucus, according to Poitras' empirical study, does not lead to an increase in the likelihood of reaching an agreement.[77] Some mediators use private caucus as a matter of course; it is an official step in each of their mediation sessions, never to be missed. Other mediators use it whenever they feel uncomfortable or when they do not want to deal with the tension in the room.[78] Currently there is a growing trend of using caucus very frequently. Two of the Canadian mediation rosters I am a member of use caucus in every mediation; it is expected by all parties. In Ontario's Mandatory Mediation Program, civil, non-family cases begin in joint session, then the disputants typically separate and the mediator shuttles back and forth between rooms. The caucuses continue until the matter settles or concludes, and the session finishes jointly.

Shuttle mediation or caucus-heavy mediation is more open to mediator power abuse – hence the concern about deception in caucus. In private meetings the mediator can obtain more information and then, as the conduit between both rooms, can choose which information is shuttled back and forth; or, as we saw in *The Good Wife*, even distort that information or lie about it. Moore cautions that: "Private meetings and controlled communications can give the mediator considerable power over the settlement."[79] In such scenarios there is increased opportunity for mediators to actually set the terms of settlement, which of course is not mediation but, rather, arbitration. While we do not exclusively see shuttle mediation in real life, John Wade describes "single issue monetized shuttling with limited intake and lawyer controlled"[80] as what mediation has begun to look like in many centres. In other words, the kind of mediation Will and Celeste participated in in *The Good Wife* exists in real life. Edward Brunet

74 Ibid., at 200.

75 Richard M. Calkins, "Caucus Mediation – Putting Conciliation Back into the Process: The Peacemaking Approach to Resolution, Peace and Healing" (2005–2006) 54 *Drake Law Review* 259 at 320.

76 Jean Poitras, "The Strategic Use of Caucus to Facilitate Parties' Trust in Mediators" (2013) 24 *International Journal of Conflict Management* 23–39.

77 Ibid., 23 at 36.

78 John Curtis, "Caucusing: Help or Hindrance in Mediation?" (May 23, 2012) www.johncurtis.ca/mediation/caucusing-help-or-hindrance-in-mediation/

79 Christopher W. Moore, "The Caucus: Private Meetings That Promote Settlement" (1987) 16 *Mediation Quarterly* 87 at 100.

80 John Wade, "Evaluative Mediation – Elephants in the Room?" (February 20, 2019), www.mediate.com/pfriendly.cfm?id=14034 at 5.

says, "this process of filtering and conveying ideas to get negotiation movement and to transfer new information from a disputant lies at the heart of the mediation process"[81] and is essential to settlement. Brunet says many mediators "leak the forbidden and learned fruits of private caucusing."[82] Jennifer Brown and Ian Ayres describe this as "noisy mediation," wherein mediators collect and distribute private information disclosed in private caucus.[83] This is likely why James R. Coben and Peter N. Thompson warn that mediation parties must retain their adversarial vigilance,[84] the exact posture we typically prefer mediation disputants to avoid.

Whether the caucus occurs as part of shuttle "mediation" or as part of regular mediation, the private and confidential meeting within the mediation presents the best opportunity for deception. John W. Cooley makes the broad statement that "consensual deception is the essence of caucus mediation"[85]; that is what we saw in *The Good Wife*. Lying is simply easier when the disputants are not face to face. Krivis notes that "caucused mediation provides a breeding ground for deceptive techniques because the risk of being caught are substantially reduced."[86] In Welton, Pruitt and McGillicuddy's study they asked questions about how behaviour in caucus differs from behaviour in the joint mediation session.[87] More criticisms of the other's behaviour and character and more put-downs happened during private caucus. Disputants praise themselves in caucus and criticize their opponents,[88] brag and lie,[89] or make statements that are "less than truthful."[90] Will, Alicia and Celeste were all guilty of making less than truthful statements. Regrettably, so was their mediator.

In private caucus the other side is not present to correct misstatements. This means that mediators could be misled or even co-opted into believing one side over the other. Or the mediator could inadvertently become a messenger who delivers a lie. The situation is exacerbated if mediators are making their own

81 Edward Brunet, "Reevaluating Complex Mediation Generalizations" (2011) 18:1 *Connecticut Insurance Law Journal* 279 at 286.

82 Ibid., at 285.

83 Jennifer Brown & Ian Ayres, "Economic Rationales for Mediation" (1994) 80 *Virginia Law Review* 323 at 326.

84 James R. Coben & Peter N. Thompson, "Disputing Irony: A Systematic Look at Litigation about Mediation" (2006) 11 *Harvard Negotiation Law Review* 43 at 81.

85 John W. Cooley, "Mediation Magic: Its Use and Abuse" (1997) 29 *Loyola University of Chicago Law Journal* 1 at 5.

86 Jeffrey Krivis, "The Truth About Deception in Mediation" (2004) 4:2 *Pepperdine Dispute Resolution Law Journal* 251 at 255.

87 Gary L. Welton, Dean G. Pruitt & Neil B. McGillicuddy, "The Role of Caucusing in Community Mediation" (1988) 32 *The Journal of Conflict Resolution* 181.

88 Ibid., at 193.

89 D. Pruitt, G. Welton, W. Fry, N. McGillicuddy, L. Castrianno, C. Ippolito & J. Zubeck, "The Process of Mediation: Caucusing, Control and Problem Solving," in Rahim M. Afzalur, ed., *Managing Conflict: An Interdisciplinary Approach* (Westport, CT: Praeger, 1989) at 207.

90 Gary L. Welton, Dean G. Pruitt & Neil B. McGillicuddy, "The Role of Caucusing in Community Mediation" (1988) 32 *The Journal of Conflict Resolution* 181 at 193.

suggestions or proposing their own solutions based on incomplete, erroneous or deceitful information provided by only one disputant in private. Dallaire says: "If a mediator trying to facilitate discussion and cooperation based on his knowledge of each side's situation is misinformed as to one party's interests, his mediation role is reduced to merely a pawn of deceit and exploitation."[91] Wade says that in mediation with many caucuses:

> the mediator routinely carries lies and deception. (S)he is deceived by the sender and distrusted by the receiver ... the usefulness of the mediator as a trusted adviser decreases and each party carefully hides any life or business goals from the mediator, fearing that (s)he will "leak" in his/her role as persuader in the other room.[92]

Will and Alicia were definitely worried about this. They explicitly told the mediator they would not share their bottom line with him. Moore asks, "Is it possible that a mediator will inadvertently reveal information that a party considers to be confidential?"[93] He argues that while this is possible, "the experience of hundreds of mediators indicates that confidentiality can be maintained, with only a few accidental revelations."[94] While that may be true, there are certainly anecdotal and pop cultural examples of mediators using confidential information. Shapira says: "Separate meetings with parties provide mediators with ample opportunities to manipulate information and deceive parties."[95]

In popular culture we see mediators manipulating and deceiving disputants, especially in caucus. Kate Reed, the mediator protagonist in *Fairly Legal*, uses deceptive techniques in every mediation she conducts. Kate, Vianne Rocher in *Chocolat*, Amélie in *Amélie* and the mediator in *The Good Wife* all use evaluative and deceptive mediation techniques, take away party self-determination and direct the disputants toward their preferred outcomes. Benjamin actually argues that the Trickster figure or archetype offers promise as a professional role model for mediators.[96] He notes that creativity, analytical skills and intuitive sensibilities are part of the Trickster's makeup.[97] Of course, the Trickster, as seen throughout history and literature, is also deceptive and manipulative, leading Benjamin to state that "a mediator must recognize the necessity, within clearly defined limits, of the

91 Michael Dallaire, "Clarifying Candor: Why the model rules should draw bright lines for attorneys' truth-telling duties in arbitration, mediation and unassisted negotiation" (2014) 12:2 *Mayhew-Hite Report on Dispute Resolution and the Courts*, Moritz College of Law, Ohio State University at 6.

92 John Wade, "Evaluative Mediation – Elephants in the Room?" (February 20, 2019), www.mediate.com/pfriendly.cfm?id=14034 at 12.

93 Christopher W. Moore, "The Caucus: Private Meetings That Promote Settlement" (1987) 16 *Mediation Quarterly* 87 at 100.

94 Ibid.

95 Omer Shapira, *A Theory of Mediators' Ethics: Foundation, Rationale, and Application* (Cambridge: Cambridge University Press, 2016) at 268.

96 Robert D. Benjamin, "The Mediator as Trickster: The Folkloric Figure as Professional Role Model" (1995) 13:2 *Conflict Resolution Quarterly* 131.

97 Ibid., at 137.

constructive uses of deception."[98] Do we believe there is such a thing as the constructive use of deception in mediation? If so, how does that impact mediator ethics? How does that change how we teach mediation? Television and the movies warn us that the privacy of the caucus can shield deception and inappropriate use of mediator power.

Mediators must examine the purpose of their caucuses. If the caucus is to calm parties down or to coach them to negotiate more productively, there should be no problems. However, if the caucus is to talk about issues one disputant wants to keep private from the other, mediators need to be more careful. Can mediators take information they obtained in confidence during caucus and use it to help push the parties closer to settlement? In the summer of 2019 I conducted a mediation and, during caucus, one side told me the other side was nowhere near her upper end. That was a potent piece of information. This is what I did with it: in private caucus with the other side I told them that, although their initial request of 25 units was met with a counter of eight units, they could likely get more than eight. They asked for 15 units and obtained them. Was my behaviour ethical? Was that an allowable use of confidential information? I did not go further and advise that side to ask for more than 15 units, but what if I did? Would that change your answer?

If the purpose of mediation is to reach an agreement that meets the needs of all parties, and if mediators employ some "benign" deception in order to effect such agreements, is that all right? If the disputants are happy, are deviations from "proper" practice allowed? How far afield of our founding definitions are we prepared to go? Are we willing to sanction Trickster-like mediation behaviour if it produces good results? Students and professors can discuss whether we can tolerate some level of bias, manipulation and deception in mediation if it leads to a good agreement. Most academics say that no type of mediator deception is permissible. I am a realist so I say mediators may hide their true feelings about the matter and make themselves appear impartial when they are not. Indeed, Welton et al. note that mediators more often do not adhere to neutrality norms during caucus.[99] Mediators may lead parties to believe they are unaware of information that they are aware of, reframe statements in ways that are not completely true to the original message but are easier to hear, suppress negative data and present offers as their own that are actually the other side's. Mediators must always make choices in terms of what, when and how much to reveal. Shapira says mediators can engage in "soft" deception[100] and make inaccurate statements if they are (a) necessary to assist the parties to communicate effectively and (b) if they are consistent with the mediator's other ethical duties, in particular the duty to ensure party self-determination.[101] I agree. *Fairly Legal*, *The Good Wife* and *Amélie* all suggest mediators do not have to be completely honest at all times in order to help parties reach good outcomes.

98 Ibid., at 136.

99 Gary L. Welton, Dean G. Pruitt & Neil B. McGillicuddy, "The role of caucusing in community mediation" (1988) 32 *Journal of Conflict Resolution* 181.

100 Omer Shapira, *A Theory of Mediators' Ethics: Foundation, Rationale, and Application* (Cambridge: Cambridge University Press, 2016) at 266 and 267.

101 Ibid., at 270.

Conclusion

Deception occurs in mediation. Disputants, lawyers and mediators have all on occasion distorted the truth in attempts to reach settlement. Popular culture explicitly demonstrates the deception that I suspect accidentally or covertly occurs in real-life private caucuses. TV shows and movies require us to acknowledge that mediation practice may not match mediation theory and education. To date no North American mediator has been found liable for negligent or deceptive mediation practice,[102] so we still do not know exactly what a mediator's legal duty is. Codes of conduct and case law provide some direction, and complete honesty is not required. Some mediators believe a totally transparent process is called for. Others believe that avoiding harm is all that is necessary. Academics and practitioners need to engage with students and colleagues about whether it is ever appropriate to sidestep proper mediation practice in order to obtain justice,[103] and whether we can fudge to help recalcitrant disputants reach settlement.

Of particular concern is the deception that may be occurring during caucus, where the other side is not present to correct misinformation. Caucuses are useful to help build rapport between the mediator and the parties and to break down emotional, procedural or substantive barriers to effective joint mediation. Brunet says that mediators can earn reputations as empathetic listeners in caucus, which enhances trust.[104] However, if mediators caucus too much there is little opportunity for good faith or understanding to grow between the disputants. The parties cannot really change their perspectives if they are not interacting with one another. Mediators from the community justice and transformative mediation traditions use caucuses far less frequently than commercial mediators, or not at all. They believe that joint sessions are always preferable. Indigenous mediation processes in Canada do not use caucusing for the precise reason that caucusing does not build trust. James H. Stark and Douglas N. Frenkel point to research on bias reduction which "suggests that inducing the parties to cooperate through face-to-face brainstorming may help the parties see each other more as individuals and less as 'types'."[105] This suggests that joint session mediation is preferable to caucus mediation. Richard Birke notes that neuroscience shows us that humans make facial expressions that are species-consistent and readily understood by

102 Jennifer L. Schulz (2001) "Mediator Liability in Canada: An Examination of Emerging American and Canadian Jurisprudence," 32 *Ottawa Law Review* 269. Two reasons North American mediators have yet to be found liable for any substandard practice are the confidentiality of the mediation process and the quasi-judicial immunity afforded many American practitioners. The instance of suits launched against mediators is extremely low in both the United States of America and Canada.

103 Robert D. Benjamin, "The Mediator as Trickster: The Folkloric Figure as Professional Role Model" (1995) 13:2 *Conflict Resolution Quarterly* 131 at 138.

104 Edward Brunet, "Reevaluating Complex Mediation Generalizations" (2011) 18:1 *Connecticut Insurance Law Journal* 279 at 293.

105 James H. Stark & Douglas N. Frenkel, "Changing Minds: The Work of Mediators and Empirical Studies of Persuasion" (2013) 28 *Ohio State Journal on Dispute Resolution* 263 at 341.

members of other cultures.[106] As such, longer joint sessions with more face-to-face contact makes sense for mediation. It stands to reason that if the disputants are speaking to one another face-to-face, in the same room, they are more likely to understand one another. The American Bar Association Section of Dispute Resolution's Task Force on Research on Mediator Techniques revealed what existing empirical evidence demonstrates about which mediator actions enhance outcomes and which do not.[107] It found that caucusing during mediation had no effect on settlement, regardless of whether the goal was to establish trust or discuss settlement proposals. The only area where caucusing generally increased settlement was in labour-management disputes. So why are we caucusing so much, especially if caucusing has no effect on settlement? Mediators must rethink caucusing and educate our disputants and their lawyers who have perhaps become too used to it. Caucusing is simply not essential to mediation, and either has no effect or a negative effect on disputants' perceptions, relationships and post-mediation conflict.[108]

Despite the knowledge that caucusing is not necessary, mediators who support the idea of long joint sessions and few-to-no caucuses appear to be in the minority.[109] For the majority of mediators who do caucus it is important for them to police themselves for honesty, and to remember to go back into joint session to work together. Mediators should also conduct background research on the lawyers that will appear in front of them to see if the lawyers have reputations for deception. If there is a possibility of an ongoing relationship between the mediator and one or both of the lawyers, that too may encourage honesty; people typically prefer to work with those whom they trust, and most mediators are interested in obtaining repeat business from lawyers (see Chapter 4). Creating a mediation atmosphere conducive to trust and rapport-building is key for mediators, as is asking counsel to provide substantiation for their claims or justifications for how they reached their numbers. Peter Reilly encourages mediators to ask "come clean" questions.[110] For example, a mediator could ask: "Is there something known to you, but not to me or the other side, that should be revealed at this point?"

Watching popular culture depictions of mediation together enables students and professors to collaborate in their discussions about proper, ethical mediation practice, mirroring the importance of collaboration to mediation. As Lawrence Raw suggests:

106 Richard Birke, "Neuroscience and Settlement: An Examination of Scientific Innovations and Practical Applications" (2010) 25 *Ohio State Journal on Dispute Resolution* 477 at 505.

107 Task Force on Research on Mediation Techniques, commissioned by the ABA Section of Dispute Resolution (June 12, 2017) www.americanbar.org/groups/dispute_resolution.html

108 Ibid.

109 Christopher W. Moore, "The Caucus: Private Meetings That Promote Settlement" (1987) 16 *Mediation Quarterly* 87 at 88–90.

110 Peter Reilly, "Was Machiavelli Right? Lying in Negotiation and the Art of Defensive Self-Help" (2009) 24 *Ohio State Journal on Dispute Resolution* 481.

> The emphasis on collaboration in terms of syllabus design, determination of course objectives, and assessment can emphasize the importance of the popular: everyone feels directly involved in their own creation, rather than listening and responding to predigested material from course books.[111]

Finally, we must remember that our popular culture, and how we teach our students, is not the only popular culture or the only way to teach. The third highest-grossing Indian film ever, *Bajrangi Bhaijaan*, directed by Kabir Khan,[112] presents an entirely different view, totally condemning deceptive conflict resolution moves.

Pawan, the film's Hindu protagonist, rescues a lost, mute Muslim girl and tries to return her to her family in Pakistan, despite constant ethnocentrism and cultural barriers. In a wonderful example of how reel life influences real life, a real Indian woman named Geeta who was lost in Pakistan found that her "story gained attention after the Bollywood film *Bajrangi Bhaijaan* was released in July with a plot similar to her case."[113] In the film, Pawan is devoted to the monkey god Bajrang Bali and, therefore, he will "never do anything on the sly." Pawan is so honest and so focused on the needs of those in conflict that not only will he never do anything on the sly, he also prioritizes disputants far above himself. Pawan puts the disputants before his own needs. For example, despite being injured, Pawan carries the girl on his shoulders, as is illustrated in the movie's poster (see Figure 5.2). He is so concerned to help the young Muslim girl that he forgets to care for himself, leading his father-in-law-to-be to explain, using the example of flying on an airplane, that Pawan must not forget himself – "you have to put your own oxygen mask on first," before helping others. Ajit Duara says that *Bajrangi Bhaijaan* follows a "story of taking the path of righteousness."[114] As a result of Pawan's righteousness and desire to always be honest he endures torture and waits three times for permission to cross the Pakistan border to return the girl; he simply will not cross, or do anything, dishonestly. Pawan is an activist, cross-cultural conflict resolver with integrity, without a deceptive bone in his body. He is described as "devout, polite, truthful to a fault, almost childlike in his enthusiasm"[115]; very different from most of the deceptive meditators found in Western popular culture and an interesting identity for Western mediators to try on. Elaine Newman says: "Ultimately, each one of us must ask, to what end do I offer my services? Who am I

111 Lawrence Raw, "Is Empathy Important in Teaching Popular Culture?" (2017) 50 *The Journal of Popular Culture* 410 at 414.

112 https://einthusan.tv/movie/watch/2737/

113 Qasim Nauman & Aditi Malhotra, "Geeta, a woman lost in Pakistan for 15 years, is to return to India" (October 16, 2015), *Dow Jones Institutional News*, http://uml.idm.oclc.org/login?url=https://search-proquest-com.uml.idm.oclc.org/docview/2061908327?accountid=14569 and Qasim Nauman, "A Hit Film May Bring a Lost Woman Home" (August 15, 2015) *Wall Street Journal* C12.

114 Ajit Duara, "Bajrangi Bhaijaan" (July 22, 2015) *OPEN* magazine, https://openthemagazine.com/cinema/bajrangi-bhaijaan/

115 Film review of Bajrangi Bhaijaan (July 17, 2015) *Mint*, http://uml.idm.oclc.org/login?url=https://search-proquest-com.uml.idm.oclc.org/docview/1696923792?accountid=14569

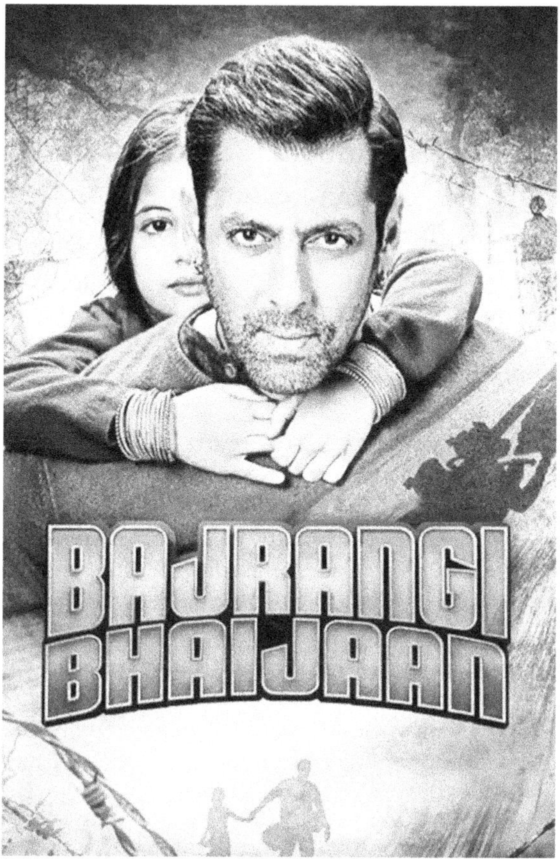

Figure 5.2 Movie poster for *Bajrangi Bhaijaan*

when I mediate?"[116] *Bajrangi Bhaijaan* demonstrates that Pawan knows exactly who he is, and that shines through in his conflict resolution endeavour. How we envision ourselves as mediators and what we allow or do not allow ourselves to do may have great impact on our identities, the subject of the final chapter.

116 Elaine Newman, "Who Are We When We Mediate?" (2012) 21 *Canadian Arbitration and Mediation Journal* 42 at 44.

6 Popular culture and mediator identity

Popular culture: *The Story of Qiu Ju* (film, China)
Research from: Australia, Belgium, Canada, China, Germany, New Zealand, Singapore, Spain, UK and USA

The research

How do mediators define themselves? The research tells us that "in terms of self-image or self-identity, studies cite a strong sense of self-confidence and self-efficacy as desirable in both mediators and negotiators."[1] Robin Wellford Slocum states that "emotional competency is integral to the exercise of good judgment and to the ability to communicate, persuade, and influence others."[2] Daniel Lieberfeld notes that mediators' self-confidence must be balanced with low egocentrism, and that patience, interpersonal skills and belief in human values are also necessary.[3] Good mediators are "both task-focused and interpersonally adept."[4] Further, mediators need to be non-judgmental, empathic and non-dogmatic. Lieberfeld goes on to say that they must have tolerance for ambiguity, be practical and have low interest in personal power.[5] Having an optimistic view of human nature and focusing on people's potential rather than their deficits certainly helps.[6] Lela P. Love says:

> The mediator's features are hazy, since the focus and light remains on the disputing parties. Her presence, however, exudes optimism, respect, and confidence in the parties' capacity. She brings an energetic and urgent sense that justice can be done by the parties' own hands.[7]

Bernard S. Mayer says mediators share common values including: being hard on the problem, easy on the people; empowering disputants; respecting diversity;

1 Daniel Lieberfeld, "Nelson Mandela: Partisan and Peacemaker" (2003) 19:3 *Negotiation Journal* 229 at 233.
2 Robin Wellford Slocum, "An Inconvenient Truth: The Need to Educate Emotionally Competent Lawyers" (2011) 11 Chapman University Law Research Paper 1 at 5.
3 Daniel Lieberfeld, "Nelson Mandela: Partisan and Peacemaker" (2003) 19:3 *Negotiation Journal* 229 at 233.
4 Ibid., at 241.
5 Ibid., at 234.
6 Ibid., at 237.
7 Lela P. Love, "Images of Justice" (2000) 1:1 *Pepperdine Dispute Resolution Law Journal* 29 at 32.

believing in communication; valuing creativity; and maintaining optimism.[8] The principles and values of mediators and mediation provide a foundation for thinking about developing the identity of the mediator. However, as Love notes, the mediator's image is still hazy.

Elizabeth E. Bader argues that the mediator's ability to deal with issues of self and identity is central to successful mediation.[9] She says mediators must have a realistic professional ego that accepts the limits of our power and knowledge and she recommends mindfulness practice to assist with mediator self-identity.[10] Trevor C. W. Farrow suggests we find out and care about what is in the head of the mediator as it may be interests other than the disputants', such as her own or the public's,[11] all of which can impact identity. Debbie De Girolamo argues that the mediator has multiple, shifting roles in any given mediation session: as neutral third party intervener, as a party and as an advisor.[12] De Girolamo says the mediator becomes an integral player in the dispute itself, basing her conclusions on a year-long ethnographic study of commercial mediation she conducted in England and Wales. De Girolamo notes that mediators can take on the identities of mediator, adviser, adversary and supporter all within the same mediation.[13] Her work highlights the difficulty of presupposing one identity per mediator, which I am decidedly not doing. Rather, in this chapter, I wish to explore how popular culture may help to shade in some of the grey areas of mediator identity and image. As John Winslade and Gerald Monk put it, "we can think of the talk we create in mediation as actually constructing experience;"[14] and I would add identity. Through mediating, mediators better understand themselves. This is depicted in popular film. Pawan, the protagonist and cross-cultural mediator in *Bajrangi Bhaijaan*, understands himself better and constructs his identity through the process of helping the mute girl. He puts it as follows: "I found myself while looking for you. I heard what you never said, and since we've met I feel capable." The mediator defines himself through the process of cross-cultural conflict resolution. In this final chapter I will argue that popular mediation images can assist with mediator identity-building.

Nadja Alexander tells us, "In terms of legal practice and legislative activity, mediation is arguably the fastest growing form of ADR in the world."[15] Globalization

8 Bernard S. Mayer, *Beyond Neutrality: Confronting the Crisis in Conflict Resolution* (San Francisco, CA: Jossey-Bass, 2004) at 289–291.

9 Elizabeth E. Bader, "The Psychology of Mediation: Issues of Self and Identity and the IDR Cycle" (2010) 10:2 *Pepperdine Dispute Resolution Law Journal* 183 at 200.

10 Ibid., at 203.

11 Trevor C.W. Farrow, "Representative Negotiation," in C. Hanycz, T. Farrow & F. Zemans, eds, *The Theory and Practice of Representative Negotiation* (Toronto: Emond Montgomery, 2008) at 22.

12 Debbie De Girolamo, "A View from Within: Reconceptualizing Mediator Interactions" (2012) 30:2 *Windsor Yearbook of Access to Justice* 103 at 105.

13 Ibid., at 127.

14 John Winslade & Gerald Monk, *Narrative Mediation: A New Approach to Conflict Resolution* (San Francisco, CA: Jossey-Bass, 2001) at 39.

15 Nadja Alexander, ed., *Global Trends in Mediation*, 2nd edn (Alphen aan den Rijn: Kluwer Law International, 2006) at 6.

and seamless transacting require the flexibility of mediation that can easily cross borders,[16] and online dispute resolution procedures and online mediation are growing every year. Yet mediators are rarely featured in popular culture, and especially not as leading protagonists. So how do we learn about mediator identity if we do not often see mediators on screen? Although mediators are outside the typical Law & Popular Culture canon, which is focused on trials and lawyers, we can learn from the fledgling images of mediators in popular culture. Elizabeth Spelman and Martha Minow correctly note: "We have as much to learn about the law from those who find themselves (in both senses of that phrase) outside it as those who enforce it, wield it, or study it."[17] Mediators are often positioned outside of the law and we can learn from them. Their images and identities are socially constructed in complex interactions played out through various discourses, including law and popular culture. As Kimberlianne Podlas notes: "Media consumption is an active process, where viewers' existing attitudes and beliefs impact how television imagery is interpreted, integrated, and acted upon."[18] Audiences are active producers of meaning.[19] I want to conclude this book by inviting readers to think about how the mediators I have discussed might help make meaning for them, thereby impacting their identities as mediators.

In this book I have recognized mediation in five television series: *Fairly Legal, The Good Wife, Orange is the New Black, Star Trek: The Next Generation* and *The Office*, and in six films: *Amélie, Face to Face, Wedding Crashers, The Break-Up, Bajrangi Bhaijaan* and *The Story of Qiu Ju* (discussed later in this chapter). The reason I know that the images of mediators I have examined in this book could shape mediation and mediators is because of the great success popular culture images of lawyers have had in influencing law and lawyers. Corie Lynn Rosen notes that "for lawyers, the media is an especially important representation of professional and personal experience."[20] Michael Asimow and Shannon Mader

16 J.G. Merrills, *International Dispute Settlement*, 5th edn (Cambridge: Cambridge University Press, 2011) at 39 notes that sometimes, in the international sphere, mediators are retained past the mediation sessions in order to ensure compliance with the agreement.
17 E. Spelman & M. Minow, "Outlaw Women: *Thelma and Louise*," in J. Denvir, ed., *Legal Reelism: Movies as Legal Texts* (Urbana and Chicago, IL: University of Illinois Press, 1996) at 276.
18 Kimberlianne Podlas, "Testing Television: Studying and Understanding the Impact of Television's Depictions of Law and Justice," in Peter Robson & Jessica Silbey, eds, *Law and Justice on the Small Screen* (Oxford: Hart, 2012) at 105. However, as Cassandra Sharp notes: "There is a void in research about the connections between television representations and the meaning-making processes of audiences in response to them, particularly in the area of in-depth empirical and ethnographic research" ("Let's See How Far We've Come: The Role of Empirical Methodology in Exploring Television Audiences," in Peter Robson & Jessica Silbey, eds, *Law and Justice on the Small Screen* [Oxford: Hart, 2012] at 112).
19 D. Morley, *Television, Audiences and Cultural Studies* (London: Routledge, 1992).
20 Corie Lynn Rosen, "Unteaching Television: Understanding the Effects of Media on Cultural Perceptions of Lawyers and Law Student Language" (June 28, 2012), http://ssrn.com/abstract=2095244. The same may be true for doctors; see Michael M. O'Conner, "The Role of the Television Drama *ER* in Medical Student Life:

note that "popular culture both *constructs* our perceptions of the law and *changes* the way that the players in the legal system behave."[21] Richard Sherwin says: "Law is not just on the books, or in the gap between books and practice. It is in people's heads in the form of scripted expectations, popular story forms, and recurrent images."[22] Sherwin describes how popular culture's characters and stories tell viewers how the law works and how people should behave; the pop culture stories stick in our memories and authorize our beliefs.[23] Steven Keslowitz states that: "Prime time television drama has the power to change – and has in fact changed – the public's perception of lawyers, the police, and the legal system."[24] Keslowitz's work with *The Simpsons* and *24* has been referenced by representatives in American congressional hearings and legislators have referred to these shows in order to shape legal and public policy debates in the United States of America.[25] Philip N. Meyer notes: "Popular cinema often directly influences trial attorneys' selection of story structure, definition of story theme, and creation of recognizable stock characters, including the identity of the storyteller/attorney."[26] J.B. Owens notes the power and influence wielded by popular culture's images of lawyers, especially the images created by John Grisham. Owens states: "A quick search on Westlaw or Lexis will reveal many opinions from courts around the country [USA] describing the facts at issue as 'Grisham-like'."[27] He further notes: "If prosecutors, defence counsel, and judges are quoting Grisham in court filings, then it is safe to say that the public, including young lawyers, must take away something about practising law from Grisham's books."[28]

Similarly, popular culture has been effective in influencing and educating students. *Journeys in Film*,[29] an American and Canadian film-based middle school curriculum, gets students to think about, discuss and relate to cultures around the world using

Entertainment or Socialization?" (1998) 280 *The Journal of the American Medical Association* 854.

21 Michael Asimow & Shannon Mader, *Law and Popular Culture: A Course Book* (New York: Peter Lang Publishing, 2004) at xxii; emphasis in original.

22 Richard K. Sherwin, "Nomos and Cinema" (2001) 48 *UCLA Law Review* 1519 at 1539 (Symposium: Law & Popular Culture).

23 Richard K. Sherwin, "Law's Screen Life: Criminal Predators and What to Do About Them: Popular Imperatives from Screen-Based Reality," in Austin Sarat, ed., *Imagining Legality: Where Law Meets Popular Culture* (Tuscaloosa, AL: The University of Alabama Press, 2011) at 107.

24 Steven Keslowitz, "*The Simpsons, 24*, and the Law: How Homer Simpson and Jack Bauer Influence Congressional Lawmaking and Judicial Reasoning" (2008) 29 *Cardozo Law Review* 2787 at 2789, note 12.

25 Ibid., at 2809–2810.

26 P.N. Meyer, "Will You Please be Quiet, Please? Lawyers Listening to the Call of Stories" (1994) 18 *Vermont Law Review* 567 at 576 (Lawyers as Storytellers & Storytellers as Lawyers: An Interdisciplinary Symposium Exploring the Use of Storytelling in the Practice of Law).

27 J.B. Owens, "Grisham's Legal Tales: A Moral Compass for the Young Lawyer" (2001) 48 *UCLA Law Review* 1431 at 1433 (Symposium: Law & Popular Culture).

28 Ibid., at 1434.

29 www.journeysinfilm.org

films such as *Bend It Like Beckham, Whale Rider* and *The Cup*. According to Martin Scott, John Street and Sanna Inthorn, 17 and 18 year-olds find entertainment television programming to be a particularly rich source of symbols for themselves, their talk, their politics and their communities.[30] Cassandra Sharp's research demonstrates that law students use "fictional legal television as a springboard for both referential and critical use."[31] According to Asimow and Mader, law and popular culture are two of the most meaningful subjects in the lives of law students, and, as such, students greatly benefit from critical examinations of their intersection.[32] Applications to California law schools in the 1990s spiked because American students were watching *LA Law* on TV and decided they too wanted to be lawyers. Today, my students often report they came to law school to be like Harvey Spector or Mike Ross, lead lawyer characters in the TV series *Suits*. When students are able to see future professional versions of themselves on TV they experience pleasurable identification. My students like Mike and Harvey and aspire to be lawyers like them. I think this means that students who like Kate Reed or other popular culture mediators might want to be mediators like her. Quite simply, based on popular culture's great success in disseminating images of lawyers, we may extrapolate its success in promulgating information about and for mediators.[33]

As a law professor specializing in mediation and as a practising mediator, I know that how we teach mediation to new generations of practitioners is important. I also know that having popular culture examples of mediation to reference with students, such as those described in this book, are useful in the classroom. And, as mediation becomes more prevalent in popular culture, references to it will also be helpful with disputants during pre-mediation. Popular culture mediators can and will shape attitudes about mediation and how it is taught. In Chapter 1 I noted it is impossible to definitively prove that popular culture creates people's views on mediators, or mediators' views on themselves. As Sharp notes, "there is a void in research about the connections between television representations and the meaning-making processes of audiences in response to them."[34] Despite this empirical void, however, it is equally impossible to deny popular culture's influence on idea

30 M. Scott, J. Street & S. Inthorn, "From entertainment to citizenship: A comparative study of the political uses of popular culture by first-time voters" (2011) 14 *International Journal of Cultural Studies* 499 at 503.

31 Cassandra Sharp, "Let's See How Far We've Come: The Role of Empirical Methodology in Exploring Television Audiences," in Peter Robson & Jessica Silbey, eds, *Law and Justice on the Small Screen* (Oxford: Hart, 2012) at 123.

32 Michael Asimow & Shannon Mader, *Law and Popular Culture: A Course Book* (New York: Peter Lang Publishing, 2004) at xxiv.

33 Jennifer L. Schulz, "Settlement and Mediation in Canadian Legal Television" (2011) 1 *Journal of Arbitration and Mediation* 77 at 102.

34 Cassandra Sharp, "Let's See How Far We've Come: The Role of Empirical Methodology in Exploring Television Audiences," in Peter Robson & Jessica Silbey, eds, *Law and Justice on the Small Screen* (Oxford: Hart, 2012) at 112. She identifies a need for more qualitative ethnographic research into the "vexed area of audience research" (at 118).

formation and meaning-making.[35] The entire field of advertising would not exist unless there is truth to the statement that what is shown on screens influences viewers. Popular culture depictions of mediators and other conflict resolvers can influence mediators' own self-definitions. Mediation, in the rare instances when we glimpse it in our popular culture, can mirror, criticize or project alternative dispute resolution realities. It can allow us, as Austin Sarat suggests, to imagine mediation anew.[36] As academics we can create room within mediation education for new insights, gleaned from popular culture, about impartiality, self-determination, fair outcomes, feelings, expert intuition, conflicts of interest, repeat business, deception, caucusing and mediator identity.

Identification

When looking to TV shows and movies to help inform thoughts about mediator identity, there are at least three things to consider: (i) the process of identification; (ii) our definitions; and (iii) the role of popular culture. I will discuss each in turn. First, mediators and mediation students need to identify with on-screen mediators. This is certainly possible due to filmic techniques that encourage certain viewer identifications and responses. Television and Netflix shows, for example, through their narrative arcs and seriality, draw us to their characters, helping us to identify with them.[37] Especially as portrayals of mediation and mediators increase, mediators will begin to recognize themselves in popular culture. When we recognize ourselves in a character or in a story we become a participant and co-creator of that story. We identify with it. As Jeffrey E. Thomas states: "When the experience depicted resonates with the experience or beliefs of the viewer, it has a reinforcing impact that is even greater."[38] An act of identification helps make the story our own, augments its believability and opens up the possibility of influence. When we identify with the mediator in a film, see ourselves reflected in a mediation plotline, or want to be like the mediator captured on screen, we experience pleasure. Our bodies, our senses and our intellects are all involved in the process of identification.

However, what if the mediators are poorly portrayed? In the Netflix series *The Affair*, about a married heterosexual couple whose marriage breaks up due to the husband's infidelity, the husband and wife attend mediation in the first episode of the second season and the family mediator is portrayed as a doofus. Mediators may not identify with such a portrayal because the on-screen mediator is not a smart,

35 D. Morley, *Television, Audiences and Cultural Studies* (London: Routledge, 1992).

36 Austin Sarat, "What Popular Culture Does For, and To, Law," in Austin Sarat, ed., *Imagining Legality: Where Law Meets Popular Culture* (Tuscaloosa, AL: The University of Alabama Press, 2011) at 16.

37 Rebecca Johnson, "Television, Pleasure and the Empire of Force: Interrogating Law and Affect in *Deadwood*," in Peter Robson & Jessica Silbey, eds, *Law and Justice on the Small Screen* (Oxford: Hart, 2012) at 60.

38 J.E. Thomas, "Legal Culture and *the practice*: A Postmodern Depiction of the Rule of Law" (2001) 48 *UCLA Law Review* 1495 at 1515.

likable character. When we look to mediator Kate Reed from *Fairly Legal* we see that sometimes she is positioned on the edge or fringes of the legal system – as a cool, renegade woman we might like to identify with – and sometimes as completely conventional or co-opted by the legal system – someone with whom mediators may or may not identify. As Margaret Davies and Nan Seuffert describe it, Kate is "situated sometimes on the fringes and sometimes closer to the centre of mainstream productions."[39] The process of identification with popular culture mediators will depend on how they are portrayed and whether those portrayals resonate with real mediators. As mediators we do not want to find ourselves in the situation Margaret E. Montoya describes:

> As we struggle to construct our own identities, to be recognizable to ourselves through the narratives we tell, others are at the same moment constructing our identities by telling other narratives (i.e. in legal opinions, movies, newspaper articles), revealing that we are not recognizable to them.[40]

In this book I have provided examples of TV and movie mediators who dispense with impartiality and party self-determination. Some privilege feelings and fair outcomes while others privilege their own repeat business. Some mediators are unethical, mediating despite conflicts of interest or mediating deceptively. This may not be what mediators want to see, and they definitely may not identify with it. However, these images may help mediators and mediation scholars think about themselves and mediation differently. How we utilize our intuition, operate in caucus and use our power must be surfaced and theorized. We need to discuss the fact that popular culture could authorize non-neutral, evaluative, deceptive mediation approaches. Rebecca Johnson suggests that the seriality of television shows can work to create a structure of feeling where practising mediators identify with and cheer for protagonists, even if they do things, such as mediate, incorrectly.[41] In series like *Fairly Legal*, *The Office* and *The Good Wife* we become affectively attached to Kate, Michael and Diane, respectively, over weeks, months or even years of watching. We like them and, as a result, we come to support their methods, even when they are contrary to proper mediation theory and practice. As Johnson explains, viewers' attachment to TV conflict resolvers happens not simply through time spent watching them on TV, but also through active work done by

39 M. Davies & N. Seuffert, "Knowledge, Identity, and the Politics of Law" (2000) *Hastings Women's Law Journal* 259 at 261.

40 M.E. Montoya, "Border/ed Identities: Narrative and the Social Construction of Legal and Personal Identities," in A. Sarat, M. Constable, D. Engel, V. Hans & S. Lawrence, eds, *Crossing Boundaries: Traditions and Transformations in Law and Society Research* (Evanston, IL: Northwestern University Press, 1998) at 133.

41 See Rebecca Johnson, "Television, Pleasure and the Empire of Force: Interrogating Law and Affect in *Deadwood*," in Peter Robson & Jessica Silbey, eds, *Law and Justice on the Small Screen* (Oxford: Hart, 2012) at 45 where she describes how the seriality of *Deadwood* works to support a structure of feeling that sustains colonial orderings.

viewers to make sense of the characters and the events they are involved in.[42] As we understand popular culture mediators and mediation processes better we are more apt to forgive deviations from proper mediation practice.

When mediators are featured in popular culture it brings more profile to mediation. When viewers see Kate Reed mediate on *Fairly Legal*, or watch the mediators in *Wedding Crashers* and *The Break-Up*, mediation's profile is increased just by being portrayed on screen. On the other hand, the vast majority of mediators and mediation scholars would not endorse these mediators' actions. Kate intervenes when she has not been invited to do so, she employs deception and she is very evaluative, sometimes crossing over to med/arb without informing her disputants. The male co-mediators in *Wedding Crashers* sing and swear and suggest being unethically compensated. The realtor-mediator in *The Break-Up* is not impartial and has a clear conflict of interest. Therefore, while these mediators enhance the profile of mediation in terms of public awareness, and could lead to viewer identification, they may not enhance the image of the mediator. (We cannot forget that popular culture is a commercial, for-profit, entertainment commodity. It is not an educational manual. The inaccurate mediation techniques and outlandish storylines are designed to appeal to the consuming, or viewing, audience.) Every television show and movie discussed in this book undermines proper mediation practice and therefore, perhaps, the image of mediation. However, they all also enhance mediation's profile by bringing mediation to viewers' attention – indeed, right into their living rooms. I believe it is more important that greater numbers of the public learn about mediation than that the popular culture "gets it right."

The popular culture examples in this book illuminate mediation differently than how we teach it and are therefore disruptive of some mediation truths. However, watching mediation deviations and deception is useful because students can *feel* mediation mistakes in ways they cannot when reading textbooks. "Films are particularly useful in the classroom, because they allow law students to see ADR processes that they might not otherwise see throughout their entire legal educations."[43] A Canadian federal report came out in 2000 recommending that law schools provide students the opportunity to develop dispute analysis and resolution skills.[44] The report stated that "in order to improve their awareness of settlement-oriented practice, law students should be exposed to various theories of social and individual conflict resolution practices as well as to materials dealing

42 Ibid., at 46.

43 Jennifer L. Schulz, "Using Film to Teach ADR," in Christine A. Corcos, ed., *The Media Method: Teaching Law with Popular Culture* (Durham, NC: Carolina Academic Press, 2019) at 382.

44 Attitudes, Skills, Knowledge: Recommendations for Changes to Legal Education to Assist in Implementing Multi-Option Civil Justice Systems in the 21st Century (Ottawa: Canadian Bar Association, 2000).

with human experiences of conflict."[45] Popular culture is the perfect vehicle to expose students to experiences of conflict and its resolution. A course can describe mediation and ethics, but watching popular culture mediators in action lets students feel and react to mediation and to breaches of process and ethics. This is an important pedagogical experience, and not just for students. The professor learns as well, which impacts her self-image and self-definition. Thomas B. McMorrow recommends the mediation professor rejects a managerial approach to teaching and embraces the vision of teacher as mediator.[46] "If the ADR professor is a mediator rather than a manager, her teaching style will better model the substance of what she is teaching, and her students will actually learn mediation better."[47] The professor's identity will also be positively impacted.

Students and viewing audiences use television narratives as "one of the many cultural resources through which they will construct meaning,"[48] so popular culture mediation, even with all its flaws, is implicated in mediation meaning-making. When we see mediation infractions in popular culture, as we do in virtually every example, if nothing else we can use those infractions as pedagogical tools to teach our students and ourselves how *not* to mediate. Quite simply, the experiences we construct together in the classroom or in the mediation chamber – even when, due to popular culture, they begin with "false" impressions of what mediation is – invite, or perhaps demand, new practice and pedagogy. Of course, it is not just professors and students who benefit from identification with popular culture mediators. Practising mediators can benefit too. Peter Eastwood argues that: "The expectations of mediation participants – formed largely from popular conceptions of cinematic and legal storytelling – must be accommodated for a session to realize its potential."[49] This suggests that there is value in mediators understanding popular depictions of conflict resolution work. A blogger wrote the following about *Fairly Legal* and disputants' expectations:

> The show has generated a huge amount of commentary from mediators – as you might imagine – ranging from wails of woe about the errors in process to whoops of joy at our profession finally making it to the TV screen. ... We might end up saying, "well, it is nothing like Kate on TV you know!" and that's OK. How different will that be from having to educate parties about what actually happens as opposed to what they have assumed happens? I

45 Ibid.

46 Thomas B. McMorrow, "Learning to Mediate Through Teaching Mediation" (2015) *Canadian Legal Education Annual Review* 49 at 69.

47 Jennifer L. Schulz, "Using Film to Teach ADR," in Christine A. Corcos, ed., *The Media Method: Teaching Law with Popular Culture* (Durham, NC: Carolina Academic Press, 2019) at 391–392.

48 Cassandra Sharp, "Let's See How Far We've Come: The Role of Empirical Methodology in Exploring Television Audiences," in Peter Robson & Jessica Silbey, eds, *Law and Justice on the Small Screen* (Oxford: Hart, 2012) at 129.

49 Peter Eastwood, "Great Expectations: Popular Culture and the Narration of Conflict in Litigation and Mediation" (2012) 2 *Masks: The Online Journal of Law and Theatre* 22.

> would rather be talking to many more people who now know that mediation exists.[50]

Without knowing what expectations of mediation disputants might have when they enter the mediation chamber, mediators will not be able to realize the session's full potential. "Mediators must be able to bridge the gap between such preconceptions and the reality of what mediation storytelling aims to accomplish."[51] Mark Pawlowsi and Sarah Greer note that "studies have shown that creating the right impression or conforming to the legal stereotype improves a lawyer's chances of building up a good clientele."[52] There is no reason to suspect otherwise for mediators.

Realistically, given the small number of mediators featured in popular culture in 2020, we do not need to be concerned that viewers will come to completely misunderstand mediation. More likely, seeing mediation in popular culture will attune viewers to the fact that this dispute resolution process exists, thereby increasing the likelihood of mediator identification and, perhaps, mediation use. Each time mediation is shown on TV or in a movie it makes viewers/potential disputants more aware of mediation and provides more opportunities for mediator identification. Identifying with a mediator's image or personality and seeing ourselves for the first time in popular culture can be a powerful force. Of course, there are also other processes of identification. Imma Armadans, Maria Munné, Xavier Serrano et al. argue that mediation training courses create a sense of belonging amongst mediation trainees. In turn, this sense of belonging creates identification with the profession of mediation.[53] "From this perspective, social identity in the case of the mediator begins with how members of the group of mediators present themselves to their own group and other groups."[54] Borrowing from Benedict Anderson, we can say that mediators are an imagined community[55] that, in order to thrive, especially against the threat of co-opted processes and the legal system, must be invoked and brought together in the minds and imaginations of its members. Popular culture can help with those invocations and identifications. Through the study of popular culture, mediators can study themselves, and that kind of critical self-reflection is necessary in order to be the best mediators we can

50 http://blog.amandabucklow.co.uk/2011/01/23/fairly-legal-a-watershed-for-mediation/

51 Peter Eastwood, "Great Expectations: Popular Culture and the Narration of Conflict in Litigation and Mediation" (2012) 2 *Masks: The Online Journal of Law and Theatre* 23.

52 Mark Pawlowsi & Sarah Greer, "Film and Literature in the Legal Classroom" (2009) 43 *The Law Teacher* 49 at 51.

53 Imma Armadans, Maria Munné, Xavier Serrano, Maria Palacin, Ana Villanueva, Andres Dimasso & Didac Selva (2012) "The Identity of the Mediator in Crisis," paper presented at the International Association of Conflict Management Conference, Spier, South Africa, http://ssrn.com/abstract=2084808

54 Ibid.

55 Benedict Anderson, *Imagined Communities: Reflections on the Origin and Spread of Nationalism* (London and New York: Verso, 1983).

be. Popular conceptions of mediation can contribute to the process of identification, provided real mediators identify with the reel mediators they see.

Definitions

When looking to popular culture to inform mediator identity, in addition to the process of identification, we must consider our definitions. A key definitional debate surrounds the word "profession." Mediation is not an official profession, so findings about professional identity and its formation may or may not be applicable to mediators. So our first definition problem is that much of the population does not know what mediation is, and our second definition problem is that we do not know whether we are professionals, or professionals in another field who are also trained in mediation.[56] Armadans, Munné, Serrano et al. say, as a result, our identity is neither consolidated nor socially recognized; as a professional identity it is still being developed.[57] Armadans, Munné, Serrano et al. did research with focus groups of researchers, teachers and mediators at the University of Barcelona in 2012. They found that the number one challenge raised by Spanish mediators was "the need to define the identity of the mediator as a professional and obtain social recognition."[58] Brian Jarrett conducted interviews with 40 well-respected American and Canadian mediator-professors and teacher-practitioners in 2009. He found that "almost all interviewees reported that mediators find themselves in a struggle for professional identity."[59] They are searching for a professional definition, label or status. Similar results were obtained in New Zealand in 2019.[60] The mediators in Jarrett's study declared their commitment to a specific mediation approach – for example, facilitative – as a way of producing meaning and coherence.[61] However, Jarrett acknowledges that "the result is that espoused theory in the mediation field may not accurately reflect actual practice."[62] Cheryl Picard's research bolsters this view, indicating that mediators, while they use the same terms – for example, facilitative and

56 Imma Armadans, Maria Munné, Xavier Serrano, Maria Palacin, Ana Villanueva, Andres Dimasso & Didac Selva (2012) "The Identity of the Mediator in Crisis," paper presented at the International Association of Conflict Management Conference, Spier, South Africa, http://ssrn.com/abstract=2084808

57 Ibid.

58 Ibid.

59 Brian Jarrett, "The Future of Mediation: A Sociological Perspective" (2009) *Journal of Dispute Resolution* 49 at 54.

60 Grant Hamilton Morris & Sapphire Petrie-McVean, "Victoria University of Wellington/Resolution Institute Commercial Mediation in New Zealand: The Mediators' Project Report" (August 2019), part of the New Zealand Commercial Mediation Study (NZCMS), asked the question, "In your opinion, what are the key challenges facing commercial mediators in New Zealand at the present time?" Most respondents said "lack of awareness of mediation and its benefits." https://papers.ssrn.com/sol3/papers.cfm?abstract_id=3474184

61 Brian Jarrett, "The Future of Mediation: A Sociological Perspective" (2009) *Journal of Dispute Resolution* 49 at 59.

62 Ibid., at 58.

evaluative – mean different things by them.[63] Mediators may seek to define themselves in terms of mediation style, and to label what they do, but it may not be accurate. (Mediators may also define themselves in response to market pressures resulting from lawyers' influence over the selection of mediators; for example, by saying "I don't do joint sessions." This is also not ideal; see Chapter 4.)

Mediators work in diverse communities of practice and they mediate in diverse ways so I am certainly not implying that there might be a mediator identity or self-image that can be covered by one definition. In the 1980s Susan Zaidel said: "Professional identity may not be problematic for the individual mediator, but it is an issue on the organizational level. Is there any common denominator among attorney-mediators, lay mediators, mental health professionals, and clergy mediators?"[64] The desire to name or define has not abated. Susan B. Goldstein's 1990s research with 90 adult volunteer mediators in a large American neighbourhood justice centre demonstrates that Asian American (31 mediators) and European American (59) mediators do not differ in terms of the degree to which they view being a mediator as important to their identity.[65] Forty-eight percent viewed being a mediator as important or very important to their identity. They also do not differ in terms of the degree to which they have a sense of commonality with other mediators (87% report that they feel a sense of commonality with other mediators) or in terms of the degree to which they believe that their cultural backgrounds influence their roles as mediators.[66] Goldstein's research suggests that mediators of different ethnicities all value their identities as mediators and have a desire to define themselves as "mediators." Unfortunately, however, that does not mean the practising pool of mediators is diverse. In 1964 American scholars conducted a study of state mediators in labour-management settings because at that time the bulk of mediation work in the United States of America, Canada and Puerto Rico was conducted by mediators employed by federal, state and provincial governments.[67] Puerto Rican and Canadian mediators were paid less than American mediators,[68] but in all cases in the 1960s the typical state mediator was a married, heterosexual man aged 45 to 54, with some college education and with more than five years' experience with the agency for which he worked.[69] Although that was more than 50 years ago, it still quite accurately describes the busiest North American commercial mediators today. In 2016 Art Hinshaw reported that most practising American mediators are still

63 Cheryl Picard, "Common Language, Different Meaning: What Mediators Mean When They Talk about their Work" (2002) 18:3 *Negotiation Journal* 251.

64 Susan Zaidel, "Identity Issues for Mediators" (Spring 1988) 19 *Mediation Quarterly* 27 at 29.

65 Susan B. Goldstein, "Responses of Asian American and European American Mediators to a Conflict Communication Scale" (1998) 15:3 *Mediation Quarterly* 181 at 184.

66 Ibid., at 184.

67 Monroe Berkowitz, Bernard Goldstein & Bernard P. Indik, "The State Mediator: Background, Self-Image, and Attitudes" (1964) 17:2 *Industrial and Labor Relations Review* 257 at 259.

68 Ibid., at 263.

69 Ibid., at 260.

white men[70] and Kendrick Lo's 2018 analysis of three reputable Canadian mediation rosters demonstrates a very low proportion of visible minority mediators.[71]

Mediators' own definitions likely relate to their training, backgrounds and favoured approaches to mediation. In 2013 a team of scholars surveyed 359 Flemish divorce mediators (166 lawyers, 68 mental health professionals and 125 mediators) and found that mediators' styles were predominantly determined by characteristics related to their professions.[72] In Flanders, mediators with psychosocial backgrounds are significantly more likely to use facilitative strategies,[73] and strengthening disputants' self-determination is more important for professionals who use an interest-based style.[74] Overall, the older the practitioner is the more settlement oriented s/he is, and the younger the practitioner the more focused on improving the quality of the disputants' relationship s/he is.[75] No stylistic discrepancy was found between mental health mediators and mental health professionals, but lawyer mediators practise in a more advisory way than mental health mediators; mental health mediators are significantly more interest-based than lawyer mediators.[76] Happily, both lawyer mediators and mental health mediators share the same goals: securing settlement, advocating for weaker parties, strengthening self-determination, improving disputants' interactions and processing emotions. However, they differ in terms of style: lawyer mediators are more advisory and mental health mediators are more interest-based.[77] Lisa Webley's research out of England and Wales also suggests that training and affiliation affect mediator identity.[78] For example, Law Society family mediators in England and Wales have first been through solicitor training and thus, according to Webley, have the identity of the imagined masculine professional. But then they add a "thick humanising cloak" that obscures that masculine identity in favour of becoming an emotionally enlightened, more feminine negotiation facilitator. The professional identity within the British College of Mediators is even more feminized, according to Webley; these family mediators adopt a full mediator identity or self-definition of facilitator and even transformer. It is not adding a cloak – it is throwing away the previous masculine

70 Art Hinshaw, "Regulating Mediators" (2016) 21 *Harvard Negotiation Law Review* 163 at 206.
71 Kendrick Lo, "Education without Representation: Cultural Fluency, Diversity, and Dispute Resolution in the Canadian Context" (2018) 7:1 *Journal of Arbitration and Mediation* 65.
72 R. Baitar, A. Buysse, R. Brondeel, J. De Mol & P. Rober, "Styles and Goals: Clarifying the Professional Identity of Divorce Mediation" (2013) 31:1 *Conflict Resolution Quarterly* 57 at 71.
73 Ibid., at 60.
74 Ibid., at 67.
75 Ibid., at 67.
76 Ibid., at 70.
77 Ibid., at 72–73.
78 Lisa Webley, "Solicitors as Imagined Masculine, Family Mediators as Fictive Feminine and the Hybridization of Divorce Solicitors," in Francesca Bartlett, Reid Mortensen & Kieran Tranter, eds, *Alternative Perspectives on Lawyers and Legal Ethics: Reimagining the Profession* (New York: Routledge, 2011) at 132–150.

identity and is thus most closely associated with the fictive feminine label. Webley states: "It is clear that both professional bodies in a family context appear to be converging on a feminized conception of professional, which shuns latent adversarialism and prizes cooperation."[79] Whether or not mediators have a distinct sense of identity, feminized or otherwise, it is undeniable that our professional backgrounds, personal identities and our lived experiences shape our self-definitions.

Despite the fact that mediation is not recognized or defined as a profession, there are many well-trained, expert mediators who carry professional liability insurance and practise as professionals in domestic and international contexts. Franziska Trede, Rob Macklin and Donna Bridges' research study on professional identity asks about the connection between professional, personal and social identities.[80] This is an important topic for further research since a "merging" of personal and professional lives seems to contribute to professional identity. Margot Paterson et al. argue that, in order to establish professional identity, professional judgment, self-evaluation and self-directed learning are necessary.[81] I would add critical self-reflection, and Sven De Weerdt et al. state that "reflection is the important mediator between experience and identity."[82] Deborah Peel says professional identity is a "personal odyssey, grounded in experiential learning from which personal meaning is derived."[83] Trede, Macklin and Bridges note that there is agreement amongst scholars that collaborative learning from practice facilitates the development of professional identity.[84] Mediators know this and most strive toward it as they make meaning and identity in their diverse communities of practice. There is also acknowledgement that the label, be it "mediator" or "professional," has an impact, especially in culturally diverse contexts. What we call our mediation endeavours (for example, facilitative, evaluative, transformative) impacts how they, and we, are understood. The definition impacts the practice and the mediator. Jane Kidner notes the importance of labels; depending on what we call our mediation styles, it influences how disputants come to our mediation tables.[85] Lee Ross and Andrew Ward asked university students to play a game. The game was identical, but with one group it

79 Ibid.

80 Franziska Trede, Rob Macklin & Donna Bridges, "Professional identity development: a review of the higher education literature" (2012) 37:3 *Studies in Higher Education* 365 at 368.

81 M. Paterson, J. Higgs, S. Wilcox & M. Villeneuve, "Clinical reasoning and self-directed learning: Key dimensions in professional education and professional socialisation" (2002) 4:2 *Focus on Health Professional Education* 5 at 7.

82 S. De Weerdt, R. Bouwen, F. Corthouts & H. Martens, "Identity transformation as an intercontextual process" (2006) 2:5 *Industry & Higher Education* 317 at 318.

83 Deborah Peel, "Peer observation as a transformatory tool?" (2005) 10:4 *Teaching in Higher Education* 489 at 495.

84 Franziska Trede, Rob Macklin & Donna Bridges, "Professional identity development: a review of the higher education literature" (2012) 37:3 *Studies in Higher Education* 365 at 378–379.

85 Jane Kidner, "Perspectives on ADR/Mediation: The Limits of Mediator 'Labels': False Debate between 'Facilitative' versus 'Evaluative' Mediator Styles" (2011) 30 *Windsor Review of Legal and Social Issues* 167.

was called the Wall Street Game and with the other group it was called the Community Game.[86] The name of the game, or its label, influenced students' perception of the game and whether they played it competitively, as they did in the Wall Street Game, or cooperatively, as they played the identical game when it was called the Community Game.

Labels and definitions also impact the goals of mediation. This is well illustrated in Zhang Yimou's 1992 film from the People's Republic of China, called *The Story of Qiu Ju*, based on a short story by Chen Yuanbin. *The Story of Qiu Ju* stars Gong Li as a pregnant peasant woman who tackles the post-Maoist bureaucratic system on her own in pursuit of justice. She is successful, but at the expense of her relationships. *The Story of Qiu Ju* was the Hundred Flowers' most popular film of the year and the National Society of Film Critics' best foreign language film. The movie was filmed in the local Shaanxi dialect, which is hard enough to understand that even most of China saw the film with subtitles. *The Story of Qiu Ju* was made in a documentary style. Director Zhang Yimou said:

> We used only four professional actors. … Fifty percent of the film was shot secretly; people did not see the cameras.[87] … This is a very ordinary story that happens all the time in China. … Most problems are not so bad to start with, they only become so because of the workings of the bureaucratic system and the ordeals you have to go through. … With this film, I wanted to say that every Chinese … should … fight for their right and discover themselves in the process.[88]

Qiu Ju and her husband dry chilli peppers on their land. Their village chief refuses them permission to do so because their land is meant for growing chilli peppers, not drying them. The chief and Qiu Ju's husband argue. Her husband insults the chief, who has three daughters and no sons (against China's one-child policy), saying "you only raise hens." The chief retaliates by kicking the husband in his crotch. Qiu Ju spends the rest of the film in search of justice for her kicked husband. She, a poor country woman, wants an apology from an older, more powerful man,[89] the village chief. Jerome Silbergeld describes Qiu Ju as a "stubborn mule … innocent, not wise … semi-literate"[90] and an "unbudgably honest peasant woman."[91] Qiu Ju is determined and does not give up; she never loses her agency. Silbergeld describes the film as a cinematic parable[92] and satire on the

86 Lee Ross & Andrew Ward, "Naïve Realism: Implications for Social Conflict and Misunderstanding (1995) 48 Working Paper, Stanford Center on Conflict and Negotiation.
87 Zhang Yimou, as quoted in Jerome Silbergeld, *China into Film: Frames of Reference in Contemporary Chinese Cinema* (London, Reaktion Books, 1999) at 126.
88 Ibid., at 129.
89 John Dragon Young, "Film Reviews: Asia: *Raise the Red Lantern* and *The Story of Qiu Ju*" (1993) 98:4 *American Historical Review* 1158 at 1160.
90 Jerome Silbergeld, *China into Film: Frames of Reference in Contemporary Chinese Cinema* (London, Reaktion Books, 1999) at 123.
91 Ibid., at 89.
92 Ibid., at 121.

legal reforms of the post-Mao era[93] that allow individuals, in theory, to proceed against the government for restitution. Qiu Ju begins locally, speaking to the chief, then a police officer, and attempts mediation, first at the district bureau and then at the city bureau. The different levels of mediation are exhausting and repetitive, both for Qiu Ju and for the viewer, and Qiu Ju is further alienated from her family and community at each ascending level. Figure 6.1 shows a despondent Qiu Ju, frustrated by her lack of progress and saddened by her physical and mental distance from her family members.

Throughout the film Qiu Ju is in search of *shuofa*, or, as it is translated in the subtitles, "justice" and "apology." Interestingly, Xudong Zhang points out that the word *shuofa* is not really a legal term but, rather, a moral term, and is closer in meaning to the English word "explanation," not "justice."[94] So we see the importance of definitions and meanings. Zhang says *shuofa* means the way things are discussed and eventually understood and accepted. "The moral-cultural point of *shuofa* is that the way things are must be accepted by those to whom it is explained."[95] Throughout the film Qiu Ju demands an explanation, and she keeps moving higher and higher up to get one. Searching for an explanation is different from searching for justice, so the frustrating mediations in the film really could

Figure 6.1 Gong Li as Qiu Ju in *The Story of Qiu Ju*

93 Ibid., at 89.

94 Xudong Zhang, *Postsocialism and Cultural Politics: China in the Last Decade of the Twentieth Century* (Durham, NC: Duke University Press, 2008) at 297.

95 Ibid.

have been better if only an explanation had been given to Qiu Ju. If she had received an explanation, that could have resolved the matter, since, once explained, morally and culturally that explanation must then be accepted. Instead, each time Qiu Ju is denied an explanation and an apology she loses, and each time the authority in question who denies her encourages her to keep trying at a higher level. Silbergeld says "Zhang Yimou reveals the authorities ironically, as seemingly benign creatures who individually assist Qiu Ju along every step of the way while assuring collectively, systematically, that she will never succeed in her quest."[96] Xudong Zhang says Qiu Ju's individual free will "is the site for discussions of gender identity and gender trouble."[97] Her husband and all the many male officials ask her to accept money and let the matter drop, but Qiu Ju will not. She wants an apology, not money, but the men she comes into contact with are afraid of losing face,[98] so Qiu Ju never receives an apology. Her subjectivity is constantly denied, yet she continues to speak to power. If Qiu Ju's need was heard and she received an explanation that made sense, together with an apology, she would have accepted the situation. Xudong Zhang notes that Qiu Ju's journey also mirrors the evolving meaning of the word *shuofa*. The word can mean speaking of law, a way of explanation, and to talk about or comment on the law.[99] First Qiu Ju speaks of the law broken against her husband. Throughout the film she seeks an explanation by attending two mediations, and ultimately her story is a comment on law and its limits. Qiu Ju's concept of *shuofa* is less rigid than the law's justice, just as mediation is less rigid than law. *Shuofa*, or explanation, is also more linguistically demanding, just as the process of mediation demands more of the defendant than law typically does. Xudong Zhang says: "Qiu Ju's is not a legal battle but a hermeneutic struggle to ensure the coherence and integrity of the world of meaning and value … she is there not so much to litigate as to heal, above all her own peace of mind."[100] Alas, coherence and meaning are not restored and she does not heal. At the end of the movie Qiu Ju sues the government and wins, but not in the way she wanted to, and her family suffers much ridicule along the way. Although the injury was to her husband's groin and his dignity, the fact that one of his ribs cracked as well elevated the event from a civil dispute to an assault. It is on this basis that Qiu Ju wins and the village chief has to go to jail for 15 days. Qiu Ju is deeply distressed by this because by the time this verdict comes she has made up with the chief, who was instrumental in saving the life of her baby boy on the night he was delivered. The sentence feels too harsh and it does not give Qiu Ju

96 Jerome Silbergeld, *China into Film: Frames of Reference in Contemporary Chinese Cinema* (London, Reaktion Books, 1999) at 121.
97 Xudong Zhang, *Postsocialism and Cultural Politics: China in the Last Decade of the Twentieth Century* (Durham, NC: Duke University Press, 2008) at 305.
98 For more on losing face in the context of *The Story of Qiu Ju*, see Ilhyung Lee, "Truth, Justice and the Shaaxian Way: Revisiting *The Story of Qiu Ju*" (2018) 19:2 *Cardozo Journal of Conflict Resolution* 229 at 243.
99 Xudong Zhang, *Postsocialism and Cultural Politics: China in the Last Decade of the Twentieth Century* (Durham, NC: Duke University Press, 2008) at 300.
100 Ibid., at 298.

the explanation or apology she truly desires. According to Silbergeld, *The Story of Qiu Ju* "presents a female embodiment of justice crusading through the imperfect Chinese justice system."[101] Qiu Ju wins, but she certainly does not feel as if she has won. Xudong Zhang says: "Qiu Ju's quest for justice is bound to fail because a general, indifferent, legalistic justice is not what she wants and does not solve her problem, and yet it is all that the modern rational social and state organization has to offer."[102] This encapsulates so much of what mediators desire to ameliorate by their diverse practices. Do we provide *shuofa* or justice in our sessions? Does our answer impact our self-definition? No matter the process' definition (directive or transformative) or the mediator's label (professional or otherwise), disputants share Qiu Ju's desire for explanation and meaning. Mediation must at least deliver that.

Popular culture's role

Finally we come to popular culture's role in developing mediator identity. Mediation students and mediators already know about mediation. Many citizens, however, do not, because mediator images and identities are still in the process of becoming. There is little doubt that mediation will more easily enter into popular awareness through popular culture than through academic texts. Television and movies simply reach a much larger audience than legal and conflict resolution writings do. Kimberlianne Podlas notes that popular culture's depictions constitute much of what the public knows about law and mediation, so it is important to analyse whether those depictions affect members of the public and mediators.[103] Television can influence and its depictions reinforce one another.[104] Unfortunately, as both Podlas and Sharp point out, there is not yet enough empirical research regarding the connections between popular culture representations and viewer interpretations.[105] What we do know is that the more audiences see a behaviour the more they will believe the behaviour is normal.[106] One of the primary effects of watching TV and movies for legal processes such as mediation is familiarization: we begin to know more about mediation because we see it presented.[107] So

101 Jerome Silbergeld, *China into Film: Frames of Reference in Contemporary Chinese Cinema* (London, Reaktion Books, 1999) at 154.
102 Xudong Zhang, *Postsocialism and Cultural Politics: China in the Last Decade of the Twentieth Century* (Durham, NC: Duke University Press, 2008) at 299.
103 Kimberlianne Podlas, "Testing Television: Studying and Understanding the Impact of Television's Depictions of Law and Justice," in Peter Robson & Jessica Silbey, eds, *Law and Justice on the Small Screen* (Oxford: Hart, 2012) at 88.
104 Ibid., at 95.
105 Cassandra Sharp, "Let's See How Far We've Come: The Role of Empirical Methodology in Exploring Television Audiences," in Peter Robson & Jessica Silbey, eds, *Law and Justice on the Small Screen* (Oxford: Hart, 2012) at 112.
106 Kimberlianne Podlas, "Testing Television: Studying and Understanding the Impact of Television's Depictions of Law and Justice," in Peter Robson & Jessica Silbey, eds, *Law and Justice on the Small Screen* (Oxford: Hart, 2012) at 93.
107 Stefan Machura, "Law and Justice in German Film and Television" (June 20, 2019), Law, Film & Society Panel, Oñati International Institute for the Sociology of Law, Oñati, Spain.

we can put popular culture to work in service of mediator identity by watching it. Johanna Schmertz says "'seeing' is a kind of 'reading' – a set of internalized interpretive strategies that, once made conscious, could be better put to work."[108] As law professors, we can do this in our mediation classrooms, using the popular culture examples provided in this book. Schmertz describes using a film clip "to encourage reflective and recursive looking. By focusing on their own interpretation, students continually asked themselves throughout the semester, 'How do I know what I know?'"[109] Asimow and Mader have long argued that many people know most of what they know about the legal system because of popular culture.[110] Mediators, students and academics can be more deliberate about their seeing and viewing practices, account for the movies in their minds,[111] and acknowledge the role of popular culture in creating knowledge.

While we know that popular culture influences us and creates meaning, we are still speculating about mediator identity. We do not know for sure how age, ability, nationality, gender, culture, race, ethnicity, sexual orientation and economic background shape viewer engagement with popular culture texts, or how they shape mediator identity, but we can make educated guesses. Just as Margaret Russell convincingly argues that Hollywood myths about race shape our images of ourselves,[112] Hollywood images of conflict resolvers could shape mediators' images of themselves. Increased numbers of mediator images and mediation storylines in popular culture will do much to increase mediation awareness, and will also help mediators in their own processes of self-reflection and self-definition. Mediators could employ popular culture to help understand the professional lives they have chosen.[113] Alexander Scherr and Hillary Farber argue that popular culture representations of lawyers can expand notions of professionalism beyond codes of conduct.[114] Correspondingly, popular culture depictions of mediators can expand notions of professionalism to include reflections upon identity. Mediation stories on TV and in film can provide opportunities for self-reflection and career contemplation because, as Montoya notes, narrative is "a mediating force in the re/construction of personal and collective identities."[115] Thus it is possible

108 Johanna Schmertz, "Movies of the Reader's Mind: Re-Mediating Interpretation with Film" (2007) 36:2 *Modern Language Studies* 88 at 93.
109 Ibid., at 100.
110 Michael Asimow & Shannon Mader, *Law and Popular Culture: A Course Book* (New York: Peter Lang Publishing., 2004)
111 Johanna Schmertz, "Movies of the Reader's Mind: Re-Mediating Interpretation with Film" (2007) 36:2 *Modern Language Studies* 88 at 102.
112 M.M. Russell, "Law and Racial Reelism: Black Women as Celluloid 'Legal' Heroines," in M.A. Fineman & M.T. McCluskey, eds, *Feminism, Media & Law* (New York: Oxford University Press, 1997) at 138.
113 James R. Elkins, "Reading/Teaching Lawyer Films" (2004) 28 *Vermont Law Review* 813 at 876.
114 Alexander Scherr & Hillary Farber, "Popular Culture as a Lens on Legal Professionalism" (2004) 55:2 *South Carolina Law Review* 351 at 353.
115 M.E. Montoya, "Border/ed Identities: Narrative and the Social Construction of Legal and Personal Identities," in A. Sarat, M. Constable, D. Engel, V. Hans & S. Lawrence, eds, *Crossing Boundaries: Traditions and Transformations in Law and Society Research* (Evanston, IL: Northwestern University Press, 1998) at 142.

that the narrative power of popular culture could be harnessed by mediators and used in the construction of their identities. Sharp says law students do this with TV images of lawyers; they use them to "begin constructing a professional identity of themselves and to generate expectations of their future careers."[116] David Ray Papke notes that "professionals … rely on self-images to picture themselves, guide their work, and preserve their status. Certain self-images are dominant in certain professions, and, indeed, without those dominant self-images a given profession would struggle to maintain its coherence."[117] It is no wonder then that mediators, who have no overriding images in popular culture, must struggle to create awareness of their field and to maintain images of themselves, especially in the face of so many popular culture lawyer images. As Papke notes in the context of law professors: "Critically contemplating the self-images of law professors in the Hollywood cinema can assist law professors, lawyers, and members of other professions as well in consciously tending to their professional self-imagery."[118] Similarly, contemplating the image of mediators in popular culture can help mediators do the same.

Right now mediators may only be able to work on image and identity construction by asserting their differences from more powerful and more visible legal characters. This is similar to how Canadians differentiate and define themselves by saying they are not like more powerful and more visible Americans. Ummni Khan has noted that more than one Canadian theorist is anxiously consumed by discerning Canadian identity as distinct from American.[119] In Canada's subordinate context, our national identity is comprised of what we are not. We define ourselves as "not American" and a sense of our Canadian identity seems to come from the absence of a national identity.[120] Just as Canadians are different from Americans, and operate in their shadow, mediators are different from lawyers and operate in their shadow. Mediators, like Canadians, may currently be a group that works on identity construction by asserting its difference, most specifically, from lawyers. Patricia Cormack and James F. Cosgrave state that "Canadians have enthusiastically supported an

116 Cassandra Sharp, "Scarlet Letter or Chastity Belt? What Legal Dramas of the Twenty-First Century are 'Telling' Law Students about a Career in Law" (2002) 5:1 *Legal Ethics* 90 at 91.

117 David Ray Papke, "Crusading Hero, Devoted Teacher, and Sympathetic Failure: The Self-Image of the Law Professor in Hollywood Cinema and in Real Life, Too" (2004) 28 *Vermont Law Review* 957 at 973.

118 Ibid.

119 Ummni Khan, "Bordering on Identity: How English Canadian Television Differentiates American and Canadian Styles of Justice," in Peter Robson & Jessica Silbey, eds, *Law and Justice on the Small Screen* (Oxford: Hart, 2012) at 311. Patricia Cormack & James F. Cosgrave, *Desiring Canada: CBC Contests, Hockey Violence, and Other Stately Pleasures* (Toronto: University of Toronto Press, 2013) at 61 state: "It is widely accepted in English Canada that Canadian things – especially cultural things – need to be collected and preserved because they are endangered by American cultural imperialism."

120 Jennifer L. Schulz, "Canada: ADR and *The Associates*," in Peter Robson & Jessica Silbey, eds, *Law and Justice on the Small Screen* (Oxford: Hart, 2012) at 438.

industry of narratives – books, contests, debates, surveys – that are premised on the impossibility of achieving an identity."[121] And this is "identified as the country's signal strength."[122] This is likely why many Canadians cannot actually articulate what it is that defines Canada. In the same vein, mediators too do not have one collective identity. All we know for sure is that what we offer is different from what lawyers offer, and we are proud of that; just like Canadians are proud they are not Americans. Mediators' lack of a homogeneous identity may also be our strength, especially as the founders of our field warn us to maintain our flexible, creative natures.[123]

Cormack and Cosgrave go on to describe a theme of humility which "renders Canadians moral agents when set against the mythically overbearing, ever-present Americans."[124] When transposed to the mediation context, however, we must ask whether mediators really are more humble than lawyers, or just quieter. Most mediators certainly believe their method, mediation, is superior to lawyers' method, litigation, so it is not clear that we are actually humbler. Edward Morgan's comments about Canadians apply to mediators too:

> The discovery may have come late in the day, but it turns out that Canadians [mediators] live in a world characterized as much by disorder as order, as much by alienation from the law as adherence to it, and as much by debate about who they are *not* as by confidence in the knowledge of who they actually are.[125]

Just as diversity is essential to Canadianness, so too is diversity essential to mediator identity. If mediators, like Canada, exist "by way of diversity, difference, and tolerance, then no value judgment [or style of mediation] can outweigh another."[126] If identity is a gap we are desirous of filling, we may use popular cultural imaginings to help us do so. Cormack and Cosgrave note that the idea of gap or incompleteness "supports democratic ideas of inclusion, change, diversity, and temperance,"[127] just as it should for mediator identity. Mediators must recognize that the value of

121 Patricia Cormack & James F. Cosgrave, *Desiring Canada: CBC Contests, Hockey Violence, and Other Stately Pleasures* (Toronto: University of Toronto Press, 2013) at 12.

122 Ibid.

123 Stephen B. Goldberg & Margaret L. Shaw, "The Past, Present, and Future of Mediation as Seen through the Eyes of Some of Its Founders" (April 2010) 26:2 *Negotiation Journal* 237.

124 Patricia Cormack & James F. Cosgrave, *Desiring Canada: CBC Contests, Hockey Violence, and Other Stately Pleasures* (Toronto: University of Toronto Press, 2013) at 53. At 55 the authors state: "Presumably, Americans [lawyers] practise a cultural and political life of export, conquest, and domination, whereas Canadians [mediators] practise a cultural and political life of self-consumption, border vigilance [remaining separate from law], and administration [process]."

125 Edward Morgan, "The Mild, Mild West: Living by a Code in Canadian Law and Film" (2006) 2 *Law, Culture and the Humanities* 115 at 117; emphasis in original.

126 Patricia Cormack & James F. Cosgrave, *Desiring Canada: CBC Contests, Hockey Violence, and Other Stately Pleasures* (Toronto: University of Toronto Press, 2013) at 61.

127 Ibid., at 219.

diversity means we may have to defer knowing who we are. If we continue to embrace different styles and approaches we may never have a definitive sense of "who is a mediator" or "what is mediation," and that may be okay. It will take time before mediators are able to assert themselves in more complex, nuanced ways.

One of Canada's well-known personalities, a journalist, broadcaster, historian and prolific author, Pierre Berton, explained the power of popular culture: "It was not the National Film Board that gave us our image of ourselves and it was not the National Film Board that gave the rest of the world its image of Canada. It was Hollywood."[128] Thus, if national image can be created by Hollywood, so might mediator image also be created. Popular culture makers bear the responsibility for popular culture visual images – both positive and negative. J.B. Colson states that, because most of the power is in the hands of the image makers, "they have the responsibility of producing media that recognizes the diversity and complexity of human experience."[129] Yet of course we know they do not do that. For example, the top legally themed television shows watched in Canada in 2017 featured police officers, not lawyers, and certainly not mediators.[130] Two of the three shows were American (*NCIS* and *Bull*) and one show was a Canadian mini-series (*The Indian Detective*). None of the shows had LGBTQ2, disabled or poor characters and in all three shows the protagonists were men.[131] A United Nations-backed study found that the film industry perpetuates gender discrimination. The 2014 study, from the Annenberg School for Communication and Journalism at the University of Southern California,[132] was supported by United Nations Women, the Rockefeller Foundation and the Geena Davis Institute on Gender in Media. It revealed "deep-seated discrimination and pervasive stereotyping of women and girls by the international film industry." The study analysed popular movies from Australia, Brazil, China, France, Germany, India, Japan, Russia, South Korea, the United States of America and the United Kingdom. Male characters outnumbered their female counterparts as lawyers and judges (13 to 1), professors (16 to 1), medical practitioners (5 to 1) and in STEM fields (7 to 1). It found women were more likely to be depicted in a hypersexualised manner than men; girls and women were twice as likely as boys and men to be shown either in

128 Pierre Berton, *Hollywood's Canada* (Toronto: McClelland and Stewart, 1975) at 237.

129 J.B. Colson, "Images That Heal," in P.M. Lester, ed., *Images that Injure: Pictorial Stereotypes in the Media* (Westport, CT: Praeger, 1996) at 220.

130 Jennifer L. Schulz, "Canada: Women, People of Colour, and Diversity on Top Law Shows," in Peter Robson & Jennifer L. Schulz, *Ethnicity, Gender, and Diversity: Law and Justice on TV* (London: Lexington Books, 2018). In our earlier study Peter Robson and I found that in 14 countries almost 95% of the law and justice TV programming was about police (Peter Robson & Jennifer L. Schulz, eds, *A Transnational Study of Law & Justice on TV* [Oxford: Hart Publishing, 2016]).

131 Jennifer L. Schulz, "Canada: Women, People of Colour, and Diversity on Top Law Shows," in Peter Robson & Jennifer L. Schulz, *Ethnicity, Gender, and Diversity: Law and Justice on TV* (London: Lexington Books, 2018) at 82.

132 Study conducted by Stacy L. Smith, Marc Choueiti & Katherine Pieper at the Media, Diversity & Social Change Initiative at the Annenberg School for Communication and Journalism, University of Southern California, 2014.

sexualised attire, in the nude, or thin. Filmmakers worldwide are perpetuating gender discrimination by failing to find strong roles for women on the big screen.[133] The report found that fewer than one third of all speaking roles went to women, who were also largely absent from positions of power. Only 22.5% of the overall fictional big-screen workforce was shown to be made up of female employees. Geena Davis commented, "In the time it takes to make a movie, we can change what the future looks like." Similarly, one blockbuster film about mediators would do much for mediator identity. The United Nations Women Executive Director called the study a "wake-up call" for the global film industry. "With their powerful influence on shaping the perceptions of large audiences, the media are key players for the gender equality agenda," she said. "With influence comes responsibility." Until such time as the makers of popular culture accept their responsibility to be more representative of everyone, women, people of colour and mediators will still be marginalized in popular culture.

The current political context also has an exacerbating effect. Scholars have noted that President Donald Trump has influenced mediation. Jennie Huang and Corinne Low's lab findings demonstrate that men exhibit more aggressive negotiation behaviour toward women since the 2016 election in the USA than before.[134] Deborah Kolb concurs, noting that "Trump's hypermasculine behaviours – his aggression and misogyny and the fallout from them, could affect women and their place at the negotiating table."[135] Carrie Menkel-Meadow says that Trump's adversarial, brutish, "win-all-you-can" negotiation approach is "nearly the polar opposite of problem-solving negotiation."[136] She points out that, after all the work mediation scholars have done over the past decades, the last thing we need is a return to understanding mediation as a process of bullying. Gail S. Packer aptly sums it up, saying it is time to build bridges, not walls.[137] Peter Robson and I believe that "we can work to negotiate, resist, change, and develop depictions of marginalized characters on television and that this will enrich the legal academy, student experience, the practice of law, and society generally."[138]

133 www.forbes.com/sites/melissasilverstein/2014/09/22/geena-davis-institute-new-research-shows-that-girls-and-women-are-missing-onscreen-and-behind-the-scenes-worldwide/#3197ba1289c7

134 J. Huang & C. Low, "Trumping Norms: Lab evidence on aggressive communication before and after the 2016 U.S. Presidential Election" (2017) 107:5 *American Economic Review* 120–124.

135 Deborah M. Kolb, "Her Place at the Table: Gender and Negotiation after Trump" (2019) 35:1 *Negotiation Journal* 185 at 185.

136 Carrie Menkel-Meadow, "The Culture of Negotiation: Trumpian Imprints on the Future?" (2019) 35:1 *Negotiation Journal* 221 at 221.

137 Gail S. Packer, "Conflict, Culture, and Community: Dispute Resolution after Trump" (2019) 35:1 *Negotiation Journal* 173 at 176.

138 Peter Robson & Jennifer L. Schulz, "Ethnicity, Gender, and Diversity on TV in Context," in Peter Robson & Jennifer L. Schulz, eds, *Ethnicity, Gender, and Diversity: Law and Justice on TV* (London: Lexington Books, 2018) at 13.

More popular culture featuring mediator protagonists could have an enormous influence on the public's general appreciation of mediation, on mediation students' learning, and on mediators' identities. Simply by showcasing mediation in popular culture we enhance its profile. Increasing mediator profile is a goal of many mediators, who hope for raised profiles within their community organisations, the legal profession and in society generally. It stands to reason that a successful film featuring a mediator protagonist could have an enormous influence on the public, lawyers, mediators, law students and mediation students. As Richard Sherwin notes, "known character and story types may serve as vehicles for shared beliefs and expectations."[139] Therefore there is great power in making a character type – the mediator – known. Doing so enhances mediation's profile and creates the possibility of shared understandings of mediation. Just as journalists can create a crime wave by reporting on all the crimes in a given time frame, and end the wave simply by not reporting on crimes,[140] waves of enthusiasm for mediation could be created by the makers of popular culture. This is not as far-fetched as it sounds. Nadja Alexander says that "mediation represents the emergence of a new form of informal and consumer-oriented justice possessing a universality not typical of legal processes."[141] Mediation is truly a worldwide process, so it is not fanciful to imagine that we will begin to see more and more instances of it in popular culture. And, when we do, we will begin to fill the gaps between mediation in theory, mediation in popular culture and mediation in real life. It is there, in those interstitial spaces, where we are most likely to find the identity of the mediator.

Image, identity and self-definition are always creative, invented, historical, contingent, situational, dynamic and related to social structure and asymmetries of power. As Margaret Davies and Nan Seuffert note:

> identity formation is a complex and ongoing process which takes place within both largely determined dominant discourses and more fluid resistant discourses over which we have some control. Self-definition is therefore always political, and identity and politics are co-constructing and mutually reproductive.[142]

Therefore images of mediators must be understood to be fluid, political and existing in relation to other images. Our selves, our practices and our identities are contingent, multiple and actively constructed.[143] Due to the narrative composability of

139 Richard K. Sherwin, *When Law Goes Pop: The Vanishing Line between Law and Popular Culture* (Chicago, IL: The University of Chicago Press, 2000) at 69.

140 C. McCormick, *Constructing Danger: The Mis/Representation of Crime in the News* (Halifax: Fernwood, 1995).

141 Nadja Alexander, ed., *Global Trends in Mediation*, 2nd edn (Alphen aan den Rijn: Kluwer Law International, 2006) at 35.

142 Margaret Davies & Nan Seuffert, "Knowledge, Identity, and the Politics of Law" (2000) *Hastings Women's Law Journal* 259 at 275.

143 This is important because, "at the level of practice, the mediation field is pluralistic rather than homogeneous, and this is well acknowledged" (Robert A. Baruch Bush & Joseph P. Folger, *The Promise of Mediation: The Transformative Approach to Conflict*, 2nd edn [San Francisco, CA: Jossey-Bass, 2005] at 259).

self, mediators can show and tell their stories, and, through consuming popular culture, social images can be tried on and tried out. When mediators see rare signs of themselves on TV or in film they can begin to develop more nuanced professional self-images, even if they do not agree with all aspects of the portrayals. The task of future researchers will be to explore how mediation discourse is then constituted and challenged by viewers as they talk about popular culture mediators and perceive the dispute resolution world.[144] What is important is how viewers and mediators use what they see to make meaning and create identities. Paul W. Kahn states: "We can know more about ourselves. This is all that a cultural study of law can promise. What we do once we have that knowledge is a question for practice, not theory."[145] Mediation, in the rare instances when we glimpse it in our popular culture, can mirror, criticize or project alternative dispute resolution realities. We must try to understand television and film as arenas of performance that both profane ADR and, at the same time, open up new imaginings of mediation.[146] I will conclude with the words of Lynsee Swisher blogging about *Fairly Legal*:

> Here is why I liked the show. Simply, it mentions mediation. It mentioned "Alternative Dispute Resolution," "win-win" (maybe one too many times), and my favourite, "mediators build bridges." Not all bad in my opinion. It makes mention of a field that many people have never even heard of. The accuracy of it, the sensationalism of it, well that's TV. It may just do what I hope it does, make people hear the word "mediation" for the first time, create others who have a healthy interest about the field, and then it is up to us, the working professionals, to show people what we are about.[147]

Let's do that.

144 Cassandra Sharp, "Let's See How Far We've Come: The Role of Empirical Methodology in Exploring Television Audiences," in Peter Robson & Jessica Silbey, eds, *Law and Justice on the Small Screen* (Oxford: Hart, 2012) at 122.

145 Paul W. Kahn, *The Cultural Study of Law: Reconstructing Legal Scholarship* (Chicago, IL and London: The University of Chicago Press, 1999) at 40.

146 Austin Sarat, "What Popular Culture Does For, and To, Law," in Austin Sarat, ed., *Imagining Legality: Where Law Meets Popular Culture* (Tuscaloosa, AL: The University of Alabama Press, 2011) at 16.

147 Posted by Lynsee Swisher on January 21, 2011 at 4p.m., http://adrhub.com/profiles/blogs/mediation-in-prime-timei-like

Index

For Product Safety Concerns and Information please contact our EU representative GPSR@taylorandfrancis.com
Taylor & Francis Verlag GmbH, Kaufingerstraße 24, 80331 München, Germany

www.ingramcontent.com/pod-product-compliance
Lightning Source LLC
LaVergne TN
LVHW021111300926
849160LV00009B/690

* 9 7 8 1 0 3 2 2 3 8 1 3 5 *